THE WOMEN'S VOLUNTEER COMMITTEE

of the

NEW ORLEANS MUSEUM OF ART

PRESENTS

ARTIST'S PALATE
COOKBOOK

CLASSIC CREOLE &

NEW ORLEANS

RECIPES

NEW ORLEANS, LOUISIANA

The Artist's Palate is the Café
in the New Orleans Museum of Art

The raison d'être of the Women's Volunteer Committee is to encourage community support for the New Orleans Museum of Art. In turn, the Museum provides educational programs in creativity and appreciation, a gem of an art collection exhibited in its galleries and shared in loan programs with other museums, and exhibitions of rare and precious objects from major collections in the USA and abroad. All proceeds from this publication will benefit the New Orleans Museum of Art.

COVER

PITCHER AND THREE CROISSANTS

Oil on canvas, 18¼ x 23¾ inches, c. 1910-1912

ALFRED MAURER

Gift of Ella West Freeman Matching Fund

The American painter, Alfred Maurer, lived in Paris from 1890-1914. The *Pitcher with Three Croissants* shows his fascination with Fauve ideas of color and hints at Cubist influence in the flattened planear composition.

For additional copies, use order blanks on the back page.

Also, copies may be obtained from the New Orleans Museum of Art Gift Shop, City Park—Lelong Avenue, New Orleans, Louisiana.

Copyright © 1986
by
Women's Volunteer Committee
New Orleans Museum of Art

Diamond Jubilee Edition   November 1986   5,000 copies

ISBN 0-89494-026-0
Library of Congress Catalog Card Number 86-51124

Printed in the USA
Wimmer Brothers Books
P.O. Box 18408
Memphis, Tennessee 38181-0408

Typography and Design by GLS Graphic Productions

Alfred Boisseau (American, born in France, 1823-1901)
LOUISIANA INDIANS WALKING ALONG A BAYOU *1847*
oil on canvas
Gift of Mr. William E. Groves.

In this painting details of the hair and basket styles indicate that the Indians depicted are Choctaws. The locale is thought to be somewhere along the Tchefuncta River on the north shore of Lake Pontchartrain. Choctaws were frequently seen in the markets of New Orleans where they sold baskets, goods woven from palmetto leaves and filé, a root condiment used in the preparation of Creole foods.

History of New Orleans Creole and French Cooking

Food. it's one of the main topics of conversation in New Orleans. Friends share recipes and tips on where to dine as part of everyday conversation. And while the famous local chefs and restaurants receive national attention, all of the good cooks are not in professional kitchens. Cooking is an art in New Orleans. Our food is different. We think it is better than any other food in the world.

There has never been a time when Creole cooking has been more popular than today. Creole restaurants have sprung up in even the smallest towns, not to mention major cities such as New York and San Francisco.

What is Creole cooking? It's a special style of cooking that was originated in Louisiana by the Creoles—descendants of the first settlers, the Spanish and the French. The Acadians, who came later and were known as Cajuns, actually were of French heritage and refugees from Nova Scotia, where they had lived for 150 years before they were driven out by the British.

It was the Spanish who brought their love of highly seasoned food to the area; the French added their sauces and the use of roux—a fat and flour thickening used in many dishes. The blending was further heightened with the addition of herbs, especially filé powder, a thickening agent made from sassafras leaves that was used by the Choctaw Indians, and it was the African slaves who brought okra and a genius for blending everything together.

Today the Creole style of cooking is still taking on refinement with the development of recipes. However, New Orleans cooking involves much more than just Creole dishes. The melting pot of cultures continues today in our interesting city and especially in our kitchens as evidenced in this personalized cookbook that brings it all together from our kitchen to yours. Bon appetit!

by Bonnie Warren
Food critic and
contributing editor to
many prestigious magazines

"Way Down Yonder In New Orleans"

There's a song that goes "Way down yonder in New Orleans . . . in the land of those dreamy scenes . . . there's a Garden of Eden . . . ."

Yes, New Orleans is an Eden, with bountiful fresh trout, redfish, shrimp, crayfish, crabs, succulent oysters, mirlitons that ripen on backyard vines, Creole tomatoes, native strawberries, yams, rice and cane sugar grown on up-river plantations. Louisiana's natural ingredients have soaked up the *mélange* of our Anglo-Latin origins and produced a cuisine as distinctive as our history, architecture, customs and patterns of speech.

Dreams are the necessary resting place of creativity, and the slow tempo and ambience of New Orleans have made this old port city a favorite of great chefs, writers, artists and musicians for over one hundred years.

Try to say New Orleans fast. It doesn't sound right, does it. You can't hurry our name any more than you can rush a great dish like shrimp creole or stuffed mirlitons, the Monday red beans, or a Creole gumbo (which is often an all-day family affair).

Look at the works of authors who have written here, like George Washington Cable, Kate Chopin, Tennessee Williams, Walker Percy and Shirley Ann Grau—works that have evolved from generations of Southern story-telling handed down like good recipes from grandmother to mother to daughter.

The French Impressionist Edgar Degas visited here for several months in 1872/73. Enchanted by the city and the warm family life of his maternal relatives he painted several portaits and a masterpiece, *Le Bureau dè coton a la Nouvelle Orléans.* Our wildlife lured the great artist/naturalist John James Audubon, our history sculptress Angela Gregory, and the plantation country gave Clarence John Laughlin his photographic essay *Ghosts Along the Mississippi* . . . speaking of dreams.

Our music springs from Caribbean rhythms, and the dichotomy of Storyville jazz and religious ceremony. The same special blend of Crescent City flavor that produced L. M. Gottschalk, Louis Armstrong, Al Hirt, Pete Fountain and Wynton Marsalis. Jazz pianist Ellis Marsalis, Wynton's Daddy, says "musicians stand on street corners in New Orleans giving away gold."

It's all around us, this rich exotic strain that has seeped into our cooking, our writing, our art and our music. It's in our nostrils, on our tongues, under our feet and in our blood. We are the keepers in this land of dreamy scenes, this Garden of Eden, this New Orleans.

"When an artist creates a picture he is painting a much more accurate portrait of the state of his soul, mind and heart than he is his subject matter."

I feel sure that the American artist Leon Kroll, who wrote the above words, would feel as I do, that this exemplary and beautiful **Artist's Palate Cookbook** is a true reflection of the souls, hearts and minds of the Women's Volunteer Committee of the New Orleans Museum of Art.

I offer these ladies my most sincere thanks. Their dedication in putting 300 classic Creole and New Orleans recipes together with the paintings of contemporary artists who have worked in New Orleans has produced a choice cookbook that will enrich the lives of all of us.

E. John Bullard
Director
New Orleans Museum of Art

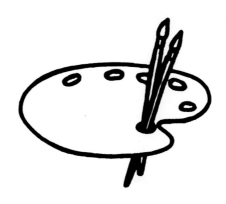

TABLE OF CONTENTS

History of the New Orleans Museum of Art

In 1986 the New Orleans Museum of Art (NOMA) celebrates its 75th Anniversary. Founded by Jamaica-born New Orleans philanthropist Isaac Delgado, the original neo-classic building, surrounded by lagoons, rests in City Park, one of the largest urban parks in America.

Three new wings were added to the Museum in 1971 tripling its original size and providing space for its permanent collections which offer a survey of Western Civilization from the pre-Christian era to the present. The name was changed from the Isaac Delgado Museum of Art at this time.

Among NOMA's storehouse of treasures are an internationally acclaimed survey of Edo Period Japanese Art, the fourth largest glass collection held in public ownership in America, a permanent exhibition of works by Peter Carl Fabergé including three Imperial Easter Eggs and the famous jeweled Basket of Lilies of the Valley, along with outstanding collections in photography, African Art, pre-Columbian Art, portrait miniatures, Spanish Colonial Art and, reflecting its own heritage, a comprehensive survey of French paintings and sculpture including works by Renoir, Monet, Degas, Redon, Braque, Picasso and Dufy, among others.

During the past decade NOMA has hosted many fine international art exhibitions including *Treasures of Tutankhamun, The Search for Alexander, The Gold of El Dorado* and *The Precious Legacy,* as well as special exhibitions of its own works and those of other institutions.

Since its opening in 1911, NOMA has received its operating funds from the City of New Orleans. Membership dues, private donations, foundation and corporate grants and Federal and State grants support exhibition and education programs and provide funds for art acquisitions.

Last year the Museum embarked on an expansion program to coincide with its 75th Anniversary. Through a national competition, an architect was selected to design an addition that will double the present facility.

History of the Women's Volunteer Committee
of the New Orleans Museum of Art

I suppose it was all Edgar Degas' fault. If he hadn't stayed in New Orleans for a time, painted a "Portrait of Estelle," his cousin, and sparked excitement for the painting among several New Orleans ladies, then the force that is now the Women's Committee would likely never have come to be. Cementing their determination to raise the money to keep the portrait where it belonged, this "force to be" swept over the city in 1964 raising money and sparking a new kind of enthusiasm in the community. Even grammar school children sent in dollar bills to help buy the "Portrait of Estelle."

Then, at a meeting at the late Edith Stern's home on an auspicious spring morning in 1965, a small group of women, including many of those involved in the successful purchase of Estelle, met and decided that if a group of determined ladies could generate this much excitement for one painting, who knows what they could do for a whole museum! And so, Mrs. Samuel Logan having gained the Museum Board's blessing, the Women's Committee was born. This group of twenty-five women dedicated to working for museum needs was officially accepted by the Delgado Board of Trustees as "Delgado Dames." They were to become the Charter Members of the Women's Volunteer Committee.

The first test of the "mettle" of the new group was the Art Auction in 1965 which raised an astounding $35,000! Then followed the first Odyssey Ball the next year. (What? A *charity ball* in New Orleans? A city of Carnival Balls! Who will ever go?) The excitement swirling around the museum was strong because 750 people came to the first Charity Ball in the city that anyone could remember. And it cleared an amazing $25,000!

To quote the popular commercial, "You've come a long way, baby!!"

Edgar-Hilaire-Germain Degas (French, 1834-1917)
PORTRAIT OF ESTELLE MUSSON DEGAS *1872*
oil on canvas
Museum Purchase through Public Subscription.

    Degas arrived in New Orleans October, 1872 for a five month visit. New Orleans was the birthplace of his mother and grandmother as well as the home of his uncle, a cotton broker, and two brothers, who had established a wine importing business in the city. During his visit, Degas painted an estimated fifteen to seventeen works. Due to his poor eyesight, these were restricted, for the most part, to indoor portraits of his immediate family. However, Degas grew testy at his family's lack of awareness of his role as an artist. Perhaps it was due to their impatience to sit for him that he painted his blind cousin and sister-in-law, Estelle Musson, three times.

    The two other paintings of Estelle are now in the Louvre and in the National Gallery of Art, Washington, D.C.

I. Museum Exhibition Preview Party

Chinese, Canton
FAN c. 1840
silk with painted appliqué and ivory, tortoise shell sticks
Gift of Mrs. Harry H. Hall.

I. Museum Exhibition Preview Party

Glögg

Serves 8 to 10

2   fifths dry red wine
1   cup sweet vermouth
2   sticks cinnamon
8   whole cloves
1   cup raisins
6   whole cardamoms, crushed
    peel of 1 orange in continuous spiral

In a large pot combine above ingredients, heat almost to a boil and simmer 20 minutes.

1   cup whole blanched almonds
1   cup brandy
1   cup sugar cubes

Put almonds in bottom of a large punch bowl. Heat brandy, pour over sugar cubes in a copper frypan and ignite. Pour while burning, into bowl. Add hot spicy wine preparation while brandy is still burning. Serve in stemmed glasses.

Mint Julep

Yield: 1 serving

2   ounces Bourbon
1   tablespoon confectioners sugar (or more to taste)
2   medium-size sprigs fresh mint

Place sugar and 1 sprig of mint in bottom of Julep glass or large Old Fashion glass. Crush mint into sugar, using bar pestle or bar spoon. Fill glass with crushed ice and pour in Bourbon. Mix with bar spoon in an up-and-down motion until glass is frosted.

Garnish with remaining sprig of mint which has been moistened and sprinkled with confectioners sugar. Serve with a sipping straw.

Vodka Slush

Yield: 5 quarts

7   cups Seven-Up (56 ounces)
1   46-ounce can pineapple juice
1   cup water
1   cup sugar
1   6-ounce can frozen orange juice concentrate
2   6-ounce cans water
1   10-ounce jar cherries and juice
1½   cups vodka

Thoroughly mix Seven-Up, pineapple juice, 1 cup water and sugar. Defrost orange juice, mix with two 6-ounce cans water and add to Seven-Up mixture. Add cherries and cherry juice, stir in vodka and freeze.

Remove from freezer about 3 hours before serving. For higher alcohol content, increase vodka to 3 cups. The more vodka, the less time it takes to thaw.

White Sangria

Serves 6

1   fifth chilled sauterne
½   cup chilled brandy
¼   cup superfine sugar
1   cup sliced fruit, any combination of orange, lemon, strawberries, cherries or pineapple
2   cups chilled club soda

In a 2-quart pitcher, preferably glass to show off pretty colors of the fruit, combine sauterne and brandy. Stir in sugar until dissolved, add fruit and chill for at least 1 hour. Just before serving, add club soda.

For an attractive garnish, add ice cubes with small pieces of fruit frozen in them.

Scarlett O'Hara Cocktail

Yield: 1 serving

1½ jiggers Southern Comfort
1½ jiggers cranberry juice
    juice of ¼ lime

Stir ingredients together with a few ice cubes in a large Old Fashion glass. Strain into a stemmed cocktail glass and serve.

Rhett Butler Cocktail

Yield: 1 serving

1   jigger Southern Comfort
    juice of ¼ lime
    juice of ¼ lemon
1   teaspoon Curaçao
½   teaspoon confectioners sugar

Combine all ingredients in shaker with ice cubes, shake well and strain into stemmed cocktail glass.

Ramos Gin Fizz

Henry Ramos concocted this famous drink in the late 1880's.

Yield: 1 serving

2   teaspoons superfine sugar
1   egg white
1   dash vanilla
2   dashes orange flower water
1½ teaspoons lemon juice
2   ounces half and half
1   ounce gin

Combine all ingredients in a shaker with ice, shake well and strain into an Old Fashion glass to serve.

Whiskey Sour Punch

Yield: 45 to 50 4-ounce cups

6   6-ounce cans frozen lemonade concentrate
1   6-ounce can frozen orange juice concentrate
2   6-ounce cans frozen lemon juice concentrate
1   fifth bourbon whiskey
60 ounces Seven-Up
28 ounces club soda
1   large bottle stemmed cherries

Defrost lemonade, orange juice and lemon juice, mix together and freeze. Place fifth of bourbon in freezer until ready to serve. Refrigerate Seven-up and club soda until ready to serve.

About 2 hours before serving, place frozen juices in a large punch bowl. Just prior to serving, pour in refrigerated Seven-Up, club soda and "frozen" bourbon. Garnish with stemmed cherry.

Mimosa

Yield: 1 serving

2   ounces freshly squeezed orange juice
4   ounces chilled domestic champagne

Place a cube of ice in a large wine glass, add orange juice and pour in chilled champagne. Garnish with a fresh strawberry.

Spicy Nuts

Great with cocktails!
Serves 6 to 10

1	pound nut halves, pecan or walnut
¼	pound butter, melted
¼	teaspoon celery salt
¼	teaspoon garlic salt
	ground red pepper to taste
	salt and white pepper to taste

Preheat oven to 200 degrees.

Toast nuts in oven for 20 minutes, stirring every 5 to 10 minutes. Pour butter over the nuts, toss thoroughly and sprinkle with celery salt, garlic salt and red pepper to taste. Toast 20 minutes longer, stirring occasionally. Drain on brown paper and season to taste with white pepper and salt.

Serve hot or at room temperature.

Tapenade

Serves 12

2	4½-ounce cans ripe olives, slivered
2	2-ounce cans anchovy fillets with oil
2	7-ounce cans solid pack tuna, drained
½	cup capers, drained
2	large garlic cloves, crushed
2	tablespoons Dijon mustard
1	teaspoon leaf thyme, crushed
	juice of 1 lemon
6	tablespoons minced parsley
6	tablespoons mayonnaise
	fresh ground pepper

In food processor with steel blade, finely chop first 5 ingredients. Add remaining ingredients, mix well and chill. May be molded and used as a spread, or stuffed in hollowed cherry tomato halves.

Caviar Pie

A beautiful, delicious party pleaser.
Serves 14 to 16

6	hard boiled eggs
1	8-ounce package cream cheese, softened
1	cup sour cream
1	medium onion, grated
1	dash Tabasco
1	large jar black caviar
	juice of 1 lemon
	Garnish: lemon, parsley, paprika
	crackers

Mash egg whites and yolks separately. Mix one-third of cream cheese and one-third of sour cream with egg whites and spread on the bottom of a clear glass bowl.

Mix egg yolks with one-third of the cream cheese and one-third of the sour cream and spread on top of first layer.

Mix remaining cream cheese, sour cream, Tabasco and grated onion for the third layer. Cover and chill until ready to serve.

Place caviar in a strainer and squeeze lemon juice over it. Drain on paper towels to remove all black liquid. Just before serving, spread caviar on top.

Garnish with lemon, parsley and paprika. Serve with crackers.

Layered Cheese Loaf

Your guests will think it took hours, but it's quick, easy and delicious!

Serves 10 to 12

1	stick butter
1	8-ounce package cream cheese
½	teaspoon grated onion
½	teaspoon horseradish
	garlic powder
	Tabasco to taste
1	6-ounce oblong package sliced natural Swiss cheese with holes
	paprika for top and sides of loaf

Mix at room temperature: butter, cream cheese, grated onion, horseradish, garlic powder and Tabasco to taste.

Cut Swiss cheese down the center lengthwise. On a large piece of aluminum foil, place one slice of Swiss cheese, spread with cream cheese, top with Swiss and continue alternating Swiss slices with cream cheese mixture. Spread front, sides and top with cream cheese mixture. Sprinkle with paprika.

Wrap loosely, but air-tight, and refrigerate overnight.

Will keep a week in the refrigerator or may be frozen. Serve with crackers.

Mushrooms Stuffed with Herbed Boursin Cheese

Yield: 2 dozen

1	pound medium-sized mushrooms
3	tablespoons lemon juice
1	cup water
1	package herbed Boursin cheese, softened
	fresh parsley sprigs for garnish

Remove mushroom stems and save for soups or sauces. Mix water and lemon juice and use to wash each cap. Dry immediately on paper towels.

Mash cheese and fill mushroom cavities, smoothing cheese flush with edges of mushroom caps. Decorate each with a sprig of parsley.

Boursin Cheese

Serves 8 to 10

8	ounces cream cheese
½	stick butter, not margarine
½	teaspoon Beau Monde seasoning
1	large garlic clove, minced
¼	teaspoon fines herbes, or pinch each of thyme, oregano, rosemary, marjoram, basil, dill and sage
1	teaspoon dried or fresh parsley
1	teaspoon water
1	teaspoon wine vinegar
¼	teaspoon Worcestershire sauce

Beat cream cheese and butter until fluffy, add remaining ingredients. Chill in a container, letting it mellow 12 hours.

Freezes well.

Cheese Ball

Serves 12 to 20

8	ounces cream cheese
5	ounces extra sharp Cheddar cheese
¾	pound blue cheese
1	clove garlic, minced
1	tablespoon Worcestershire sauce
⅛	teaspoon hot pepper sauce
1	teaspoon liquid smoke
½	cup chopped pecans
½	cup chopped parsley

Soften cheeses at room temperature. Mix all ingredients, except pecans and parsley, in a food processor. Form cheese mixture into a ball and chill. Roll ball in pecans and parsley before serving.

Freezes well.

Anchovy Butter

Yield: 1½ cups

4	hard cooked eggs
2	tubes anchovy paste OR 2 2-ounce cans anchovy fillets, well drained on paper towels and mashed
3¼	teaspoons lemon juice
½	cup softened butter
¼	teaspoon white pepper
¼	cup basic mayonnaise

Put eggs through ricer or chop fine in food processor. Mix lemon juice with anchovy paste. Beat butter until light and fluffy. Add anchovy-lemon mixture and beat well. Gradually add chopped eggs, mixing well. Stir in pepper and mayonnaise and beat until well blended.

To serve, mound on a serving plate, using knife to smooth sides and top. Chill overnight to blend flavors. Garnish top and sides with full blown rose buds of savory paprika butter and leaves made of green tinted butter.

Serve with small crackers or toast rounds.

Blue Cheese Butter

Yield: 3 cups

12	ounces blue cheese, crumbled
1½	cups butter
¼	teaspoon white pepper
	pistachio nuts, ground

Whip blue cheese until light and smooth. Whip butter until fluffy. Combine cheese and butter, blend well, and add pepper.

Line a 3-cup mold with cheesecloth. Press cheese mixture into mold, fold cheesecloth over top and refrigerate overnight.

Lift mold with cheesecloth, turn onto a serving dish, and sprinkle with pistachio nuts. Serve with crackers.

Savory Paprika Butter

½	cup softened butter
1	teaspoon paprika
1	teaspoon chablis

Cream butter until light and fluffy. Add paprika and chablis and blend well. Store tightly covered in refrigerator until ready to use. After forming rose atop anchovy butter, tint balance with green food coloring and pipe-on stems and leaves.

Blue Cheese Mousse

Delight your guests with this impressive cheese mousse!
Serves 8 to 10

2	tablespoons unflavored gelatin
¼	cup cold water
2	cups dairy sour cream
½	cup chopped green onions
1	.6-ounce package dry Italian salad dressing mix
½	cup blue cheese, crumbled
2	cups small curd cottage cheese
1	4-ounce can chopped black olives, drained
½	cup chopped cucumbers
⅓	cup chopped tomatoes

Oil a 9½-inch porcelain quiche dish or flan tin with indented bottom.

In a 1-quart saucepan, sprinkle gelatin over cold water, let stand 5 minutes to soften. Cook over moderate heat until gelatin is dissolved, stirring constantly.

In food processor with metal blade, combine dissolved gelatin, sour cream, green onions, salad dressing mix, blue cheese and cottage cheese until smooth. Pour mixture into prepared mold, cover with plastic wrap and refrigerate until firm.

Before serving, unmold onto platter by running knife tip around edge, dipping bottom of mold into warm water and inverting. Arrange olives, cucumbers and tomatoes in separate concentric circles on top of mold.

Baked Brie

A must for cheese lovers!
Serves 6

1	4½-ounce wheel of Brie cheese
6	teaspoons butter
6	tablespoons slivered almonds, lightly toasted
	sliced apples and strawberries

Preheat oven to 400 degrees.

Place brie in baking dish, top with butter and slivered almonds. Bake for about 5 minutes or until cheese is crusty on outside and runny on the inside.

Place baking dish on a large platter and garnish with sliced apples and strawberries. Serve with hot French bread rounds.

This cannot be frozen or made in advance.

Stuffed Mushrooms

Serves 15

2	pounds fresh mushrooms
½	stick butter
3	tablespoons finely chopped onion
1	pound raw shrimp, peeled, deveined and chopped or 1 pound crabmeat
¼	teaspoon cayenne pepper
½	cup Italian bread crumbs
¼	cup water
¼	cup grated Parmesan cheese

Wash mushrooms, remove stems and reserve. Steam caps 15 minutes.

Sauté onion in 1/2 stick butter for 5 minutes until clear. Add seafood, cook 5 minutes, then add pepper, bread crumbs and chopped mushroom stems. Add 1/4 cup water and cook 10 minutes.

Preheat oven to 350 degrees.

Cool mixture and stuff into mushroom caps, top with Parmesan cheese and bake 15 minutes.

Miniature Mushroom Pies

Yield: about 75

Dough:

8	ounces cream cheese
8	ounces butter, melted
2½	cups flour

Combine ingredients in food processor with on/off motion until mixture forms a ball. Wrap in plastic wrap and chill.

Filling:

3	tablespoons butter
1	cup chopped onions
½	pound fresh mushrooms, finely chopped
¼	teaspoon thyme
½	teaspoon salt
	dash of pepper
2	tablespoons flour
¼	cup sour cream

In a skillet, melt butter, add onions and brown lightly. Add mushrooms and cook about 3 minutes, stirring often. Add thyme, salt and pepper, sprinkle in flour. Stir in sour cream and cook slowly until thickened.

Roll out chilled dough on a cookie sheet until 1/4 inch thick. Cut in 2½-inch circles with a cookie cutter. Place 1/2 teaspoon of mixture on each dough circle, fold circle in half and press together with fork tines. Pierce tops with fork for steam to escape. Freeze.

Preheat oven to 350 degrees.

When ready to serve, place frozen on a cookie sheet and bake 25 to 30 minutes.

Miniature Quiches

Yield: about 50

Dough:

½	**cup butter**	
3	**ounces cream cheese**	
1	**cup flour**	

Blend ingredients together in food processor with on/off motion until a ball forms. Chill in plastic wrap until firm. Press chilled dough into mini muffin tins and chill again until ready to fill.

Filling:

1	**egg**	
½	**cup half and half**	
	dash of nutmeg	
	dash of cayenne pepper	
¼	**teaspoon seasoned salt**	
½	**cup grated Swiss cheese**	
½	**cup grated Cheddar cheese**	
1	**tablespoon shallots OR 2 green onions, white part only, chopped**	
5	**strips bacon, cooked and crumbled (optional)**	

Preheat oven to 350 degrees.

Beat egg, half and half, nutmeg, pepper and salt together and set aside. Blend cheeses, shallots or green onions and bacon and place small amount in each mini muffin tin. Pour blended liquids over cheese/onion mixture until tins are two-thirds full. Bake 25 minutes and cool before serving.

Baked quiches may be frozen until ready to serve.

Gougère (Cheese Puff)

Serves 6

½	**cup butter**	
1	**cup water**	
1	**cup flour**	
½	**teaspoon salt**	
4	**eggs**	
1	**cup plus 2 tablespoons shredded natural sharp cheese**	
1	**egg, beaten**	

Preheat oven to 375 degrees.

In a medium saucepan, combine butter and water, cook over moderate heat until mixture comes to a boil. Combine flour and salt and add all at once to pan. Cook over low heat, stirring constantly, until mixture leaves sides of pan and forms a ball. Remove from heat. Beat in 4 eggs, one at a time. Stir in 1 cup cheese and blend thoroughly. On a buttered cookie sheet drop cheese batter in heaping tablespoons in a circle (12 to 14 tablespoons). Brush with beaten egg and sprinkle with remaining cheese. Bake 40 minutes. Turn off oven and remove after 10 additional minutes. Break puffs apart rather than cutting them.

Recipe may be used to make 2 smaller rings. Reduce baking time to 30 minutes.

Alwyn Scott Turner (American, born 1936)
UNTITLED (OLYMPIA PARADE)
gelatin silver print
8½ x 11"
Collection of New Orleans Museum of Art.

Shrimp Toast

With these delicious frozen canapés,
you are always ready for unexpected guests!
Yield: 90 pieces

2	eggs
2	tablespoons melted butter
2	green onions cut in 1/2-inch lengths
2	teaspoons salt
1	teaspoon sugar
1½	pounds raw shrimp, shelled and deveined
4	water chestnuts, finely chopped
1	loaf thin-sliced day old bread
	vegetable oil

Process first 6 ingredients in blender or food processor, until paste is formed. Remove to a bowl and stir in chopped chestnuts.

Trim crust from bread. If it is very soft, dry in a warm oven until firm. Spread shrimp mixture on bread and cut each slice diagonally into quarters. *The sauce might be green before cooking, but the toast turns golden when cooked.*

In a medium skillet, heat 1 inch of oil to 400 degrees or until very hot. Fry 4 to 6 canapés, shrimp side down, until golden brown, turn and brown on other side. Remove with slotted spoon and drain on paper towels. Repeat until all are cooked. May be made in advance and frozen up to 8 weeks. To reheat, place frozen canapés on a cookie sheet and bake 15 to 20 minutes in a preheated 325 degree oven.

Jumbo Shrimp with Bacon

A delicious treat worth your effort!
Yield: 40 to 60 pieces

3	pounds large raw shrimp
1	pound bacon
2	eggs
¼	cup water
	salt and pepper
2	sticks butter or 1 cup oil

Dehead, peel and devein shrimp, leaving shell on tails.

Cut bacon in half and wrap around shrimp, secure with toothpick. Dip each shrimp in a mixture of beaten eggs, water, salt and pepper to taste. Fry in hot butter, turning once, or deep-fry in oil. Serve hot.

Be careful not to let butter burn with too hot a fire. Oriental rice (page 122) is suggested as an accompaniment for a main dish.

Hot Crab Dip

Serves 12

¼	stick butter, melted
4	green onions, chopped
1	8-ounce package cream cheese
1	pound lump crab meat
½	teaspoon horseradish
	juice of 1 lemon
1	tablespoon Worcestershire sauce
½	cup chopped almonds

Preheat oven to 350 degrees.

Cook chopped onions in melted butter for 5 minutes, uncovered, over low heat. In a casserole, mix onions and the remaining ingredients, except almonds. Sprinkle almonds on top and bake 20 to 30 minutes.

Tangy Crab Mold

Serves 8 to 10

2	8-ounce packages cream cheese, softened
2	tablespoons Worcestershire sauce
2	tablespoons fresh lemon juice
¼	cup chopped green onions
1	cup bottled chili sauce
1	pound fresh crab meat
¼	cup chopped parsley

Mix the first 4 ingredients and shape into a rectangle on a shallow glass dish. Cover the top of the cheese mixture with chili sauce. Spread crab meat on top of chili sauce and press down lightly. Sprinkle chopped parsley on top.

Serve with wheat crackers.

Marinated Shrimp

*Serves 4 as an entreé or
12 as an appetizer*

4	pounds cooked shrimp, peeled and deveined
1½	cups salad oil
½	cup white vinegar
4	tablespoons capers with juice
2	bay leaves
3	teaspoons celery seed
1	teaspoon dried dill
1½	teaspoons salt
½	teaspoon pepper
½	teaspoon Tabasco
	juice of 1 lemon
1	medium onion, sliced

Combine all ingredients, except shrimp. Pour over shrimp in a large glass or non-metal bowl. Cover and refrigerate 24 hours, spooning marinade over shrimp occasionally.

Marinated shrimp will keep at least 1 week in the refrigerator.

Salmon Ball

*A quick dish that will receive raves from all your guests.
Serves 8 to 10*

1	8-ounce package cream cheese
1	15-ounce can pink salmon
1	tablespoon liquid smoke
1	cup chopped pecans
2	tablespoons chopped parsley

Beat cream cheese until smooth, add mashed salmon, liquid smoke and nuts. Blend until all ingredients are well mixed. Form into a ball and refrigerate until firm. Remove from refrigerator and roll in chopped parsley.

Serve with crackers.

Shrimp Spread

*Something special for your next party.
Yield: 2 cups*

1	8-ounce package cream cheese at room temperature
1	pound cooked, peeled and deveined shrimp, finely chopped
¼	cup mayonnaise
2	tablespoons fresh lemon juice
1	teaspoon chopped parsley
½	teaspoon dried dill
½	teaspoon salt
	thinly sliced black bread
	crackers

In a mixing bowl, combine all ingredients, except bread and crackers, and beat until well blended. Transfer to a serving dish, cover and chill until ready to serve.

Spread on black bread or crackers.

Crawfish à la Rockefeller

A delicious change from Oysters Rockefeller.
Serves 8 as an appetizer, or 4 as an entreé

2	10-ounce packages frozen chopped spinach, uncooked
4	tablespoons butter
1	teaspoon celery seed
2	teaspoons Worcestershire sauce
½	teaspoon salt
1	cup chopped lettuce
¼	cup chopped green onions
1	small clove garlic, minced
¾	cup light cream
1	egg, beaten
4	dashes Tabasco
1	pound cooked and peeled crawfish tails

Topping:

¼	cup fine dry bread crumbs
¼	cup grated Parmesan cheese
2	tablespoons butter

Preheat oven to 375 degrees.

Thaw and drain spinach thoroughly, purée and set aside.

In a medium saucepan combine butter, celery seed, Worcestershire and salt. Stir in lettuce, green onion and garlic. Cover pan and simmer 2 to 3 minutes. Add spinach, cream, egg and Tabasco. Cook and stir until mixture begins to bubble.

Divide 1/2 pound of the crawfish tails equally among 8 individual ramekins, or place in a 2½-quart casserole. Add hot spinach mixture and top with remaining crawfish tails. Combine breadcrumbs with grated cheese and sprinkle over mixture. Dot with butter and bake for 15 minutes, or just until hot.

Crawfish Cardinale

A delicious first course.
Serves 8

5	tablespoons butter
½	cup chopped green pepper
½	cup chopped onions
2	tablespoons flour
1	cup light cream
½	cup tomato ketchup
2	teaspoons lemon juice
1	pound cooked and peeled crawfish tails*
1½	teaspoons salt
¼	teaspoon pepper
¼	teaspoon mace
¾	cup dry sherry
	paprika for garnish

Preheat oven to 350 degrees.

Heat 3 tablespoons butter in a skillet and sauté green pepper and onions for 5 minutes.

In a saucepan combine flour, remaining butter, cream , ketchup and lemon juice. Heat, stirring constantly, until mixture is smooth and slightly thickened. Combine contents of both pans, add crawfish, salt, pepper, mace and sherry, stirring to thoroughly mix ingredients. Divide mixture into 8 ramekins and bake approximately 12 to 15 minutes, until warm. Garnish with lemon slices and top with a sprinkle of paprika.

Dish may be prepared 1 day in advance, refrigerated and baked prior to serving for 15 to 20 minutes, until bubbly.

*1 pound cooked, peeled and deveined shrimp may be substituted for crawfish tails.

Spinach Balls with Mustard Sauce

Yield: 100 bite-size pieces

2	10-ounce packages frozen chopped spinach
2	cups herb stuffing mix, crushed
1	cup firmly packed freshly grated Parmesan cheese, 5-ounce wedge
1½	sticks butter, melted
4	small green onions, finely chopped
3	eggs
1	teaspoon garlic salt
½	teaspoon thyme
	dash freshly grated nutmeg

Thaw and squeeze spinach dry, or cook it slightly and drain well. Combine all ingredients in a large bowl and mix thoroughly. Shape into individual bite-size balls. Cover and refrigerate, or freeze until ready to bake. *To prepare in a food processor, place green onions, eggs, garlic salt, thyme and nutmeg in container, pulse briefly, then add other ingredients in order listed.*

Preheat oven to 350 degrees.

Place spinach balls on a greased baking sheet and bake until golden brown, about 10 to 15 minutes. Serve with Mustard sauce dip.

Mustard Sauce:

½	cup dry mustard
½	cup white vinegar
¼	cup sugar
1	egg yolk

Combine mustard and vinegar in a small bowl. Cover and let stand at room temperature for 4 hours.

Mix sugar and egg yolk in a small saucepan. Add mustard-vinegar mixture and cook over low heat, stirring constantly until slightly thickened. Cover and chill.

Remove from refrigerator and serve at room temperature as a dip for spinach balls.

Egg Rolls

Yield: 52

2	16-ounce cans bean sprouts
4	cups cooked chicken or lean pork, shredded
3	cups cooked shrimp, finely diced
2	tablespoons peanut butter
2	10-ounce cans water chestnuts, drained and finely chopped
4	teaspoons peanut oil
8	teaspoons sesame seeds, browned in hot skillet
8	teaspoons soy sauce
2	cups finely chopped green onions
2	packages noodle dough*
	peanut oil for deep-frying

Combine all ingredients, except dough and peanut oil. Place a teaspoon of mixture on each noodle dough wrapper. Fold in each end and roll up. Can be frozen at this stage.

Deep fry in peanut oil heated to 350 degrees, until golden brown.

*Noodle dough square may be purchased at Oriental or Gourmet shops.

Kreatopeta

Traditional Greek miniatures.
Yield: about 40

Filling #1

1	cup minced fresh mushrooms
1½	cups minced green onions
1½	cups minced onions
1½	cups minced ham
5	cloves garlic, pressed
1	cup butter
6	tablespoons flour
	black and cayenne pepper to taste
1	cup beef stock
½	cup claret
	salt to taste
2	eggs, beaten
1	package phyllo pastry sheets
1	pound butter, melted

Lightly sauté mushrooms, green onions, onions, ham and garlic in butter until soft. Stir in flour, pepper and cayenne. Brown lightly for 10 minutes, stirring constantly. Blend in stock, claret and salt to taste. Cover and simmer 15 minutes over low heat, stirring occasionally. Remove from heat and stir in eggs. Refrigerate until ready to use. Mixture may be made several days ahead.

Phyllo Pillows:

Preheat oven to 350 degrees.

If phyllo dough is frozen, defrost in its package overnight in the refrigerator. Cut phyllo into 3-inch wide strips. Take 1 strip out at a time, keep the others covered with a damp cloth. Brush on butter. Place a scant teaspoon of filling on one end, fold dough over filling to make a triangular pillow and continue folding to end of strip. Brush again with butter. Continue forming triangles until all the dough and filling are used. Bake about 20 minutes, until puffed and very light golden brown. May be frozen before baking. If frozen, do not thaw, add 5 minutes to baking time.

Spanakopetes:

Filling #2

8	ounces frozen chopped spinach, defrosted and well drained
8	ounces feta cheese, crumbled
8	ounces cream cheese, softened
1	egg, well beaten
1	onion, finely chopped
1	tablespoon dill
1	stick unsalted butter, melted
½	package phyllo pastry sheets
	dash of pepper

Combine first six ingredients. Refrigerate at least 1 hour or overnight. Follow instructions above for making phyllo pillows.

Oysters Rockefeller

A famous New Orleans Specialty!
Serves 6

Sauce:

4	tablespoons oil
1	very large onion, chopped
2	ribs celery with leaves, chopped
5	cloves garlic, chopped
4	tablespoons chopped fresh parsley, OR 2 tablespoons dried parsley
1	small green pepper, chopped
6	drops Tabasco
4	tablespoons Herbsaint liqueur
	salt and pepper to taste
	bread crumbs to thicken
5	boxes chopped frozen spinach, cooked and well drained
3	dozen oysters and their shells which have been well scrubbed
	Parmesan cheese

In a large skillet, sauté vegetables in hot oil until very soft. Remove excess oil, add Tabasco, Herbsaint, salt and pepper. Add a few bread crumbs to thicken, then add cooked spinach.

Preheat broiler.

Cook oysters in a small pan until edges curl; drain. Place an oyster in each shell and top with Rockefeller sauce. Place oyster shells over rock salt in pie pans, sprinkle with Parmesan cheese and run under broiler until brown.

This may also be served from a glass baking dish. Place oysters in a single layer in an oven proof dish, top with spinach sauce and Parmesan cheese and bake in a 350 degree oven 15 to 20 minutes.

Oysters Albert

Serves 4

1	stick butter
1	bunch green onions, chopped
3	tablespoons chopped parsley
3	cloves garlic, chopped
	pinch of rosemary
3	dozen oysters, drained
¼	cup strained oyster water
¼	cup Italian bread crumbs
2	tablespoons Worcestershire sauce
¼	cup dry white wine

Preheat oven to 350 degrees.

In a skillet, melt butter and sauté onions, parsley, garlic and rosemary for 10 minutes. Add oysters and oyster water and cook 2 minutes. Stir in bread crumbs, Worcestershire and wine, mixing well. Divide mixture into ramekins and bake for 10 minutes.

Recipe may be made a day in advance.

Mixture may be served hot from a chafing dish with toast points as an appetizer.

Escargots en Casserole

Serves 6

36	canned snails
½	stick butter
1	tablespoon chopped garlic
1	green onion, chopped
2	tablespoons diced bacon
1	teaspoon flour
1	cup white wine
1	tomato, diced
	salt and pepper to taste

Sauté snails in butter 5 minutes, add garlic, green onion and bacon. Sprinkle with flour, add white wine, tomato, salt and pepper, mix well and cook an additional 5 minutes. Serve in small ramekins.

Clarence John Laughlin (American, 1905-1985)
THE ENIGMA (Windsor Plantation)
gelatin silver print
43.1 x 35.6"
Collection of New Orleans Museum of Art.
©Historic New Orleans Collection

Liver Pâté Supreme

A wonderful pâté to serve with cocktails!
Serves 20

½   **pound butter**
1   **medium apple, peeled, cored and chopped**
1   **medium onion, chopped**
1   **pound chicken livers, cleaned**
¼   **cup apple brandy**
2   **tablespoons whipping cream**
1   **tablespoon lemon juice**
     salt and pepper to taste
1   **cup chopped pecans**

In a skillet melt 2 tablespoons butter and sauté apple and onion until clear. Add chicken livers, stir lightly, add brandy and flame. When flame dies, remove from pan and cool.

Place chicken liver mixture in food processor with cream, lemon juice, salt and pepper to taste. Add pecans and blend. Place ingredients in a bowl and cool to room temperature. Soften remaining butter and blend into mixture. Spoon into a crock, cover and refrigerate.

If kept more than one day before serving, clarify 2 tablespoons butter (page 211) and seal top of mixture.

Almond Mushroom Pâté

An unusual, different pâté.
Serves 8 to 10

½   **small onion, quartered**
1   **small clove garlic**
½   **pound fresh mushrooms, halved**
2   **tablespoons butter**
¼   **teaspoon salt**
¼   **teaspoon tarragon, crushed**
     dash of white pepper, or to taste
1   **10-ounce package blanched whole almonds, toasted**
2   **tablespoons dry sherry**
1   **tablespoon whipping cream**

In a food processor with metal blade, process onion and garlic with on/off bursts until coarsely chopped; set aside. Coarsely chop mushrooms in the same manner.

Melt butter in a skillet, add onion, garlic, mushrooms, salt, tarragon and pepper. Cook, stirring occasionally, until most of the liquid has evaporated.

Reserve 2/3 cup whole almonds for garnish. Process remaining almonds until coarsely chopped, reserve 2 tablespoons. Continue processing remaining almonds to form a paste. Add mushroom mixture, sherry and cream, processing until smooth. Add reserved 2 tablespoons chopped almonds, process with on/off burst. Cover and chill.

Mound pâté on serving plate, garnish with whole almonds.

Steak Diane

So tasty it will disappear fast!
Yield: 50 hors d'oeuvres

5	pound beef tenderloin or rib eye
2	sticks butter
¾	cup finely chopped chives
2	tablespoons chopped parsley
	salt and pepper to taste
1	cup finely chopped shallots
1	pound fresh mushrooms, sliced
1	cup cognac or brandy
1	cup sherry
9	tablespoons Worcestershire sauce

Remove all membrane and fat from beef. Slice thinly, flatten with a mallet and cut into 1/2 inch strips.

Cream 2/3 cup butter with chives, parsley, salt and pepper. Set aside.

Melt 1/3 cup butter. Sauté shallots and mushrooms until softened, but not browned. Remove from pan. Increase heat and sauté beef strips quickly, just enough to sear on each side. Remove from pan and keep warm. After all beef is seared, flame pan with cognac or brandy. Reduce heat, add seasoned butter, sherry and Worcestershire sauce. Return beef and shallot/ mushroom mixture to pan.

Serve in hollowed out loaf of bread, or chafing dish. May also be served over rice as a main course.

Dill Dip in Rye Loaf

Quick, easy and a great party starter!
Serves 15 to 20

1½	cups mayonnaise
1⅓	cups sour cream
3	tablespoons finely chopped green onions
2	tablespoons fresh parsley
2	heaping teaspoons dill weed
2	teaspoons garlic salt or seasoned salt
	several shakes Beau Monde seasoning
1	round loaf rye bread, unsliced

Mix together and blend well the first seven ingredients. Prepare dip a day ahead and refrigerate.

Slice the top off the loaf and put aside. Pull bread from inside the loaf and tear it into bite-sized pieces. Fill the inside with dill dip. Place filled loaf on a platter surrounded by bread pieces, raw vegetables and/or chips.

Sliced top can be used as a decoration by leaning against loaf, and can be cut up later if additional bread is needed for dipping.

Curried Broccoli Dip

Serves 6 to 8

1	bunch broccoli-flowerets only
¼	cup sour cream
2	tablespoons Parmesan cheese
2	tablespoons lemon juice
1	teaspoon minced onions
¼	teaspoon curry powder

Cook flowerets in boiling salted water until tender. Drain. Place broccoli and remaining ingredients in food processor and blend until smooth. Chill.

Serve with fresh vegetables or crackers.

Cheese and Green Chili Crustless Quiche

Serves 15 to 20

1	pound Monterey Jack cheese, grated
1	pound sharp Cheddar cheese, grated
6	eggs, lightly beaten
	cayenne pepper to taste
1	5-ounce can evaporated milk
2	4-ounce cans whole green chilis

Preheat oven to 350 degrees.

Combine cheeses, eggs, cayenne and milk. Line a 9 x 13-inch pyrex dish with chilis and cover with cheese mixture. Bake 40 minutes. Cool and cut into bite-sized squares.

May be frozen and reheated.

Jellied Seafood

Serves 6

1	envelope unflavored gelatin
¼	cup cold water
2	egg yolks, slightly beaten
1	teaspoon salt
1	teaspoon Creole mustard
¼	teaspoon paprika
1 ½	tablespoons butter, melted
¾	cup milk
2 ½	tablespoons fresh lemon juice
2	cups canned seafood (tuna, salmon or crabmeat)
¼	cup chopped pimiento olives
	watercress for decoration

Prepare a 9-inch pie plate by rinsing it in cold water and chilling in the refrigerator.

Sprinkle gelatin over cold water to soften.

Mix egg yolks with salt, mustard and paprika. Add butter, milk and lemon juice. Cook over boiling water in a double boiler, stirring constantly until mixture thickens. Add softened gelatin to hot mixture and stir until dissolved.

Drain seafood of your choice, remove skin, bones or shells and separate into flakes. Stir olives and seafood into gelatin mixture.

Line chilled pie plate with wax paper and spoon gelled mixture into it. Refrigerate 4 hours or more. Unmold and decorate with watercress.

Joan Miró (Spanish, 1893-1983)
PORTRAIT OF A YOUNG GIRL *1935*
oil with sand on cardboard
Bequest of Victor K. Kiam

II. Lunch In The Artist's Palate

Okra Seafood Gumbo

Classic New Orleans dish!
Serves 10 to 12

Stock:

4	**quarts water**
	heads and shells of 3 pounds raw shrimp
1	**carrot**
½	**cup celery**
1	**quartered onion**
1	**tablespoon liquid crab boil**

Fill a 6-quart stock pot with 4 quarts of water, shrimp heads and shells, carrot, celery, onion and crab boil. Simmer for 1½ hours. Strain stock and reserve liquid.

Gumbo:

4	**pounds fresh okra**
6	**gumbo crabs***
1	**cup plus 2 tablespoons bacon drippings**
1½	**cups chopped onions**
1	**cup chopped green onions**
3	**cloves garlic, finely chopped**
1	**28-ounce can peeled tomatoes, reserve liquid**
3	**tablespoons flour**
1	**cup cubed ham**
1	**tablespoon Worcestershire sauce**
2	**bay leaves**
½	**teaspoon thyme**
½ to 1	**tablespoon crushed red pepper**
3	**quarts or more of shrimp stock**
3	**pounds raw shrimp, peeled and deveined**
3	**tablespoons chopped parsley**
	salt and pepper to taste
	Tabasco to taste
1	**pound fresh claw or white crabmeat**
2	**cups cooked rice**

Wash and remove both ends from okra; cut into 1/2 to 3/4 inch slices and let dry.

Salt and pepper hard crab halves. In a large pot, heat 3/4 cup of bacon drippings. Add crab halves, stir until golden brown, then remove them from pot.

In a large skillet, sauté onions and garlic in 1/4 cup drippings until soft. Put okra in pot, cook over medium heat, stirring constantly, about 45 minutes, until okra is soft and ropy texture is gone. More bacon grease may be added if okra sticks.

Drain and chop tomatoes, reserving liquid. In a separate skillet make a roux by cooking 2 tablespoons of bacon drippings with 3 tablespoons of flour until brown, stirring frequently. When flour is brown, add the sautéed vegetables, ham, and chopped tomatoes; cook until tomatoes are lightly browned. Transfer to a large stock pot. Add tomato liquid, Worcestershire sauce, bay leaves, thyme, red pepper, okra, crab halves and 3 quarts of stock. Stir until heated. Cover and cook on low heat for 1 hour. Add more stock to produce desired consistency. Check seasoning, add salt, pepper and Tabasco to taste. Add raw shrimp to gumbo and cook an additional 15 to 20 minutes. Remove bay leaf. Gumbo can be frozen at this stage.

Before serving gumbo, heat crabmeat in a saucepan in a small amount of gumbo liquid. In individual soup bowls, place rice, warm crabmeat and fill with heated gumbo. If serving from a soup tureen, crabmeat can be added directly to the gumbo. Rice may be served from a separate bowl.

*Gumbo crabs can be purchased at most seafood markets in the New Orleans area. These are hard crabs, usually small to medium size, which have been put into boiling water for only a minute or two. Then the back shells and gills are removed, middles cleaned and the crabs broken in half, leaving the legs and claws attached. Crabs that have been fully boiled, and not left partially raw as described here, will not impart the flavor that "gumbo" crabs will.

Shrimp Corn Soup

Serves 12 to 16

¼ cup flour

¼ cup shortening or vegetable oil

2 dozen ears of corn, cooked and kernels scraped from ears (OR 2 cans whole kernel corn and 1 can cream style corn)

2 pounds raw shrimp, peeled and deveined

1 cup diced tomatoes

½ cup chopped onions

½ cup chopped shallots

½ cup chopped celery

3 quarts hot water (more if you like a thin soup)

sprig of parsley, chopped

salt and pepper to taste

Make a roux with flour and shortening. When roux is golden brown, add corn, shrimp, tomatoes, onions, shallots and celery and cook over medium heat, stirring often, until wilted. Add hot water, parsley and simmer for about 45 minutes or longer on a low fire. Add salt and pepper to taste.

Vichyssoise

Serves 6

3 cups boiling water

1½ cups chopped onions

3 cups peeled, cubed potatoes

4 chicken bouillon cubes

1 cup milk

3 tablespoons butter

1 cup whipping cream

½ teaspoon salt

½ teaspoon white pepper

Add onions, potatoes and bouillon cubes to boiling water and cook until potatoes are tender. Cool. Pour into a blender container, add remaining ingredients and purée. Chill before serving.

Oyster Okra Filé Gumbo

Serves 10 to 12

3 tablespoons bacon fat

3 tablespoons flour

4 cups chopped okra

3 quarts rich homemade turkey or chicken stock

3 tablespoons butter

1 medium yellow onion, chopped

1½ cups chopped celery

¼ cup chopped hot red peppers

2 cloves garlic, minced

salt to taste

cayenne pepper to taste

2 pints oysters with their liquor

2 tablespoons filé powder

Make a roux in a heavy pot by stirring together the bacon fat and flour. Cook the roux for about 15 minutes, stirring frequently, until it is caramel-colored. Do not let it burn.

Add the okra and cook over medium heat until it is no longer stringy, about 45 minutes. Stir occasionally, adding a little stock if the mixture seems too dry.

In a separate pan, melt the butter and sauté the onion, celery, red pepper and garlic together until they are tender-crisp. Add to the roux mixture.

Heat the stock and slowly stir it into the vegetable mixture. Simmer for 15 minutes. Add salt and cayenne pepper to taste. Add oysters and their liquor. Simmer for 10 minutes or until edges of the oysters curl. Ladle into a tureen or individual bowls and sprinkle filé just before serving. Do *not* add filé to boiling liquid. Serve with lemon rice or plain cooked rice.

Note: Filé is always added after cooking to avoid gumminess.

Curried Apple Soup

An elegant soup for a very special occasion.
Serves 4 to 6

3   medium apples, unpeeled
1   tablespoon curry powder
1   pint half and half
1½ cups clear chicken stock
1   ounce apple brandy
1   apple, thinly sliced

Blend 3 apples, curry powder, half and half and chicken stock in blender or food processor. Put in a sauce pan and heat to boiling point. When cool, add apple brandy and refrigerate. When ready to serve, float apple slices on top of each serving. Can be served warm or cold.

Arty Cheese Tureen

Serves 10 to 12

2   packages frozen chopped spinach
1   stick butter
1   bunch green onions, chopped
3   cans mushroom soup, undiluted
2   8-ounce bottles clam juice
2   cups water
1   can artichokes, drained and chopped, liquid reserved
2   tablespoons Worcestershire sauce
3   tablespoons sherry
    salt to taste
    Tabasco to taste
12 slices American cheese

Cook spinach according to package directions, retaining liquid. Sauté green onions in butter. Add soup, clam juice, water and artichoke liquid, heat and stir until smooth. Add cooked spinach with liquid, stir and blend in thoroughly. Add chopped artichokes, Worcestershire sauce, sherry, salt to taste and Tabasco. Water may be added if mixture is too thick. Add cheese slices and cook until cheese is melted.

Easy to make. May be made 1 or 2 days in advance. Freezes well.

Duck and Sausage Gumbo

Serves 6 to 8

1   pound smoked sausage, cut in half inch rounds
    vegetable oil
4   Mallard ducks, skinned and deboned*
    Creole seasoning to taste
½   cup vegetable oil
½   cup flour
1   cup chopped onions
½   cup chopped green onions
1   cup chopped celery
1   cup chopped green pepper
¼   cup chopped parsley
3   quarts warm water
2   teaspoons salt
    Tabasco to taste
1½ teaspoons red pepper
1½ cups cooked rice

Fry sausage to render all fat, drain. There should be 1/2 cup fat in the skillet; if not, add oil to make 1/2 cup. Dry ducks well and rub with Creole seasoning. Dip each duck in flour to coat and shake off any excess. Brown ducks in hot fat and drain well.

In a heavy skillet heat 1/2 cup oil, add flour, stirring to blend. Cook the roux slowly over low heat stirring until it is a golden brown. Add onions, green onions, celery and cook until vegetables are soft. Add green pepper, parsley, warm water and bring to a boil. Add sausage, duck, salt, Tabasco and red pepper. When mixture returns to a boil, reduce heat and simmer for 2 hours. Serve over rice.

Bones should be left in for a wilder taste. Most men prefer this.

Soupe au Pistou

For a really different good soup, try this!
Serves 12

Pistou: Prepare ahead.

5	**cloves garlic, finely chopped**
½	**cup fresh basil, cut fine, OR 5 tablespoons dried basil**
2	**tablespoons tomato paste**
½	**cup grated Parmesan cheese**
6	**tablespoons olive oil**

With a large mortar and pestle, or back of a wooden spoon, pound garlic cloves and basil, working in tomato paste and Parmesan cheese. Beat in olive oil, one tablespoon at a time. Reserve while preparing stock.

Stock:

3	**cups water**
¾	**cup white beans**
¼	**cup olive or vegetable oil**
1	**cup diced onions**
1	**pound peeled tomatoes, seeded and coarsely chopped; or a 16-ounce can tomatoes**
3	**quarts water**
1½	**cups diced carrots**
1½	**cups diced boiling potatoes**
1	**cup coarsely chopped leeks**
1	**teaspoon salt**
½	**teaspoon pepper**
½	**cup coarsely chopped celery leaves**
1½	**cups fresh green beans cut in 2 inch pieces**
½	**cup uncooked vermicelli**
2	**threads or 1/2 teaspoon saffron**
1½	**cups unpeeled zucchini cut into 1/2-inch cubes**
	Pistou, recipe above

Bring water to a boil and drop in white beans. Boil 2 minutes, remove from heat and let stand 1 hour. Return to heat and simmer uncovered until beans are tender. Drain, reserving liquid.

In a heavy saucepan heat oil, stir in onions and cook over moderate heat until tender and golden. Add tomatoes and cook 3 to 4 minutes longer. Pour in 3 quarts water and bring to a boil over high heat. Add carrots, potatoes, leeks, salt and pepper. Stir in white beans with their liquid, celery leaves, green beans, vermicelli broken into 2 inch pieces and saffron. When all vegetables are tender, adjust seasonings and add zucchini, cooking just until tender.

When ready to serve, thin pistou with 1/2 cup soup stock and stir into soup. Pass additional grated Parmesan·cheese with soup.

Cream of Carrot Soup with Fresh Mint

A refreshing, cooling summer soup.
Serves 8

1	pound pared and sliced carrots
4½	cups chicken stock
¼	teaspoon salt
	dash white pepper
2	tablespoons butter
1	cup chopped onions
1½	teaspoons curry powder
1½	cups plain yogurt
1	pared coarsely grated carrot
	fresh mint sprigs

In a large saucepan combine sliced carrots, chicken stock, salt and pepper. Bring to a boil and reduce heat. Simmer 10 minutes or until carrots are fork tender.

In a skillet heat butter, sauté onions and add curry powder, stirring occasionally until onions are tender, about 5 minutes. In a processor or blender purée half of the cooked carrot mixture at a time, until smooth. Add onion mixture, yogurt and mix until smooth. Pour into a serving bowl and refrigerate until well chilled. Before serving mix well and sprinkle with grated carrot. Garnish with mint sprigs.

Cauliflower Soup

Serves 8

1	large cauliflower, water to cover
2	leeks, chopped
4	tablespoons butter
3	tablespoons flour
1	pint light cream
1	cup cauliflower liquid
4	cups chicken broth
	salt and white pepper to taste
1	cup chopped water cress
¼	cup sherry

Chop cauliflower and boil in water to cover until tender. Drain and reserve liquid. Purée cauliflower in blender and set aside.

In a large saucepan sauté leeks in 4 tablespoons butter until clear. Add flour and stir. Add cream, cauliflower liquid and cook over low heat 3 minutes, making a thick cream sauce. Add chicken broth, salt, white pepper, chopped water cress and cauliflower. Purée about 1 cup of the mixture at a time in a blender or food processor with steel blade. Return to the saucepan and add sherry. Serve hot.

Cream of Squash Soup

Serves 12

1   stick butter
2   cups chopped onions
1   clove garlic
1   cup carrots, scraped and sliced
2   cups sliced potatoes
2   cups sliced yellow squash
4   cups chicken stock
1   cup heavy cream
     salt and cayenne pepper to taste
     paprika

Sauté onions and garlic in butter until translucent. Add carrots, potatoes, squash, chicken stock and cook until vegetables are tender, about 45 minutes. Remove from heat. When cool enough to handle, purée in food processor or blender, about 1 cup at a time. Return to pot, add cream and heat thoroughly. Add salt and cayenne pepper if desired.

At serving time, sprinkle each bowl with paprika. Can be served hot or cold.

Fresh Mushroom Soup

Serves 8

¾   cup butter
15   green onions, chopped fine
½   cup flour
7   cups chicken stock
1½   pounds fresh mushrooms, washed, trimmed and sliced
1   cup half and half
     salt and white pepper to taste

In a 3-quart pot, sauté onions in butter for about 3 minutes. Add flour and cook for 10 minutes, stirring constantly. Slowly add heated chicken stock and bring to a boil. Stir in mushrooms, reserving some for garnish, and cook 10 more minutes. Put through a blender or food processor until smooth. Return to stove and stir in half and half. Season to taste with salt and pepper. Heat, but do not boil. Garnish each serving with reserved mushroom slices.

Season with a dash of lemon and hot pepper sauce, if desired.

Cream of Lettuce Soup

An excellent soup hot or cold.
Serves 6

2   pounds romaine lettuce
¾   cup fresh or frozen green peas
3   tablespoons butter
½   cup chopped onion
4   tablespoons flour
1   quart heated chicken stock, preferably homemade
     salt and pepper to taste
     generous pinch chervil
½ to ¾ cup whipping cream
½   cup sour cream for topping

Wash, trim, chop and blanch lettuce in salted water until wilted, saving a little lettuce for garnish. Add peas to blanching lettuce for a few minutes, drain.

Melt butter and sauté onions until soft. Add lettuce/pea mixture, then add flour and blend well. Stir in chicken stock and cool for 10 to 15 minutes. Taste to correct seasoning.

Put mixture in a blender and process to desired texture. Add chervil and stir in whipping cream. Serve hot or cold with a dollop of sour cream, or a bit of reserved lettuce.

Tomato and Cheese Soup

Serves 12

3	tablespoons butter
1	cup chopped onions
1	clove garlic, chopped
2	green onions, chopped
2	tablespoons flour
	salt to taste
2	pounds fresh tomatoes peeled, seeded, chopped OR a 29-ounce can Italian plum tomatoes with basil, drained and chopped
	Bouquet garni*
½	cup dry white wine
7	cups chicken stock
	freshly ground pepper

Garnish:

½	cup Gruyère cheese, cut in small pieces
	coarsely cracked pepper

Heat butter in a soup pot, add onion, garlic, green onion and sauté over medium heat until translucent. Add flour and cook for 5 minutes. Salt very lightly, add tomatoes, toss well and cook an additional 5 minutes. Add the bouquet garni, white wine, stock, and bring to a boil. Add juice drained from tomatoes and a dash of pepper and bring to a second boil. Lower heat to a simmer and cook until tasty, about 45 minutes. Remove bouquet garni. Ladle soup into bowls and to each bowl add 1 teaspoon of Gruyère and coarsely cracked pepper to taste. Serve piping hot.

*Make a bouquet garni with 10 parsley stems, 1 bay leaf and 2 sprigs fresh thyme wrapped into one another and tied with a string. If fresh thyme is not available, add 1/4 teaspoon dried thyme.

Leek Soup

This soup has a delicious, velvety flavor!
Serves 4 to 6

1	bunch leeks
1	quart chicken stock
½	onion, diced
½	stick butter
¼	cup flour
1	bay leaf
1	whole clove
⅛	teaspoon thyme
	salt and pepper to taste
1	cup half and half

Wash leeks thoroughly, separate green parts from white. Combine the green parts with chicken stock and simmer 1/2 hour in a large pot. Remove greens, reserving liquid. Slice the white part of the leeks about 1/8 inch thick.

In medium saucepan, over low heat, sauté white leeks and onion in butter. Add flour and blend for 2 minutes. Add 1 cup hot stock and stir until smooth. In a large pot add remaining chicken stock, vegetable sauce mixture, bay leaf, clove, thyme and simmer 1½ hours. Add salt and pepper to taste, then stir in half and half. Remove bay leaf and clove, serve at once.

May be made a day in advance. Freezes well.

Cream of Zucchini Soup

Serves 4

1	pound tender young zucchini
2	tablespoons butter
2	tablespoons finely chopped shallots or green onions
1	clove garlic, minced
½	teaspoon salt
½	cup half and half
2	cups chicken stock
¼	teaspoon dry mustard
⅛	teaspoon nutmeg
2	teaspoons curry powder (optional)

Scrub and slice zucchini very thin or slice in a food processor.

Melt butter in a medium-size saucepan, add shallots, garlic and zucchini. Cover tightly and simmer 1/2 hour, but do not let mixture brown.

Spoon zucchini mixture into a blender or food mill, then add salt, half and half and stock. Add mustard, nutmeg and curry powder, stirring lightly to blend.

Serve hot with croutons, or cold with chopped chives.

Oyster Soup

A very simple old fashioned Southern oyster soup.
Serves 8 to 10

¼	cup all purpose flour
¼	cup water
4	teaspoons salt
4	teaspoons Worcestershire sauce
3	dozen oysters with their liquid
¼	cup chopped green onions
8	cups half and half
3	tablespoons butter
2	tablespoons chopped fresh parsley

In a 4-quart saucepan combine flour, water, salt and Worcestershire sauce. Add oysters, liquid and green onions. Cook over medium heat 10 minutes, or just until oysters curl, stirring constantly. Add half and half and butter. Heat, but do not boil. Garnish with parsley and serve.

Oyster Artichoke Soup

Serves 8 to 10

1	stick butter
2	tablespoons olive oil
½	cup flour
1	chopped carrot
1	cup chopped onions
1	cup chopped celery
1	cup chopped green onions
4	cups chicken stock
2	tablespoons butter
1	cup sliced fresh mushrooms
1	can artichokes, drained, chopped and liquid reserved
2	cups milk
2	dozen oysters
2	egg yolks

In a saucepan melt the stick of butter, add olive oil, stir in flour and cook until smooth. Add carrot, onions, celery, green onions and cook until vegetables are tender. Place mixture in a food processor, add 1 cup chicken stock and purée until smooth.

Sauté mushrooms in 2 tablespoons butter until tender. Add them with artichoke hearts and their liquid to vegetable mixture. Stir in milk and remaining chicken stock, cook on low heat 5 minutes. (Soup may be prepared a day ahead to this point.) Add oysters and cook 10 minutes over low heat.

In a small bowl, combine egg yolks with 1/2 cup hot soup and stir rapidly into soup. Cook over low heat 5 minutes. If soup seems too thick, additional stock may be added.

Oysters Rockefeller Soup

A deliciously unique soup.
Serves 6

1	10-ounce box frozen chopped spinach, thawed
½	cup coarsely chopped onion
2	stalks celery with leaves, coarsely chopped
¼	cup chopped parsley
2	green onions, coarsely chopped
½	cup coarsely chopped iceberg lettuce
4	tablespoons butter
2	tablespoons anchovy paste (1 tube)
1	teaspoon seasoned salt
½	teaspoon pepper
	juice of 1/2 lemon
3	tablespoons flour
3	dozen small oysters, reserve liquid
1¼	cups chicken stock OR 1 can chicken broth, undiluted
2	teaspoons Worcestershire sauce
2	cups half and half
2	tablespoons grated Parmesan cheese
2	tablespoons Italian seasoned bread crumbs
1	tablespoon Herbsaint bitters

Squeeze spinach dry and purée it along with onion, celery, parsley, green onions and lettuce, in a food processor fitted with the steel blade.

Melt butter in a 3-quart pot, add puréed vegetables and sauté 8 minutes over medium heat, stirring frequently. Stir in anchovy paste, salt, pepper and lemon juice, blend in flour. Stir in oysters and 1/2 cup of their liquid, or more if needed. Simmer 3 minutes and gradually add chicken stock and Worcestershire sauce. Bring to a boil, lower heat and simmer 2 minutes. Add half and half, Parmesan cheese, seasoned bread crumbs and heat to serve. Just before serving add 1 tablespoon Herbsaint.

Creole Bouillabaisse

Serves 6

2	tablespoons margarine or butter
2	tablespoons olive oil
¼	cup flour
2	cups chopped onions
½	cup chopped celery
2	cloves garlic, minced
6	cups fish stock (page 206)
1	28-ounce can tomatoes, undrained and cut up
½	cup dry white wine
2	tablespoons chopped parsley
1	tablespoon lemon juice
2	bay leaves
	salt and cayenne pepper to taste
¼	teaspoon saffron (optional)
2	pounds fresh fish fillets, cut into 1½-inch chunks
½	pound fresh raw shrimp, peeled and deveined
½	pint fresh oysters

In a large soup pot over medium heat, melt margarine and add olive oil. Prepare roux by slowly blending in flour, stirring constantly, until mixture is light brown. Add onions, celery, garlic and continue stirring until vegetables are tender. Gradually stir in fish stock. Add tomatoes, wine, parsley, lemon juice, bay leaves, salt, pepper and saffron. Bring to a boil and simmer 30 minutes. Add fish and shrimp, simmer 15 minutes more. Add oysters and cook 5 minutes more or until all seafood is done.

Crabmeat Bisque

Easy and delicious!
Serves 8 to 10

1	16-ounce can peeled tomatoes, drained, liquid reserved
1	can artichoke quarters, drained
1	pint half and half
2	cans mushroom soup, undiluted
1	teaspoon salt
¼	teaspoon pepper
4	tablespoons dry sherry
½	teaspoon Worcestershire sauce
6	drops Tabasco, or to taste
¼	teaspoon basil
1	pound fresh lump crabmeat

Purée half the tomatoes and cut up the remainder. Purée the drained artichoke quarters.

In a large pot combine reserved tomato liquid, half and half, cut and puréed tomatoes and artichokes. Add soup, salt, pepper, sherry, Worcestershire sauce, Tabasco and basil. Heat for 5 minutes over low heat then fold in lump crabmeat and heat an additional 10 minutes. If too thick, add 1/2 cup milk or chicken stock.

Serve with French bread and salad.

Crawfish Soup

Serves 6 to 8

½	stick butter
½	cup flour
7	cups water
8	ounces tomato sauce
6	green onions, chopped
½	cup chopped celery
2	whole cloves garlic
1	tablespoon Worcestershire sauce
1	teaspoon thyme
1	bay leaf
½	cup white wine
1	pound cooked and peeled crawfish tails
1	tablespoon fresh parsley
	salt and cayenne pepper to taste
1½	cups cooked rice

Make a dark brown roux by cooking flour and butter over medium heat until brown. Add water gradually, stirring constantly to keep mixture smooth. Stir in tomato sauce. Add onions, celery, garlic, Worcestershire sauce, thyme and bay leaf; cook on a low fire for 30 minutes. Add wine, crawfish tails and parsley to mixture and cook soup 15 minutes. Remove garlic pods and bay leaf before serving. Season to taste with salt and pepper. Serve over rice.

Henri Cartier-Bresson (French, born 1908)
NEW ORLEANS, 1947
gelatin silver print
9½ x 14³⁄₁₆"
Collection of New Orleans Museum of Art.

Chinese Chicken Salad

A delicious, different salad.
Your guests will ask for the recipe.

Serves 10 to 12

½   cup soy sauce
½   cup dry sherry
1   tablespoon finely chopped ginger
1   clove garlic, minced
2   pounds boned skinned chicken breasts, split, trimmed and flattened
¼   cup peanut oil
¾   ounce Chinese rice noodles
½   cup cornstarch
½   cup flour
½   teaspoon salt
1   large head iceberg lettuce
1   bunch green onions, thinly sliced
¾   cup toasted slivered almonds
     Sweet and Sour Dressing

Mix the soy sauce, sherry, ginger and garlic to make a marinade. Place chicken breasts in a bowl and pour on the marinade, coating well. Cover and refrigerate several hours or overnight. Prepare Sweet and Sour Dressing and refrigerate.

Heat oil to 350 degrees and fry the noodles a handful at a time. As soon as they puff up, but before they brown, remove and drain well on paper towels. They will stay crisp for several days in an airtight container.

Mix cornstarch, flour and salt. Remove chicken from the marinade and dip in the cornstarch mixture. In the same oil used to fry the noodles (add more oil if necessary), fry the chicken just until brown and crispy, 2 to 4 minutes. Drain on paper towels. When cool, cut into bite-size shreds.

Shred the lettuce. Toss the chicken pieces, lettuce, sliced green onions and almonds with enough dressing to coat them well. Surround with Chinese noodles and serve.

Sweet and Sour Dressing

1   cup salad oil
¾   cup distilled white vinegar
½   cup sugar
2   tablespoons soy sauce
½   teaspoon dry mustard
¼   teaspoon freshly ground black pepper

Mix ingredients together; refrigerate until ready to use. It will keep several days.

Combination Chicken Salad

An interesting and delightful salad.

Serves 8 to 10

Salad Ingredients:

2   cups cooked, cubed chicken, approximately 4 breasts
1   4-ounce can pineapple chunks, drained
½   cup fresh bean sprouts
2   cups shredded romaine lettuce
2   cups shredded bibb lettuce
1   medium avocado, diced
2   medium tomatoes, diced
8   slices crisp bacon, crumbled
¼   cup crumbled blue cheese
¼   cup chopped green onions
1   medium cucumber, diced
¼   cup toasted sesame seeds

Vinaigrette Dressing:

½   cup salad oil
⅓   cup wine vinegar
1   teaspoon salt
1   teaspoon sugar
2   cloves garlic, crushed
     pepper to taste
½   teaspoon dry mustard
1   teaspoon dill seed

Combine all dressing ingredients in a jar, cover, shake well and set aside.

Combine chicken, pineapple and bean sprouts. Add a small amount of dressing and marinate several hours.

Before serving, arrange lettuce in bottom of a glass or lucite bowl. Place remaining ingredients over lettuce, add marinated chicken mixture and additional dressing, toss and serve.

California Salad

Serves 8

1	bunch spinach leaves
½	bunch green, red or other lettuce
½	pound grated Monterey Jack cheese
1	small red onion, sliced into rings
1	small or ½ large avocado cut in pieces
1	small can pitted prunes, drained
1	small can mandarin orange slices, drained

Curry Dressing:

½	cup salad oil
¼	cup rice vinegar
½	teaspoon curry powder
1	teaspoon sugar
	salt and pepper to taste
2	hard boiled eggs, sliced for garnish

Wash, pick and tear spinach leaves and lettuce into bite-size pieces to make about 6 cups. Add remaining ingredients, stir together and chill.

Just before serving, toss with dressing and garnish with egg slices.

Grapes Glazed with Creme de Menthe

You can decorate any tray with these delicious, beautiful grapes!

1	pound large red seedless grapes
¾	cup white creme de menthe
1	cup confectioners sugar, sifted

Divide grapes into small bunches. Wash and dry them on paper towels.

Pour creme de menthe into a flat soup plate and dip each bunch of grapes into it. Dust a baking sheet with some of the sugar. Place bunches of grapes on the sheet and coat them with the remaining sugar. Freeze for at least 45 minutes, but do not let ice form on the grapes. Transfer to the refrigerator. Remove and decorate platter.

Natchez Salad

A delightful summer salad.
Serves 8 to 10

Dressing:

⅜	cup rice wine vinegar
⅝	cup mild olive oil
½	cup chopped pecans or walnuts
½	cup white raisins

Whisk vinegar and oil together in a small bowl, add nuts and raisins to the dressing and soak for 1 hour.

Salad Ingredients:

16	cups Boston or red leaf lettuce, torn into pieces
1	cup Swiss cheese strips
1½	cups ham or prosciutto strips

Arrange the lettuce in layers in a crystal or glass serving bowl. Add a layer of cheese, then a layer of ham; top with dressing mixture. Bring to the table and toss just before serving.

Artist's Palate Chicken Salad

Serves 10 to 12

1	quart cooked, deboned chicken
1	cup sliced celery
1	pound seedless grapes
10	ounces water chestnuts, sliced
1½	cups mayonnaise
1	teaspoon curry
1	tablespoon soy sauce
1	tablespoon lemon juice
	salt and pepper to taste
¾	cup toasted almond slivers

Combine all ingredients and chill. Serve on bed of lettuce.

Divine Chicken Salad with French Basil Dressing

Serves 6 to 8

4   whole chicken breasts
1   onion
       salt and pepper to taste
1   onion, quartered
       red leaf lettuce
8 to 10 carrots, peeled and sliced
1   bunch broccoli florets
1 to 2 avocadoes
1   can pitted ripe black olives,
       drained and sliced
1   red bell pepper, sliced into rings
¼   pound feta cheese, crumbled

Poach chicken with salt, pepper and onion. Remove skin from poached chicken and cut meat into bite-size pieces and chill. Discard onion.

Steam carrots and broccoli until just barely tender. Refrigerate vegetables.

Sauce:

1   egg
½   cup red wine vinegar
¼   cup Dijon mustard
2   tablespoons chopped shallots
1   teaspoon fresh ground pepper
¼   teaspoon salt
2   tablespoons chopped fresh basil
1½   cups salad oil

Place all ingredients except oil in a food processor. Turn machine on and slowly pour the oil through the feed tube. Chill.

Arrange lettuce on individual plates. Mound chicken in center and surround with carrots, broccoli, avocado and olives. Top with a slice of red bell pepper. Pour dressing over chicken and sprinkle with feta cheese.

This recipe is lovely on a hot summer evening or for lunch. Serve with a chilled white wine.

Layered Salad

Serves 10

½   head iceberg lettuce
1   bag fresh spinach
4   eggs, hard cooked and chopped
2   red onions, sliced thin
1   20-ounce package frozen tiny peas
2   cups sliced fresh mushrooms
¼ to ½ pound Gruyere cheese,
       cut in small cubes
6   slices bacon, crisply fried and crumbled
       (reserve some to sprinkle on top)
2   teaspoons sugar
       salt and pepper

Dressing:

1½   cups sour cream
1½   cups mayonnaise
       paprika
1   tablespooon fresh dill

Wash, drain and tear lettuce and spinach into pieces. Layer one half of lettuce, spinach, eggs, onions, peas, mushrooms, cheese and bacon. Sprinkle with 1 teaspoon sugar, salt and pepper. Frost with half the dressing. Repeat layers and frost with remainder of dressing. Sprinkle top with some of the bacon. Cover with plastic wrap and refrigerate overnight. Do not toss.

Is especially attractive layered in a deep glass or clear plastic bowl.

Artichoke Rice Salad

Great to make ahead for your next luncheon.
Serves 6 to 8

1	**package chicken flavored rice mix**
½	**finely chopped green pepper**
2	**medium onions, thinly sliced**
10	**pimiento stuffed green olives, sliced**
1½	**cups marinated artichoke hearts**
¼	**teaspoon curry powder**
⅓	**cup mayonnaise**
½	**cup slivered almonds**

Cook rice as directed on package, but omit addition of butter. Remove from heat, turn into a bowl and let stand until cooled to room temperature. Add green pepper, onions and olives.

Drain artichoke hearts, reserving marinade. Combine marinade with curry powder and mayonnaise, mix well. Add artichoke hearts and marinade mixture to rice, add almonds and mix lightly. Cover bowl and chill.

Serve, garnished with spinach leaves and tomato wedges.

Three skinned and deboned cooked chicken breasts may be chopped and added to the rice mixture for a main dish.

Shrimp Remoulade

Serves 4 to 6

6	**tablespoons wine vinegar**
3	**tablespoons Dijon mustard**
3	**tablespoons Creole mustard**
½	**cup chopped green onions**
¾	**cup salad oil**
1 or 2	**tablespoons paprika**
3	**pounds cooked shrimp, peeled and deveined**
1	**head of lettuce, washed, drained and broken in small pieces**

Mix vinegar, mustards and onions. Add oil and paprika, mix well. Marinate shrimp in sauce overnight.

To serve as a salad, add to lettuce and mix well. As an hors d'oeuvre, serve from a lettuce-lined platter with toothpicks.

Vegetarian's Delight Salad

Serves 6 to 8

4 or 5	**medium potatoes, boiled in jackets, peeled and chopped**
3	**tablespoons vinegar**
	salt, pepper and garlic powder to taste
1	**teaspoon fresh oregano**
1	**tablespoon dill weed**
2	**tablespoons chopped parsley**
3	**green onion tops, chopped**
⅓	**cup each chopped onions, carrots, celery and other vegetables of your choice**
1	**medium cucumber, seeded and sliced**
6	**sweet pickles, sliced**
3	**hard boiled eggs, chopped**
¼	**cup mayonnaise (add a few tablespoons milk if mixture is too dry)**
	paprika

While potatoes are still warm, pour vinegar over them and toss with salt, pepper, garlic powder, oregano, dill weed, parsley and green onion. Add vegetables, pickles, eggs, mayonnaise and mix well. Serve either hot or cold on a bed of crisp lettuce. Sprinkle with a little paprika.

May be decorated with ripe tomatoes, parsley and sliced hard boiled eggs, if desired.

Add salt to water when boiling eggs to prevent shell from cracking.

To easily unmold a mousse or gelatin mold, run pointed tip of knife around top edge, dip bottom of mold into warm water, place platter or serving plate on top and invert mold.

Avocado Mold

The pink and green colors make this dish especially appealing.
Serves 10

½   package unflavored gelatin
½   cup cold water
1   package lemon flavored gelatin
1   cup boiling water
3   tablespoons lemon juice
1   teaspoon salt
1   cup mayonnaise
1   cup mashed ripe avocado
½   pint whipping cream, whipped

Soften unflavored gelatin in cold water. Dissolve lemon gelatin and unflavored gelatin in boiling water and chill until partially set.

Remove gelatin mixture from refrigerator and whip. Add lemon juice and salt to mayonnaise, blend together, fold into whipped gelatin, then fold in avocado and whipped cream. Place mixture in a greased 5½ or 6-cup mold, and refrigerate 8 hours or until firm. Unmold and garnish with fresh strawberries. Serve with Strawberry Yogurt Dressing.

Strawberry Yogurt Dressing

1   8-ounce container strawberry yogurt
½   cup sour cream
3   tablespoons powdered sugar

Thoroughly blend all ingredients together.

DECORATIVE BASE FOR MOLDS
Dissolve one 6-ounce package of lime gelatin following package directions. Cool until very slightly thickened. Pour onto a large serving platter and refrigerate until firm.
To serve, invert mold on top of gelatin base.

Corned Beef Mold

Serves 10 to 12

1   envelope unflavored gelatin
1¼   cups cold water
1   6-ounce package lemon flavored gelatin
2   cups boiling water
1½   cups mayonnaise
1   pound cooked corned beef, OR 1 can corn beef, chopped
1   cup chopped celery
½   cup chopped green pepper
1   cucumber, seeded and chopped
2   hard-boiled eggs, chopped
½   cup chopped green onions

Soften unflavored gelatin in 1/4 cup cold water and combine in a bowl with lemon gelatin. Pour 2 cups boiling water over gelatins, stirring to dissolve. Add 1 cup cold water, mayonnaise and beat until blended. Combine beef with remaining ingredients, fold into mixture and chill 8 hours or overnight.

May be put into a decorative mold, or an oblong casserole dish and cut into squares. Serve on crisp lettuce.

Lemon Salmon Mold

Easy and good.
Serves 8 to 10

1   6-ounce package lemon gelatin
2   cups hot water
½   cup cold water
3   teaspoons vinegar
½   cup mayonnaise
1   can (15½-ounces) pink salmon, drained and flaked
1   cup chopped celery
1½   tablespoons minced onion
1   cucumber, peeled, seeded and cut in cubes

In a large bowl, dissolve gelatin in hot water. Add cold water and vinegar. Using a rotary beater, blend in mayonnaise. Refrigerate for 30 minutes. Remove from refrigerator and fold in salmon, celery, onion and cucumber. Pour into a lightly greased 9 x 13 x 2-inch rectangular dish or decorative mold and chill overnight.

Molded Chicken Salad

Serves 12 to 16

2	2½-pound chickens OR 8 chicken breasts
1	teaspoon salt
2	ribs celery, quartered
¼	teaspoon pepper
1	onion, quartered
2	envelopes unflavored gelatin
½	cup reserved chicken broth
1	8-ounce package cream cheese
1	10-ounce can cream of chicken soup, undiluted
2	cups chopped celery
¾	cup homemade mayonnaise (page 55)
4	tablespoons fresh lemon juice
¼	cup chopped black olives

In a large pot cover chicken with water and add next 4 ingredients. Bring to a boil, reduce heat, simmer about 1 hour or until chicken is tender. Strain and reserve broth. When chicken is cool, skin, debone and cut into small pieces.

In a large bowl, soften gelatin in reserved chicken broth. In a saucepan blend the cream cheese and chicken soup over low heat and add to gelatin mixture. Combine gelatin mixture, chicken and remaining ingredients, mix well.

Pour into a 9 x 13 x 2-inch pan, or an 8-inch decorative mold and refrigerate 8 hours or overnight.

Shrimp Mold

Serves 8 as a salad
10 to 12 as hors d'oeuvre

2	tablespoons unflavored gelatin
1	cup consommé
1	8-ounce package cream cheese, softened
¾	cup homemade mayonnaise (page 55)
2	cups boiled shrimp, peeled, deveined and chopped in small pieces
1	cup finely chopped celery
2	finely chopped pimientos
1	bottle capers, drained
2	tablespoons finely grated onion
½	cup chili sauce
2	tablespoons lemon juice
2	teaspoons Worcestershire sauce
1	teaspoon salt
¼	teaspoon pepper
4 or 5 drops Tabasco	
	dash each of thyme, oregano and garlic salt
¼	cup finely chopped fresh parsley OR 1 teaspoon dried parsley flakes

Soften gelatin in 1/4 cup consommé. Heat remaining consommé and add the softened gelatin, stirring until dissolved. Set aside to cool. Blend mayonnaise and softened cream cheese. Add cooled consommé/gelatin mixture, remaining ingredients and blend well. Place in a lightly greased 2-quart ring or fish mold. Chill thoroughly until firm. Serve on lettuce with French dressing, as a salad.

For use as an hors d'oeuvre, unmold on a decorative plate and serve with small crisp crackers.

May be molded in individual salad molds and served as a luncheon dish. Should be prepared 1 or 2 days before serving.

Spinach Ring

Serves 8 to 10

1	6-ounce package lemon flavored gelatin
1	teaspoon salt
2	cups boiling water
½	cup cold water
2	tablespoons vinegar
1	8-ounce bottle creamy cucumber salad dressing
1	cup small curd cottage cheese
2	cups chopped fresh spinach
¼	cup chopped fresh parsley
2	tablespoons chopped green onions

Dissolve gelatin and salt in boiling water. Add cold water and vinegar. Allow mixture to cool. Stir in cucumber dressing and chill gelatin mixture until partially set. Fold in cottage cheese, spinach, parsley and green onions, pour into a 6-cup ring mold which has been lightly brushed with oil, chill until set.

May be served with Egg Mustard Dressing page 54.

Mandarin Orange Salad

Perfect for your next brunch.
Serves 12

1	6-ounce package orange gelatin
1	cup boiling water
1	pint orange sherbet
1	8-ounce can crushed pineapple
1	cup chopped pecans
1	cup miniature marshmallows
1	11-ounce can mandarin orange slices
½	cup whipping cream, whipped

In a large bowl, dissolve gelatin in boiling water. Add orange sherbet and stir until melted. Add remaining ingredients and mix well. Spoon mixture into a crystal bowl. Refrigerate until firm.

Serve garnished with mint leaves.

Crabmeat Mousse

Serves 6 to 8

1	8-ounce package cream cheese
1	cup homemade mayonnaise (page 55)
⅓	teaspoon paprika
¼	teaspoon garlic powder
1	pound special white or lump crabmeat, picked over for shells and cartilage
1	ounce unflavored gelatin
¼	cup cold water
½	cup milk, heated
⅓	cup chopped parsley
4	tablespoons capers
1	teaspoon salt
1	tablespoon Worcestershire sauce
6	dashes Tabasco

Mix cream cheese and mayonnaise until smooth. Add paprika and garlic powder. Fold in crabmeat.

Soften gelatin in cold water. Add 1/2 cup of hot, not boiled, milk. Add parsley, capers, salt. Worcestershire sauce and Tabasco to crabmeat mixture and fold in. Add gelatin and mix well. Put into a cold, oiled 4-cup fish mold and refrigerate 8 hours or until firm.

When ready to serve, unmold, sprinkle paprika on mousse, garnish with lettuce, tomatoes, olives and parsley.

Curried Chicken Mousse

Serves 8

1	3-pound broiler or fryer
	water
	salt and pepper to taste
2	tablespoons salad oil
2	medium-size celery stalks, chopped
1	medium-size onion, chopped
2	tablespoons curry powder
2	envelopes unflavored gelatin
	dash of salt
½	cup mayonnaise
¼	teaspoon pepper
1¾	teaspoons salt
1	cup whipping cream
¼	cup flaked, toasted coconut
8	large kiwis, peeled and sliced
2	large mangoes, peeled

Place chicken, breast side down, in a 3 to 4-quart size pot. Cover with water and season to taste. Bring to a boil over high heat. Reduce heat to low, cover and simmer 35 minutes or until chicken is tender. Remove chicken to a large bowl and refrigerate 30 minutes. Reserve 1½ cups of the chicken broth, cover and refrigerate until cool.

In a 10-inch skillet over medium fire, heat salad oil and cook celery and onion until tender, stirring occasionally. Stir in curry powder and cook 1 minute.

Discard skin and bones from chicken. Coarsely chop meat. Place 1 cup chopped chicken in a small bowl. Sprinkle lightly with salt. Place remaining chicken in food processor or blender.

In a 2-quart saucepan, sprinkle gelatin evenly over reserved 1½ cups chicken broth. Let stand 1 minute. Cook over low heat until gelatin is completely dissolved, stirring occasionally.

Add celery, gelatin mixtures, mayonnaise, pepper and 1¾ teaspoons salt to chicken in food processor, cover and blend. Pour mixture into a large bowl, cover and refrigerate until mixture mounds slightly when dropped from a spoon, about 45 minutes, stirring mixture occasionally.

At medium speed, beat whipping cream until soft peaks form. Gently fold reserved chopped chicken and whipped cream into gelatin mixture. Grease a 2-quart mold. Spoon chicken mousse into mold. Cover and refrigerate until set, at least 2 hours.

To serve, carefully unmold mousse onto a platter, sprinkle top of mousse with toasted coconut. Arrange kiwi slices and bite-size mango chunks around mousse.

Crawfish Mousse

Serves 12 to 14

2	cups sour cream
2	8-ounce packages cream cheese, softened
1	cup mayonnaise
2	pounds cooked and peeled crawfish tails, chopped
4	tablespoons lemon juice
½	cup minced red bell pepper
½	cup minced green bell pepper
½	cup minced celery
½	cup minced onion
½	cup minced green onion
¼	cup minced parsley
5 or 6	cloves garlic, minced
½	cup bottled chili sauce
1	tablespoon Worcestershire sauce
⅛	teaspoon pepper
	Tabasco to taste
2	envelopes unflavored gelatin
6	tablespoons brandy

In a mixer cream together sour cream, cream cheese and mayonnaise. Add crawfish tails, lemon juice, minced vegetables and seasonings. Mix well.

Soften gelatin in brandy and very carefully heat to dissolve. Stir into crawfish mixture, mixing well. Season to taste and pour into a lightly oiled decorative springform mold. Chill at least 8 hours before unmolding. Serve with crackers or toast points.

Salmon Mousse

Serves 6

1	envelope unflavored gelatin
¼	cup white wine
½	cup boiling water
½	cup mayonnaise
1	tablespoon lemon juice
1	tablespoon grated onion
½	teaspoon Tabasco
½	teaspoon paprika
1	teaspoon salt
1	15-ounce can salmon, drained
1	cup whipping cream
2	tablespoons snipped fresh dill
	watercress
	fresh dill sprigs

In medium bowl, sprinkle gelatin over wine and let stand 5 minutes to soften. Add boiling water, stirring until gelatin is dissolved. Let cool.

Add mayonnaise, lemon juice, onion, Tabasco, paprika, salt and stir to mix well. Set bowl in a large bowl of ice cubes, let stand. Stir gelatin mixture occasionally until consistency of unbeaten egg white for about 10 minutes.

Lightly grease a 4-cup mold. Remove any skin and bones from salmon. Place salmon and 1/2 cup of the cream in blender or food processor, blending to a purée.

Beat remaining 1/2 cup cream until stiff. Using a wire whisk, fold salmon purée, whipped cream and 2 tablespoons dill into slightly thickened gelatin mixture, using an under and over motion to combine thoroughly. Turn into mold and refrigerate until well chilled and firm enough to unmold, about 8 hours, or overnight.

Unmold on platter and garnish with watercress and fresh dill sprigs.

Cold Pasta Salad

For a special luncheon, as it's a crowd pleaser!
Serves 6 to 8

Pasta Sauce:

¼	cup fresh basil
½	cup olive oil
2	cloves garlic, minced
8	sprigs parsley
¼	cup chopped pecans
2	tablespoons dill
1	tablespoon Worcestershire sauce
½	cup fresh, grated Romano cheese

Place all ingredients, except Romano cheese, in a food processor and pulse until finely chopped. Remove from blender and add cheese.

Salad:

½	pound fresh corkscrew pasta, cooked
2	tomatoes, cut in wedges
2	cloves garlic, crushed
2	tablespoons chopped walnuts or pecans
3	tablespoons chopped fresh parsley
¼	cup olive oil
¼	cup fresh lemon juice
1	15-ounce can artichokes, drained and chopped
1	2½-ounce jar pimento-stuffed olives, sliced
2	pounds cooked and peeled fresh crawfish tails*
1	10-ounce box frozen green peas, thawed
¼	cup pasta sauce

Toss salad ingredients with 1/4 cup of sauce, mix well and refrigerate until ready to serve. Add additional pasta sauce if needed.

*Shimp may be substituted for crawfish.

Eugene J. Bellocq (American, 1873-1949)
BEDROOM MANTLE, STORYVILLE
gelatin silver print
35.6 x 27.8"
Collection of New Orleans Museum of Art.

Mock Avocado Dressing

Yield: 1 quart

5	green onions
3	tablespoons yellow mustard
1⅓	teaspoons salt
⅓	cup wine vinegar
⅓	cup white vinegar
⅔	cup water
1½	teaspoons Worcestershire sauce
3	dashes Tabasco
1⅓	cups peanut oil
1	cup olive oil

Place green onions, mustard, salt, vinegars and water in blender. Blend until smooth. Add Worcestershire sauce, Tabasco, peanut oil and olive oil and blend until well mixed. Store in refrigerator.

Roquefort Cheese Dressing

Yield: ½ cup

½	teaspoon sugar
½	teaspoon salt
⅛	teaspoon black pepper
¼	teaspoon dry mustard
	dash of paprika
3	tablespoons salad oil
3	tablespoons vinegar
2	tablespoons Roquefort cheese, crumbled

Mix together all ingredients except cheese in a food processor until blended. Add cheese and serve over lettuce wedges.

Cooked Dressing for Chicken Salad

Yield: 1 cup

1	tablespoon butter
1	teaspoon sugar
1	tablespoon flour
1	tablespoon prepared yellow mustard
1	egg, beaten
¼	cup vinegar
¾	cup water
	salt and pepper to taste

Melt butter in a saucepan, add sugar, flour and mustard. Cook 1 minute while stirring. Add egg, vinegar, water, salt and pepper. Cook 2 minutes or until thick.

Egg Mustard Dressing

For salad or cold fish.
Yield: ¾ cup

2	hard-boiled eggs
½	teaspoon salt
¼	teaspoon celery or onion salt
½	teaspoon garlic powder
½	teaspoon Worcestershire sauce
2	tablespoons cider vinegar
1	tablespoon Creole mustard
1	tablespoon mayonnaise
½	cup safflower oil
6	slices bacon, cooked and crumbled for garnish (optional)

Separate hard-boiled egg whites and yolks. Finely chop whites and set aside for garnish.

In blender or food processor, add egg yolks, seasonings, Worcestershire sauce, vinegar, mustard and mayonnaise. Blend until egg yolks are well mixed. Slowly add safflower oil. Process until thoroughly combined and the mixture has a smooth consistency.

May be served over fresh cooked chilled asparagus, or assorted mixed greens or spinach salad. Garnish with chopped egg whites and bacon bits.

Basic Mayonnaise

Yield: 1 cup

1	**egg**
½	**teaspoon salt**
1	**teaspoon dry mustard**
2	**tablespoons lemon juice**
1	**cup vegetable oil**

With rotary beater, or in a food processor, mix egg, salt, mustard and lemon juice. Continue beating and very slowly add oil in a thin stream until the mixture becomes firm.

Hot Dill Mustard

This is a very nice accompaniment to cold meats. Use sparingly, it is hot!
Yield: 1½ cups

2	**1.5-ounce tins dry mustard**
¾	**cup cider vinegar**
¾	**cup sugar**
¼	**cup water**
2	**teaspoons salt**
2	**teaspoons dill seed**
2	**eggs, well beaten**

Mix the first 6 ingredients in the top of a double boiler and set aside 4 hours.

Slowly blend the eggs into the mustard mixture and cook over medium heat, stirring continuously with a wire whisk until it thickens, 5 to 8 minutes. Pour into jars. Must be refrigerated.

Poppyseed Dressing

Yield: 1¼ cups

½	**cup salad oil**
¼	**cup orange blossom honey**
¼	**cup grapefruit juice**
¼	**cup red wine vinegar**
2	**teaspoons dry mustard**
½	**teaspoon salt**
2	**tablespoons poppyseeds**

Blend all ingredients in jar with a tight fitting lid. Store in refrigerator.

Excellent served on fruit salad, or grapefruit/avocado salad.

Sesame Salad Dressing

This dressing is delicious on any type salad.
Yield: 3/4 cup

4	**green onions**
½	**cup salad oil**
¼	**cup lemon juice**
½	**teaspoon garlic powder**
½	**teaspoon onion salt**
½	**teaspoon pepper**
½	**teaspoon salt**
½	**cup sesame seeds**

Cut up green onions. In a blender combine oil, lemon juice, onions and seasonings, blend well. (The dressing will have a green color.)

Heat a small frying pan and slowly toast sesame seeds.

Salad:

2	**heads of lettuce (a mixture of red leaf, romaine, etc.)**
½	**pound sliced mushrooms**

Toss washed and dried lettuce with sliced mushrooms and enough dressing to coat leaves. Mix well, add toasted sesame seeds and mix again.

Tangy Salad Dressing

Yield: 1 cup

¾   **cup corn oil**
1   **tablespoon apple cider vinegar**
1   **tablespoon tarragon vinegar**
    juice of 1 lemon (about 3 tablespoons)
1   **teaspoon Worcestershire sauce**
¼   **teaspoon sugar**
1   **teaspoon yellow mustard**
2   **cloves garlic, finely chopped**
1   **teaspoon salt**

In a mixing bowl combine ingredients one at a time, mixing after each addition. Pour into a salad dressing jar and shake. Do not make in a blender.

Will keep refrigerated for 2 weeks.

This dressing is delicious over mixed greens, spinach or as a marinade for crabmeat or shrimp.

Vermouth Dressing

Yield: 1½ cups

¼   **cup lemon juice**
¼   **cup dry vermouth**
2   **teaspoons dry mustard**
1   **teaspoon pepper**
1   **clove garlic, pressed**
2   **teaspoons salt**
¼   **cup olive oil**
¾   **cup salad oil**

Combine ingredients in a food processor or blender and mix well. Store in refrigerator.

Serve over spinach, avocado, meat or green salad.

Watercress Dressing

Delicious served over any type salad greens.
Yield: 1 cup

1   **egg**
1   **clove garlic**
1   **teaspoon salt**
½   **teaspoon paprika**
½   **cup salad oil**
6   **flat anchovies**
3   **tablespoons wine vinegar**
½   **bunch watercress**

Combine egg, garlic, salt and paprika in blender or food processor with steel blade, blend. With motor running, add salad oil in a slow steady stream, blending until consistency of mayonnaise. Add anchovies, wine vinegar and watercress. Process until watercress is chopped.

Walker Evans (American, 1903-1975)
BARBER SHOP, NEW ORLEANS
gelatin silver print
18 x 15"
Collection of New Orleans Museum of Art.

Eggs Benedict

Serves 6

2   cups Hollandaise sauce (page 78)
6   large eggs
     water and vinegar for poaching
     bowl of warm water
3   English muffins, split
6   slices baked ham

Prepare Hollandaise and keep warm in the top of a double boiler over low heat.

Poach eggs: Break eggs into individual saucers. Fill a saucepan with 1 to 1½ inches of water, add 1 teaspoon vinegar; bring to a boil, then lower heat to simmer. Gently slide egg into the water and spoon some of the water and egg white over yolk. Cook each egg for about 2 to 3 minutes. Remove with a slotted spoon, transfer poached egg into bowl of warm water. Repeat with each egg until all are poached.

Preparation:

Toast English muffins. Lay a slice of ham over each half. Lift poached egg from warm water with a slotted spoon to drain off water, then place on top of ham. Spoon Hollandaise sauce to cover each of the eggs. Serve immediately.

Eggs Sardou

Serves 6

3   cups Hollandaise sauce
6   large artichokes
6   eggs
3   cups creamed spinach

Prepare Hollandaise sauce and keep warm in the top of a double boiler over low heat.

Boil artichokes in salted water. Drain and remove and discard chokes. Scrape meat from leaves and freeze for future use in other artichoke recipes. Poach eggs as directed in Eggs Benedict.

Place 1/4 cup of warmed spinach on a warm plate and top with a warm artichoke bottom. Spoon 1/4 cup spinach in artichoke bottom, top with a poached egg and cover with Hollandaise sauce. Serve immediately.

Pain Perdu
(Lost Bread)

2   eggs
1   cup milk
½   cup sugar
½   teaspoon nutmeg
⅛   teaspoon vanilla
6   slices stale white bread
2   tablespoons butter, melted
     confectioners sugar
     honey or jam

Beat eggs, add sugar, nutmeg and vanilla and mix well. Soak bread in this mixture for a few minutes, then fry in melted butter. Remove from pan, sprinkle with confectioners sugar and serve with honey or jam.

Cheese Blintzes

A very special treat!
Yield: 2½ to 3 dozen

Batter:

4	**eggs**
1	**cup milk**
1 to 1½	**cups water**
1	**teaspoon oil**
2	**cups flour**

In a blender, beat eggs slightly, add other ingredients, adding flour last. Blend quickly until smooth. Batter should be the consistency of unwhipped cream. Let batter rest about 20 minutes.

Filling:

2	**eggs**
¼ to ½	**cup sugar or to taste**
1	**8-ounce package cream cheese**
2	**12-ounce cartons dry uncreamed cottage cheese**
1	**8-ounce package dry Ricotta cheese**

If cottage cheese and Ricotta are not dry, they must be drained to remove liquid.

In a mixer, beat eggs, add sugar, cream cheese, softened cottage and Ricotta cheeses. Blend ingredients thoroughly.

Filling may be made in advance and refrigerated.

Crêpes:

Very lightly oil a 6 or 7-inch slope-sided crepe pan. Wipe pan so only a shine of oil is left. Warm pan over medium heat about 2 minutes or until a drop of batter sizzles as soon as it hits the pan. Pick up pan and pour 2 tablespoons batter into it, quickly tilting pan so that the batter thoroughly coats the bottom and slightly up the sides. Make the crêpe as thin as possible and pour out excess batter. Cook until edges and bottom are golden, 30 to 60 seconds. Brown only one side. Remove each crepe to cool with browned side up, placing on a paper towel. Do Not Stack. Cover with waxed paper to prevent drying.

To fill blintz:

On the browned side, place 1 tablespoon of the cheese mixture about 1/2 inch from one edge of the crepe. Fold blintz over this and press or flatten slightly. Fold over both sides to center and continue rolling. Place seam side down.

Blintzes may be frozen until ready to use.

To cook on top of the stove:

Melt 2 tablespoons butter in a large skillet and slowly fry blintzes until golden brown.

To Bake:

Preheat oven to 350 degrees.

Grease bottom of baking dish, arrange blintzes and dot with butter. Bake until golden brown.

Serve with sour cream, applesauce, preserves, fruit or lightly sprinkled with cinnamon.

Brunch Eggs

Serves 4 to 6

	hard rolls crushed to yield 4 cups OR 5 slices white bread, cubed
12	**ounces grated sharp cheese**
1	**teaspoon dry mustard**
1	**teaspoon salt**
	few grains cayenne pepper
5	**eggs, beaten**
2	**cups milk**
2	**teaspoons Worcestershire sauce**
	Tabasco sauce to taste

Alternate layers of bread and cheese in a buttered 3-quart casserole. Mix dry ingredients, add to beaten eggs, milk, Worcestershire and Tabasco sauces and pour over bread and cheese. Cover with plastic wrap and let stand in refrigerator overnight.

Preheat oven to 350 degrees.

Bake casserole 1 hour.

Leftover ham or a pound of cooked sausage or crumbled bacon may be added to casserole before baking.

Basic Quiche

Serves 6

1	unbaked 9 inch pie shell (page 168)
1	cup half and half
1½	teaspoons flour
3	eggs
1	cup ham pieces*
1	tablespoon butter
1	cup sliced fresh mushrooms
½	cup chopped onions
3	cups grated Gruyère cheese
¼	cup grated Romano cheese

Preheat oven to 425 degrees.

Chill pie shell for 30 minutes so that it will bake evenly. Place sheet of lightly buttered foil across pastry, fill with rice or beans. To prevent a soggy bottom pre-bake shell in the lower middle level of the oven until bottom of pastry is set, but still slightly soft, about 10 minutes. If edges have sunk down, gently push them up with a spatula. Remove foil with rice or beans. Lower oven to 375 degrees and bake 5 more minutes, remove from oven and set aside.

Lower oven to 350 degrees.

Put half and half in blender, add flour and blend until smooth. Beat in eggs 1 at a time. Place ham pieces in bottom of pastry shell.

Sauté mushrooms and onions in butter, spread over ham, sprinkle with Gruyère cheese, and pour egg mixture over same. Sprinkle Romano cheese on top, dot with butter and bake 30 minutes.

*1/2 pound crab meat or cooked shrimp may be used in place of ham.

Crustless Quiche

Serves 6 to 8

6	eggs, beaten
2	cups sour cream
1	teaspoon Worcestershire sauce
¼	teaspoon salt
2	cups grated Gruyère cheese
2	8-ounce cans French fried onion rings
1	10-ounce package frozen broccoli or spinach, thawed, drained and chopped
1	cup sliced mushrooms

Preheat oven to 325 degrees.

Mix all ingredients and place in a well-greased 9 x 12-inch baking dish. Bake in preheated oven for 1 hour or until brown. Do not overbake.

Spinach Shrimp Strata

Serves 6

2	10-ounce packages frozen chopped spinach
10	slices white bread, cut into 1 inch cubes
2	cups cooked shrimp, peeled, deveined and chopped
2½	cups grated cheddar cheese
1	10¾-ounce can shrimp soup, undiluted
1	cup milk
5	eggs, slightly beaten
¼	teaspoon ground nutmeg
¼	teaspoon black pepper

Cook spinach according to package directions and drain well.

In a greased 2-quart shallow baking dish, 12 x 8 x 2-inches, arrange half of the bread cubes and spread spinach evenly on top. Sprinkle chopped shrimp over the spinach and add half of the cheddar cheese, then layer remaining bread and cheese.

Combine soup, milk, eggs, nutmeg, pepper and pour over bread mixture. Cover and refrigerate 4 hours or more.

Preheat oven to 350 degrees.

Uncover baking dish and bake 45 minutes or until set.

Tested in the Artist's Palate by WVC members.

Asparagus Soufflé

Serves 4 to 5

5   egg whites
1   teaspoon butter
2   tablespoons dry fine bread crumbs
¼   cup butter
¼   cup flour
1⅓ cups hot milk
1   teaspoon salt
⅛   teaspoon pepper
1   teaspoon grated onion
¼   cup shredded sharp Cheddar cheese
2   tablespoons chopped pimiento
4   egg yolks
1¼ cups finely chopped raw asparagus
    (about 1 pound) OR
    1/2 pound chopped raw broccoli

Place egg whites in a large bowl and let stand at room temperature 1 hour. Preheat oven to 400 degrees.

Butter a 1½-quart soufflé dish with 1 teaspoon butter, sprinkle crumbs to coat sides and bottom. Shake out excess crumbs.

Melt the 1/4 cup butter in a 1½-quart saucepan over low heat. When butter begins to bubble, add flour all at once and stir vigorously with a wire whisk to blend well. Cook over moderate heat, stirring constantly about 2 minutes, until mixture begins to foam and bubble. Remove from heat and pour in hot milk all at once, beating vigorously with a whisk until mixture is thickened and smooth. Return to heat and cook 1 minute, stirring constantly, until sauce begins to boil.

Remove from heat, add salt, pepper, onion, cheese and pimiento. Stir until cheese is melted. Immediately add egg yolks, one at a time, beating well after each addition. Stir in asparagus or broccoli, mix well and pour into a large bowl.

Beat egg whites until stiff peaks form. Add 1 large tablespoon of the beaten egg whites to the egg yolk mixture and stir until well blended. Spoon remaining egg whites on top, gently fold in and blend well.

Pour mixture into prepared soufflé dish, smooth surface with spatula. Run a metal spatula through the mixture, in a circle, 1 inch from side of dish. Place dish in center of oven and immediately lower temperature to 375 degrees. Bake 35 to 40 minutes or until soufflé is puffed about 2 inches above rim of dish and knife inserted in center comes out clean. Serve immediately.

Carrot Soufflé

Serves 6 to 8

4   cups peeled, sliced carrots
½   stick butter, melted
½   cup sugar
1   egg
¼   cup milk
⅓   cup flour
½   teaspoon cinnamon
1   tablespoon vanilla
1½   teaspoons baking powder
½   teaspoon salt

Preheat oven to 350 degrees.

Boil carrots until tender, drain and pureé. Add melted butter and sugar. Beat in egg, add milk, flour, cinnamon, vanilla, baking powder and salt, blending well. Bake in a greased soufflé dish 40 to 45 minutes, or until a knife inserted in center comes out clean.

Sweet Potato Soufflé

Serves 8

4   sweet potatoes*
1½   sticks butter
1   cup sugar
3   eggs
1   tablespoon vanilla
10   ounces evaporated milk
1   tablespoon all-purpose flour
2   teaspoons baking powder
1   teaspoon cinnamon

Boil potatoes approximately 25 minutes or until tender, drain, peel and mash.

Preheat oven to 325 degrees.

Using an electric mixer, cream 1 stick butter. Add potatoes and all other ingredients, except baking powder. When well blended, gently fold in baking powder. Pour into a casserole, sprinkle cinnamon on top and dot with remaining butter. Bake 40 to 45 minutes until firm.

4 cups cooked pumpkin may be substituted for sweet potatoes.

Chicken Soufflé

Serves 4

5	egg whites
1	teaspoon butter
2	tablespoons grated Parmesan cheese
¼	cup butter
2	tablespoons finely chopped onion
¼	cup flour
1	cup hot milk
⅓	cup grated Parmesan cheese
½	teaspoon salt
⅛	teaspoon pepper
4	egg yolks
¾	cup ground cooked chicken or turkey

Place egg whites in a large bowl and let stand at room temperature for 1 hour.

Preheat oven to 400 degrees.

Butter a 1½-quart soufflé dish with 1 teaspoon butter, sprinkle with 2 tablespoons Parmesan cheese to coat sides and bottom. Shake out excess cheese.

Melt 1/4 cup butter in a 1½-quart saucepan over moderately low heat, add onion and cook until transparent. Add flour all at once and stir vigorously with a wire whisk to blend well. Increase heat slightly and continue cooking, stirring constantly, for 2 minutes or until mixture begins to foam and bubble. Remove from heat and pour in hot milk all at once, beating vigorously with whisk until mixture is thick and smooth. Return to heat and cook 1 minute, stirring constantly, until sauce begins to boil. Remove from heat and stir in 1/3 cup grated Parmesan cheese, salt and pepper. Immediately stir in egg yolks, one at a time, beating well after each addition. Stir in ground chicken, mix well and pour into a large bowl.

Beat egg whites until stiff peaks form. Add 1 large tablespoon of beaten egg whites to the egg yolk mixture and stir until well blended. Spoon remaining egg whites on top and gently fold in until well blended.

Pour mixture into soufflé dish, smooth surface with spatula. Run a metal spatula through the mixture in a circle, 1 inch from side of dish. Place dish in center of oven and immediately lower temperature to 375 degrees. Bake 35 to 40 minutes or until soufflé is puffed about 2 inches above rim of dish and knife inserted in center comes out clean. Serve immediately with Mushroom Sauce.

Mushroom Sauce:

Yield: 1⅔ cups

¼	cup butter
1	cup sliced fresh mushrooms
2	tablespoons flour
1¾	cups hot milk
2	tablespoons chicken stock
¼	teaspoon salt
	pepper to taste

Melt butter in a saucepan over low heat. Add mushrooms and cook until tender, stirring frequently. Remove from heat. Blend flour into hot milk and add with chicken stock, salt and pepper to mushrooms. Return to heat, cook, stirring constantly, until sauce has thickened and is smooth.

Mushroom Frittata

A great lunch treat with salad and French Bread.
Serves 6

1	cup sliced fresh mushrooms
⅔	cup chopped onion
⅔	cup chopped green pepper
1	cup coarsely chopped zucchini
1	teaspoon minced garlic
2	teaspoons vegetable oil
5	large eggs
⅓	cup half & half
½	teaspoon salt
⅛	teaspoon pepper
1½	cups soft bread cubes
1	8-ounce package cream cheese, cut in 1/2 inch cubes
1	cup grated mild Cheddar cheese

Preheat oven to 350 degrees.

Sauté mushroom, onions, green pepper, zucchini and garlic in oil until tender. Beat eggs and cream, add salt, pepper and combine with vegetables. Add bread cubes, cream cheese and Cheddar cheese. Mix well, being careful not to break up cream cheese cubes while stirring. Put into a greased 9-inch pie pan and bake 45 minutes.

Pablo Picasso (Spanish, 1881-1973)
STILL LIFE WITH CANDLE *1937*
oil on canvas
Bequest of Victor K. Kiam.

III. Private Collections From Curators, Staff and The Woman's Volunteer Committee

Cherried Roast

Serves 6

2½ to 3 pound sirloin tip or
      boneless round roast
2   teaspoons salt
¼   teaspoon black pepper
¼   teaspoon dry mustard
2   tablespoons butter
1   tablespoon oil
¼   cup dark brown sugar
¼   cup lemon juice
⅓   cup red Burgundy wine
⅓   cup water
1   beef bouillon cube
1   package frozen black cherries
1½   tablespoons corn starch
1½   tablespoons water

Preheat oven to 325 degrees.

Rub meat with salt mixed with black pepper and dry mustard. In a heavy pot brown meat in butter and oil, remove from pan and set aside.

Add brown sugar, lemon juice, wine, water and bouillon cube to pan. Return meat to pan and bake covered for 2 hours. Add 2 cups cherries, cover and bake 1 hour more.

Remove meat to a platter. Stir corn starch mixed with 1½ tablespoons water into sauce, bring to a boil, pour over meat and serve.

Roast Filet of Beef

Serves 8 to 10

2   onions, chopped
1   carrot, chopped
1   stalk celery, chopped
2   teaspoons whole peppercorns
1   bottle Madeira wine
4 to 5 pound filet of beef
      salt and pepper to taste
2   whole cloves garlic, halved

Combine onions, carrot, celery, peppercorns and wine in a large bowl and marinate filet overnight in the refrigerator.

Preheat oven to 450 degrees.

Drain filet, reserving marinade and dry meat well. Season filet with salt and pepper and insert garlic halves. Roast 40 minutes for a medium-rare filet, basting with pan juices. Add a bit of marinade to the fat if needed. Remove filet from pan and cool before slicing. Serve warm with heated Madeira Sauce or cold with Horseradish Sauce.

Madeira Sauce:

Pour off most of fat in baking pan and add a bit of the marinade. Scrape off bits of meat clinging to pan. Pour this and remaining marinade into a small pan and simmer over medium heat until reduced to about 1½ cups. Thicken with cornstarch or flour mixed into 2 tablespoons cold water and blend to make a smooth gravy. Refrigerate after correcting seasonings. Heat before serving over sliced filet.

Horseradish Sauce

1   8-ounce container sour cream
1   tablespoon Dijon mustard
2 to 3 tablespoons horseradish
      salt, pepper and a few drops of vinegar

Combine ingredients until thoroughly blended and refrigerate overnight in a jar. To serve roast cold, remove from baking pan, cool, wrap in foil and refrigerate. Slice before serving with Horseradish Sauce.

Filet may be served with both sauces, for a choice of hot or cold.

Pepper Steak with Brandy Cream Sauce

Serves 4

4 filet steaks, at least 1 inch thick
4 teaspoons oil
4 to 6 tablespoons cracked peppercorns
2 tablespoons oil
4 tablespoons butter
1 teaspoon salt
4 tablespoons brandy
⅔ cup whipping cream
   watercress or parsley for garnish

Rub each steak on both sides with oil. Press peppercorns into both sides of steaks.

Heat butter and remaining oil in frying pan over moderate heat until very hot (do not let butter burn). Sauté steaks for 4 minutes on each side, seasoning with salt. Add brandy and light immediately with a match. When flames die down remove steaks and place on a hot plate. Keep warm while preparing sauce.

Add cream to pan juices and boil 2 to 3 minutes until reduced and slightly thickened. Pour sauce over steaks and add garnish.

Beef Tournedos with Mushrooms

Serves 6

1 stick butter
1 pound fresh mushrooms, sliced
3 tablespoons flour
2 cups beef stock or consommé
¼ cup Madeira wine
6 small beef tournedos
2 tablespoons lemon pepper
   salt and pepper to taste

Melt butter in skillet and sauté mushrooms. Blend in flour. Add beef stock, stirring until smooth and continue cooking to thicken. Stir in Madeira wine.

Season tournedos with lemon pepper, salt and pepper. Grill to suit individual taste. Place tournedos on individual plates and top with mushroom sauce.

Rouladen

Serves 6

6 slices very lean and very thin good quality beef
   salt and pepper
   prepared mustard
6 small white onions, chopped
6 slices cooked bacon, chopped
3 tablespoons chopped parsley
3 dill pickles, chopped
   all-purpose flour for coating rolls
   water

Salt and pepper meat and spread thinly with mustard. Combine onions, bacon, parsley and spread over meat. Top each slice with chopped pickles. Roll up and tie with string. Roll in flour and brown in bacon drippings. Add enough water to cover and simmer 1 hour.

Serve with hot buttered noodles.

Lemony Dill Sauce

Yield: 1½ cups

3 tablespoons mayonnaise
2 tablespoons Creole mustard
2 tablespoons lemon juice
2 teaspoons fresh dill weed

In a small mixing bowl, stir together mayonnaise, mustard, lemon juice and dill weed. Serve over grilled meats.

Natchez Grillades

Great for a brunch!
Serves 8 to 12

3	pounds beef chuck cut into ¼-inch slices
1¼	cups flour
2	tablespoons sugar
4	tablespoons black pepper
½	cup bacon fat
1	cup chopped onions
2	cups finely chopped green onions
2	cups chopped green peppers
2	cloves garlic, minced
4	cups peeled chopped fresh or canned tomatoes
1	teaspoon Tabasco
1	tablespoon tarragon
1	tablespoon ground thyme
1	cup minced parsley
3	tablespoons freshly ground black pepper
3	teaspoons salt
1	cup dry red wine
1	cup beef stock
3	cups raw shrimp, peeled and deveined

Flatten meat slices by pounding with the side of a cleaver or rolling pin until they almost fall apart. Mix 1 cup flour in a bowl with sugar and black pepper and use to dredge meat slices.

Heat 4 tablespoons bacon fat in a large Dutch oven. Add meat slices and cook over medium heat until brown. Do not crowd the slices or they will not brown properly. Remove meat and set aside. Add the onions, green onions, green peppers and garlic. Sauté over medium heat until tender but not brown. Add tomatoes, Tabasco, tarragon, thyme, parsley, ground pepper and salt. Set aside.

Make a roux by mixing the remaining bacon fat and flour in a heavy skillet over medium heat, stirring constantly until the mixture is a dark caramel color. Combine roux with the vegetable mixture. Add wine and beef stock while stirring constantly. Add meat, cover and simmer over low heat until tender, about 2½ hours. Add shrimp and simmer 20 minutes longer, or until just cooked. Serve hot with grits or rice.

This dish is better when prepared a day ahead. Freezes well.

Oriental Tenderloin with Pea Pods

Serves 4

2	pounds beef tenderloin
½	cup peanut oil
2	medium onions, chopped
½	pound fresh pea pods, sliced crosswise
2	cups sliced fresh mushrooms
1	cup drained sliced water chestnuts
2	tablespoons cornstarch
1½	cups chicken stock
½	teaspoon black pepper
1	teaspoon salt
4	teaspoons soy sauce
1	teaspoon ground ginger

Cut meat into 2 inch squares about 1/4 inch thick. Sauté in hot peanut oil until lightly browned, but not dry. Add onions, pea pods, mushrooms and water chestnuts. Continue cooking over moderate heat for 5 minutes, turning frequently.

Mix cornstarch into chicken stock and add to pan. Gently stir seasonings into mixture. Cover and cook over low heat until thick and glossy, about 5 minutes, turning gently several times.

Serve over steamed rice.

Tafelspitz
(Austrian cooked brisket of beef)

*Tafelspitz is the national Austrian meat dish
made popular by its former Emperor Franz Josef.*
Serves 8

1   16-ounce jar peach preserves
1   15-ounce can tomato sauce
    salt and pepper
2   tablespoons Worcestershire sauce
1   onion, chopped in cubes
5   pound trimmed beef brisket

Preheat oven to 350 degrees.

Mix all sauce ingredients. Place meat in a deep
roasting pan and pour sauce over it. Cover and bake
3 hours or until tender.

Remove brisket and cool. Slice to desired thickness,
cover and refrigerate. Pour sauce in a separate bowl
and refrigerate several hours. Remove any fat from
surface, pour sauce over sliced meat and heat in a
350 degree oven for 20 minutes or until hot.

*This dish may be frozen and reheated as above. Horse-
radish sauce may be served in a separate bowl if desired.*

Horseradish Sauce for Tafelspitz:

Yield: 1 cup

½   cup whipping cream
2   tablespoons creamy horseradish
2   tablespoons applesauce
1   teaspoon lemon juice
    pinch of sugar (optional)

In a small bowl whip cream until stiff. Fold in remaining ingredients and mix well. Chill for 2 hours
before serving.

Entrecôte Poivre Vert
(Steak with Green Peppercorn Sauce)

Yields 1¼ cups sauce
Serves 4

Sauce:
¼   cup minced onion
1   small clove garlic, minced
½   stick butter
3   cups sliced mushrooms
1   bay leaf
    salt and white pepper to taste
½   cup dry vermouth or white wine
¾   cup beef broth
2   tablespoons meat extract
1   cup half and half

4   rib eye steaks, 1 inch thick
2   tablespoons drained peppercorns
2   tablespoons chopped fresh parsley

In a pan sauté minced onions and garlic in butter
until vegetables are softened. Add mushrooms, bay
leaf, salt and white pepper. Sauté 5 minutes or until
mushrooms are tender. Stir in vermouth and bring
to a boil. Boil for 1 minute, stir in beef broth and meat
extract. Return to a boil, stirring constantly, for 2
minutes. *Sauce may be made in advance and refrigerated at this point.*

When ready to serve, reheat sauce, stir in half and
half and cook over low heat until sauce is reduced
by half. Remove bay leaf. Keep sauce warm while grill-
ing meat. Broil steaks, pour sauce over them, sprinkle
with peppercorns and parsley. Serve immediately.

Veal Grillades Bayou Teche

"Rich but irresistible." Your guests will be impressed.
Serves 8 to 10

12	slices veal, pounded thin
	salt and pepper to taste
2	tablespoons flour
3	tablespoons butter
1	pound cooked and peeled crawfish tails
2	cups Hollandaise sauce (page 78)
½	teaspoon dried tarragon

Salt and pepper veal and sprinkle with flour. Heat butter in a skillet and sauté veal for about 3 minutes until browned. Add crawfish and sauté another minute.

Place veal on a platter, topping it with crawfish tails. Cover with Hollandaise sauce mixed with tarragon.

Hungarian Veal

Serves 4

3	tablespoons flour
¼	teaspoon pepper
¼	teaspoon dried sweet basil
¼	teaspoon dried oregano
¼	teaspoon Hungarian paprika
1	pound well trimmed veal cutlets
2	tablespoons vegetable oil
1	tablespoon butter
1	onion, chopped
1	clove garlic, minced
½	cup white wine
½	cup water
1	cup sliced fresh mushrooms
¼	cup chopped fresh parsley
	salt and pepper to taste

Combine flour, pepper, basil, oregano and Hungarian paprika and use to coat veal cutlets. Heat oil in a pan and brown cutlets. Remove meat from pan.

Add butter to pan and sauté onion and garlic until transparent. Stir in wine while scraping pan well. Return cutlets to pan, add water, cover and cook 20 minutes over medium heat, adding more wine if necessary. Add mushrooms, parsley, salt and pepper. Cover and cook 5 minutes longer until meat is tender. Whisk in additional flour as necessary to thicken gravy.

Osso Bucco

Serves 6

8	tablespoons butter
6	veal shanks (or slices 1½-inches thick)
⅓	cup flour
1	onion, chopped
1	carrot, chopped
1	rib celery, chopped
2	cloves garlic, chopped
1	tablespoon marjoram
1	small piece lemon peel
	salt to taste
	freshly ground white pepper to taste
½	cup dry white wine
2	tomatoes, seeded and finely chopped
⅓ to ½ cup veal stock	
1	tablespoon fresh grated lemon peel
1	tablespoon freshly squeezed orange juice
	cooked rice

Melt butter in skillet. Roll meat in flour and put in skillet over moderate heat until brown on all sides. Add onions, carrot, one-half of garlic, marjoram, and small piece lemon peel. Season to taste with salt and pepper. When vegetables are light in color, pour in wine and cover. Lower heat to moderate. Cook until liquid is almost reduced completely. Add tomatoes, 1/3 cup stock. Cover pan, lower heat and simmer 1½ hours. If necessary to prevent juice from getting too thick, add a few more spoonfulls of stock a few minutes before the end of cooking time. Add remaining garlic, grated lemon peel and orange juice. Stir and cook over moderate heat for a few minutes to blend flavors. Serve over rice.

Veal Piccata

Serves 6

12	veal scallops
	salt and pepper to taste
½	cup flour to dredge veal
¼	cup olive oil
2	tablespoons butter
2	cups sliced fresh mushrooms
3	tablespoons beef stock, heated
	juice of 1 lemon
3	tablespoons fresh parsley, chopped
2	tablespoons grated Parmesan cheese

Gently pound veal until flat. Sprinkle with salt and pepper; dredge with flour. Heat oil in frying pan, add veal. Turn up heat and fry veal quickly and remove to a platter.

Drain grease from frying pan. Add butter and mushrooms and sauté a few minutes. Add beef stock, lemon juice and parsley. Stir and heat sauce thoroughly. Spoon sauce over veal and sprinkle with Parmesan cheese.

Serve with fettucini.

Voluptuous Veal Scallopini

Serves 6

1½   pounds thinly sliced veal cutlets,
     preferably baby veal
1½   cups flour
     salt, pepper and paprika to taste
6   tablespoons Parmesan cheese
1   pound fresh mushrooms, thinly sliced
1   stick butter, melted
2   beef bouillon cubes dissolved in
     1 cup boiling water
6   tablespoons Marsala wine or sherry

Pound veal with a mallet, dredge in flour seasoned with salt, pepper, paprika and Parmesan cheese. Sauté meat and mushrooms in butter until meat is golden brown on both sides. Remove to a hot plate.

Add bouillon water to pan, heat and stir in wine while scraping the pan well. Pour over veal and serve.

Vitello Tonnato
(Cold veal roast in tuna sauce)

Serves 8

3 to 4 pound baby veal roast
      flour, salt and pepper
½   cup olive oil
1   large onion, chopped
4   stalks celery, chopped
2   cups chicken broth
¾ to 1 cup white wine
1   2-ounce can anchovies
1   7-ounce can tuna
½   cup homemade mayonnaise (page 55)
      juice of 1 lemon
      capers
      Rice salad (page 47)

Rub veal with flour, salt and pepper, brown lightly in oil. Remove veal and cook onion and celery until soft but not brown. Add broth, wine, anchovies and tuna. Return veal to pan, cover and simmer in sauce until meat is tender, but still firm.

Remove veal. Purée pan sauce in a blender. When cool, add mayonnaise and lemon juice. Slice veal very thin and pour on some of the sauce. Garnish with capers. Serve extra sauce in a sauce boat.

Roast may be prepared a day ahead. Delicious served with rice salad surrounded by cold, marinated vegetables—tomatoes, broccoli and green beans.

Roast Leg of Lamb with Artichokes

A Greek specialty.
Serves 6

4 to 5 pound leg of lamb
3   cloves garlic, slivered
4   tablespoons lemon juice
2   teaspoons salt
1   teaspoon pepper
1   teaspoon oregano
3   large artichokes
2   8-ounce cans tomato sauce
1   cup water
1   lemon, sliced

Preheat oven to 400 degrees.

Make slits several places around leg of lamb. Insert garlic into each slit. Rub lamb with lemon juice, salt, pepper and oregano. Place in a shallow baking pan and cook 30 minutes. Reduce temperature to 350 degrees and cook 1 hour, basting roast with pan drippings. Skim off excess fat.

Trim artichoke stems, snip off tips of leaves. Cut in half and remove reddish prickly center with a spoon and scoop out the fuzz underneath, being careful not to dig into the meaty flesh of the artichokes. Add tomato sauce and water to roasting pan. Arrange artichokes cut side down in sauce mixture around roast. Add lemon slices. Continue cooking and basting occasionally for 1 hour.

Lamb Stew

Serves 6

4   tablespoons olive oil
**   salt and pepper to taste**
3   pounds lamb, cut in 1-inch chunks
2   tablespoons flour
2   cups chicken broth
1   clove garlic, minced
2   tablespoons tomato paste
½   cup sliced mushrooms
1   cup sliced carrots
10   small new potatoes
6   small onions
1   teaspoon sugar
1   10-ounce package frozen green peas
¼   cup sherry

Preheat oven to 350 degrees.

Heat 2 tablespoons oil in large skillet. Season meat with salt and pepper, sprinkle with flour and brown. Add chicken broth, garlic and tomato paste. Bring to a boil while stirring constantly. Pour into a 3-quart casserole, cover and bake for 30 minutes.

Heat remaining 2 tablespoons oil and add mushrooms, carrots, potatoes and onions. Sprinkle sugar over vegetables and cook only to glaze them. Put vegetables into casserole with meat. Cover and cook another 1 hour. Stir in peas and sherry and cook 10 more minutes.

Couscous Exotic Stew
(Chicken, lamb and vegetable stew)

It's a great Middle Eastern dish.
Serves 10

¾   cup oil, preferably olive
1½   pounds cubed lean boneless lamb
2 to 2½ pound broiler chicken, cut up
3   large onions, chopped
3   tomatoes, cubed
1   green pepper, sliced
2   teaspoons salt
1   teaspoon black pepper
2   teaspoons turmeric
½   teaspoon allspice
4   cups boiling water
1   10-ounce package frozen peas
1   16-ounce can garbanzo beans
1   9-ounce package frozen artichoke hearts
2   cups bulgur (cracked wheat, available at natural food and gourmet stores)

Heat oil in a deep kettle or Dutch oven. Add lamb, chicken and onions and cook until meat and chicken are browned on all sides. Add tomatoes, blend well and continue to cook over low heat for 10 minutes. Add green pepper, salt, pepper, turmeric, allspice and water and blend. Cover and simmer over low heat for 1 hour. Add peas, beans with liquid and artichoke hearts, cover and simmer 15 to 20 minutes.

Cook bulgur and put into a large serving bowl. Slowly pour meat mixture over the bulgur. Let stand 5 minutes to allow wheat to absorb some of the sauce.

Lamb Ragout

Serves 4 to 6

2½   pound leg of lamb or lamb shank, cut in cubes
¼   cup flour
⅓   cup margarine, melted
2   teaspoons salt
½   teaspoon pepper
½   teaspoon dried thyme
¾   teaspoon rosemary leaves
1   can chicken broth
1   6-ounce can tomato paste
2   tablespoons melted butter
1½   teaspoons sugar
8   small white onions
3   carrots, sliced
1   clove garlic, chopped
½   cup sliced leeks
1   can artichoke hearts, drained
2   tomatoes, peeled, quartered

Coat lamb with flour and brown in margarine in a Dutch oven. Stir in salt, pepper, thyme, rosemary, chicken broth and tomato paste. Bring to a boil, reduce heat and simmer covered, for 45 minutes.

In a skillet mix melted butter and sugar, add onions, carrots, garlic and leeks and cook until glazed. Stir glazed vegetables into lamb mixture in Dutch oven. Cook covered for 30 minutes. Add artichoke hearts, cook 20 minutes longer. Add tomatoes and cook an additional 10 minutes. Serve over noodles.

Pork Chops and Apples

Serves 4

4   1-inch thick pork chops
    salt and pepper to taste
2   large apples
½   teaspoon lemon juice
3   tablespoons brown sugar
3   tablespoons butter
⅓   cup apple juice
2   tablespoons finely chopped fresh parsley

Trim chops and parboil 15 to 20 minutes. Remove from pan, pat dry and season with salt and pepper. Core apples and slice into thick rings, sprinkle with lemon juice and toss in brown sugar.

Brown chops in butter on both sides and cook until nearly done, 25 to 35 minutes. Remove from pan. If needed, add more butter to pan and sauté apples 2 to 3 minutes until colored and slightly softened. Return chops to pan and cover with apple rings. Continue to cook 10 minutes or until chops are thoroughly cooked, turning 2 or 3 times.

Remove chops to a platter. Add apple juice to pan, turn to medium heat and bring to a boil. Scrape sides of pan with a wooden spoon and pour over chops. Sprinkle with parsley and serve.

Sweet and Sour Pork

Serves 6

2¾ pounds cooked, cubed pork
1½ teaspoons soy sauce
½   teaspoon ground ginger
1   quart salad oil

Toss pork well with soy sauce and ginger. Let stand 10 minutes. Heat oil while preparing batter.

Batter:
3   eggs
¾   cup sifted flour
3   tablespoons cornstarch

Beat eggs slightly, add flour and cornstarch and beat until smooth. Drain cubes and pour batter over them, covering well. Drop cubes into hot oil and brown on both sides. Drain on paper towels.

Sauce:
1   13-ounce can pineapple chunks
2   teaspoons soy sauce
1   cup sugar
1   cup vinegar
2   large green peppers, cut into strips
2   tablespoons cornstarch
¼   cup water
¼   teaspoon ground ginger

Drain pineapple chunks. Add enough water to pineapple juice to measure 1 cup. In a saucepan combine juices, soy sauce, sugar and vinegar. Heat until sugar is dissolved and bring to a boil. Add peppers and cook 2 minutes longer. Remove from heat. Combine cornstarch and water in a small bowl, stir until smooth. Combine with hot mixture, pineapple chunks and ginger. Cook over moderate heat until translucent. Pour sauce over hot pork cubes and serve over steamed rice.

Does not freeze well.

Pork à la Marsala

Delicious for guests.
Serves 4 to 6

2	ounces dry porcini or shiitake mushrooms (available at specialty food stores or Oriental markets)
½	cup cold water
3	tablespoons butter
3	pounds boneless pork loin roast
½	cup dry Marsala wine
¼	teaspoon salt
¼	teaspoon pepper
½	pint whipping cream

Soak dry mushrooms in cold water for 1/2 hour or until soft.

Melt butter in a Dutch oven and brown roast well on all sides. Sprinkle with Marsala and when wine has been reduced, add mushrooms with their water, salt and pepper. Cover and cook over low heat 1½ hours, adding cream periodically, and turning roast several times.

Oven Baked Pork Chops

Serves 4

8	pork chops
	salt and pepper to taste
2	medium tomatoes peeled, seeded and chopped
½	cup dry white wine
¼	cup minced green pepper
¼	cup minced onion
1	tablespoon minced garlic
1	tablespoon minced parsley
1	tablespoon dried tarragon

Preheat oven broiler.

Salt and pepper chops. Broil them under high heat on both sides until brown and set aside.

In a saucepan put tomatoes, wine, green pepper, onion, garlic, parsley and tarragon. Slowly bring to a boil and simmer for 5 minutes.

Preheat oven to 350 degrees.

Place browned chops in an oven-proof casserole and cover with tomato mixture. Cover dish and bake 12 to 15 minutes or until chops are just cooked through. Serve chops with the sauce in which they were cooked.

This recipe would work with veal chops as well.

Béarnaise Sauce

Yield: 2 cups

4 egg yolks
   juice of 1 lemon
4 sticks butter, melted
   salt and pepper to taste
¼ cup chopped parsley
1 teaspoon dried tarragon
1 tablespoon tarragon or red wine vinegar

In top of double boiler, beat egg yolks and lemon juice together, cooking slowly over low heat. Do not allow water to come to a boil. Slowly add melted butter, stirring constantly. Add salt and pepper to taste, parsley, dried tarragon and vinegar. Blend thoroughly.

Sauce Béchamel

One of the family of white sauces
Yield: 1½ cups

3 tablespoons butter
¼ cup finely chopped onion
3 tablespoons all-purpose flour
2 cups scalded half and half
¼ teaspoon salt
   dash of ground white pepper
   pinch of ground nutmeg

In a heavy 2-quart saucepan, preferably a black iron skillet, melt butter over low heat. Add onion and cook until tender but not browned. Quickly stir in flour to make roux. Cook, stirring constantly, until roux is smooth and free of lumps, about 3 minutes. Remove saucepan from heat and slowly add half of the hot liquid, stirring constantly. Add remaining liquid and continue stirring until sauce is smooth. Return saucepan to medium-low heat, add salt, pepper and nutmeg. Simmer uncovered about 20 to 30 minutes or until sauce is reduced by about one-quarter. Stir frequently with a wooden spoon while cooking, making sure to include sides of saucepan. Remove from heat and strain.

Provençale Sauce

Serve over seafood or chicken.
Yield: 3½ cups

5 tablespoons flour
½ cup safflower oil
3 cloves garlic, chopped
4 green onions, chopped
½ cup sliced mushrooms
2 bay leaves
2 cups water
1 tablespoon beef extract
½ cup tomato sauce
1 cup dry white wine
2 tablespoons chopped fresh parsley

Make a brown roux with flour and oil. Add garlic and onions. Cook until soft. Add mushrooms, bay leaves, water, beef extract and tomato sauce. Simmer 15 minutes. Add wine, parsley and cook 5 more minutes.

Creole Sauce

Delicious sauce over meat, chicken or fish.
Yield: 2 cups

4 tablespoons safflower oil
2 cups finely chopped onions
2 cups finely chopped celery
4 cloves garlic, minced
1 bell pepper, chopped
4 tablespoons flour
1 28-ounce can peeled tomatoes with basil, finely chopped
   juice from tomatoes
3 bay leaves
¼ teaspoon thyme
4 tablespoons chopped parsley
   salt and pepper to taste
   dash of Tabasco

Sauté onions, celery, garlic and pepper in oil until soft. Add flour and cook, stirring until flour turns golden. Add tomatoes, juice and remaining ingredients. Simmer 1 hour, stirring occasionally. Add water if sauce becomes too thick. Remove bay leaves before serving.

Freezes well.

Sauce for Beef Tenderloin

Yield: 2 cups

½	**cup butter**
1	**clove garlic, minced**
½	**pound mushrooms**
1½	**cups sliced onions**
¼	**pound lean ground beef**
2	**tablespoons chili sauce**
2	**tablespoons steak sauce**
⅛	**teaspoon marjoram**
⅛	**teaspoon thyme**
4	**drops Tabasco**
2	**teaspoons Worcestershire sauce**
½	**cup red wine**
½	**cup beef broth**
1	**teaspoon salt**
¼	**teaspoon pepper**
½	**teaspoon flour**

Melt butter in a saucepan and sauté garlic, mushrooms and onions for 5 minutes. Add beef and cook until brown. Add remaining ingredients, stirring until sauce is smooth. Serve over beef.

Bordelaise Sauce

Yield: 1½ cups

1	**cup Burgundy wine**
1	**cup finely chopped green onions**
1	**clove garlic, minced**
1	**cup beef gravy (page 206)**
1	**bouillon cube**
2	**tablespoons chopped parsley**

Cook wine, onions and garlic until liquid is reduced to half. Strain and add to the gravy, to which the bouillon cube has been added. Cook uncovered in a double boiler over simmering water for 2 hours, stirring occasionally. Add parsley and stir. Do not return sauce to direct heat.

Serve over steak or roast.

Crème Fraîche

Yields: 2 cups

2	**cups whipping cream**
1	**tablespoon buttermilk**

Mix cream and buttermilk in a covered jar and shake for 2 minutes. Let stand at room temperature for 8 hours, or until thick. Refrigerate.

Hollandaise Sauce

Yield: 1 cup

3	**egg yolks**
2	**tablespoons lemon juice**
⅛	**teaspoon cayenne pepper**
½	**cup butter**

Place egg yolks, lemon juice and cayenne pepper in blender, cover and process 3 or 4 seconds, using on/off technique.

Heat butter until bubbling, but do not allow to brown. Remove access cover, turn blender to high speed and add hot butter slowly, in a steady stream, blending until thick and fluffy.

Sauce may be kept warm in a double boiler over warm water until ready to serve.

Marchand de Vin Sauce

Serves 8

½	**cup oil**
2	**tablespoons flour**
5	**cloves garlic, minced**
1	**cup chopped green onions**
3	**tablespoons chopped fresh parsley**
1	**cup sliced fresh mushrooms**
2	**tablespoons beef bouillon**
2	**cups water**
⅔	**cup red wine**
	salt and pepper to taste

Heat oil in saucepan, add flour and stir until brown. Add garlic and green onions and cook about 3 minutes. Add remaining ingredients and cook another 10 minutes.

Henri Cartier-Bresson (French, born 1908)
LOUISIANA, 1947
gelatin silver print
9½ x 14³⁄₁₆''
Collection of New Orleans Museum of Art.

Coq au Vin

Coq au vin is a popular dish served in the south of France.

Serves 6 to 8

4   tablespoons butter

½   pound bacon, slice strips in half crosswise

14 to 16 small white onions

1   clove garlic, chopped fine

2   cups sliced fresh mushrooms

8 to 10 chicken breasts or pieces, skinned and excess fat removed

     pepper to season chicken

½   cup brandy

Bouquet garni:

1   sprig fresh parsley, 1 bay leaf and 2 sprigs fresh thyme tied together; 1/4 teaspoon dried thyme may be used in place of fresh

1½   cups red wine

1   can beef broth, undiluted

3   tablespoons flour

In a large heavy pot, heat 2 tablespoons butter and fry bacon slices until golden, not crisp. Transfer with slotted spoon to a bowl. Brown whole onions and garlic in same fat and remove to bowl with bacon. Sauté mushrooms in fat and place in same bowl.

Season chicken with a little pepper, but do not add salt (the bacon and beef broth provide sufficient salt). Add butter to the pot if necessary and brown chicken on both sides. Turn off heat, but keep pot of chicken on burner. Warm brandy carefully in a small pan, and pour over chicken. Gently shake pot and quickly touch lighted match to contents. Let flames die, then add Bouquet garni, bacon, onions and mushrooms to pot. Add red wine and beef broth which should almost cover chicken. Bring to a boil and simmer on a slow fire for 1/2 hour or until tender. Shake pot from time to time so all the chicken will be covered. Remove chicken from pot and set aside.

Skim fat off the top. Mix 3 tablespoons fat with flour in a cup. Drop by teaspoons into the simmering wine broth mixture, stirring until sauce reaches a velvety consistency. Place sauce in a bowl and refrigerate to allow fat to gel. Remove fat and put chicken into sauce. Reheat and serve.

May be prepared 1 day ahead.

Supremes de Volaille au Vinaigre (Chicken breasts with vinegar)

A fine mixture of flavors.

Serves 6

6   chicken breasts, skinned

     salt and pepper to taste

½   stick butter

6   whole cloves garlic

Sauce:

½   cup sherry vinegar

2   tablespoons Dijon mustard

2   ounces cognac or brandy

1   cup white wine

2   tablespoons tomato paste

½   cup half and half

2   tomatoes, seeded and diced

¼   cup chives or 1/4 cup parsley

Salt and pepper chicken. Heat butter and sauté chicken slowly on both sides without browning. Add garlic and cook 15 minutes. Remove all ingredients from pan and set aside.

Sauce: Return pan to fire, add sherry vinegar. In a separate bowl, whip mustard, cognac, wine and tomato paste. Add to pan and cook 5 minutes on a high fire.

Return chicken breasts and reserved drippings to pan. Add cream and simmer 15 minutes or until done. Garnish chicken with diced tomatoes and chives or parsley.

Poulet Marengo

Specially created for Napoleon by his cook with whatever was available around the battlefield.

Serves 6

1½	fryer chickens, cut in serving pieces, or approximately 3 pounds chicken pieces
	a little oil to cover bottom of pan
	salt and pepper
¼	teaspoon thyme
3 to 4	large ripe tomatoes, peeled
1	bay leaf
1	pound fresh mushrooms, quartered
1	onion, chopped finely
1	pound fresh crawfish tails or 1 package frozen crawfish etouffé or bisque
1	cup dry white wine
1	tablespoon butter mixed with 4 tablespoons flour
	few sprigs parsley for garnish

Heat just enough oil to cover the bottom of a large, heavy pot. Brown chicken pieces a few at a time, seasoning them with salt and pepper and a pinch of thyme as you go. Don't hurry, fix the mushrooms while the chicken browns slowly. When done, remove with slotted spoon.

In juices left in pot, quickly brown the mushrooms, reserving the largest prettiest ones for garnish. When mushrooms begin to brown, sprinkle onions over them and cook until onions are transparent.

Peel tomatoes, cut in half cross-wise and squeeze to remove seeds; chop finely. Return chicken to pot and add tomatoes and bay leaf. Stir well and moisten with just a little wine. There should be enough just to bathe the bottom of the pot. Add more if chicken seems to get dry.

If using fresh crawfish, reserve about 12 of the prettiest for garnish and add rest to chicken. If you are using prepared crawfish add to stew now. Simmer gently, covered, until chicken is tender (about 45 minutes). At this time, remove bay leaf.

Mix thoroughly the butter and flour in a small bowl. Drop teaspoonfuls of this "beurre manie" into stew, stirring gently until sauce is lightly thickened. Just add a little at a time and stop as soon as sauce is velvety-looking. You may not use all of the beurre manie. Place reserved large mushrooms on top, where you can find them. Simmer 8 to 10 minutes.

Arrange reserved crawfish, heated in own liquid, all around dish and pile chicken in center, top with mushrooms and parsley garnish.

Poulet Marin

Serves 6

3	sticks butter
6	skinless, boneless chicken breast halves
1	can artichoke hearts, coarsely chopped
1	small can pitted black olives (optional)
⅔	cup chopped green onions
½	cup dry white wine
1	pound fresh crabmeat, cleaned well or 2 cans of white crabmeat, rinsed in cool water and drained
12 to 15	small cherry tomatoes
	salt and pepper

Melt and clarify butter. Heat clarified butter and poach chicken breasts, turning once until cooked. Place breasts on a serving platter and salt and pepper to taste.

Use butter remaining in pan to sauté artichoke hearts, green onions and olives for about 3 minutes. Add crabmeat, wine and tomatoes and simmer for 1 to 2 minutes. Spoon mixture on each breast, using all of sauce.

Chicken with Champagne Sauce

Serves 6

6   chicken breasts, skinned and deboned
1   stick butter
    salt and pepper to taste
4   ounces brandy
4   ounces chicken bouillon
1   pint champagne, dry or brut
½   pint whipping cream
1   tablespoon tomato paste
1   tablespoon butter
1   truffle
¼   cup chopped fresh parsley

In a large skillet cook chicken slowly in butter without browning. Salt and pepper lightly. When chicken is half-cooked, pour off butter from pan and set aside. Add brandy to pan and ignite. Add bouillon and all but 4 ounces of the champagne. Simmer until cooking juices are reduced to half. Add whipping cream and tomato paste, continue to simmer until chicken is tender.

Arrange chicken attractively on a serving platter. Whisk butter into the reduced sauce and add remaining champagne. Pour sauce over chicken and garnish with sliced truffle and chopped parsley.

Chicken with Cranberries and Bananas

Serves 8

¼   cup butter
8   chicken breasts
½   cup chopped onion
2   cups apple cider
1   teaspoon salt
¼   teaspoon pepper
1   teaspoon grated lemon peel
1   tablespoon cornstarch
⅓   cup sugar
2   cups fresh cranberries
4   bananas, sliced

Melt butter in a large skillet over medium heat. Brown chicken breasts on all sides. Add onions and cook 5 minutes until tender. Add 1½ cups cider, salt, pepper and lemon peel, cover and simmer 30 minutes. Remove chicken.

Combine cornstarch with remaining cider and blend until smooth. Add to skillet with sugar and cranberries and cook 10 minutes, or until cranberries are tender, stirring occasionally. Add chicken and bananas and heat.

Serve with bulgur, page 120.

Chicken Almond Bourbon

Guests always ask for seconds!
Serves 6

12	**chicken breast halves, boned and rolled**
½	**stick butter**
1	**12-ounce can frozen orange juice concentrate**
½	**cup sliced almonds, sautéed and browned in butter**
¼	**cup bourbon whiskey**

In a skillet brown chicken in butter until just slightly golden, 2 to 3 minutes. Pour one-half of thawed orange juice over chicken. Cover and simmer 1/2 hour, turning chicken several times. When breasts seem tender, remove to a platter, top with almonds and keep warm in a low oven.

Add bourbon to remaining orange juice and, boiling rapidly, stir until sauce is very thick and dark in color. Pour over chicken and serve with rice.

Sauce is also delicious served over dove or other fowl.

Hawaiian Chicken

A great summer dish for around the pool.
Serves 6 to 8

¼	**cup honey**
½	**stick butter**
1	**teaspoon salt**
1	**5-pound roasting chicken or 8 chicken breasts**
2	**tablespoons sesame seeds**

Preheat oven to 350 degrees.

Combine honey, butter and 1/2 teaspoon salt in a small saucepan. Cook over low heat until butter is melted.

Rub chicken cavity or chicken pieces with remaining salt. Place chicken in a shallow roasting pan and brush generously with honey mixture. Roast 2 hours for whole chicken or 1 hour for breasts. Brush chicken frequently with mixture during baking. Sprinkle with sesame seeds 15 minutes before chicken is done.

Arroz con Pollo

An original Spanish dish.
Serves 8

1	**large tender chicken**
3	**teaspoons oil**
8	**cherry tomatoes OR 2 large tomatoes**
¾	**cup finely chopped onions**
¾	**cup finely chopped green pepper**
2	**cloves garlic, finely chopped**
2½	**teaspoons salt**
½	**teaspoon pepper**
3	**tablespoons dry white wine**
2	**cups chicken stock**
4	**shreds toasted saffron or ½ package Bijol (available at specialty food stores)**
8	**ounces short grain rice (long grain rice may be used, but short grain is typically Spanish)**
1	**can sweet red peppers**
1	**large can petit pois peas**

Clean and prepare chicken, preferably the night before. Cut into serving pieces and fry lightly in the hot oil. Pour off oil, leaving a small amount to cover bottom of pan. Add tomatoes, onions, green pepper, garlic, salt, pepper and dry wine to pan. Cook 10 minutes.

In a large pot heat chicken stock. Dissolve saffron in 1 tablespoon of hot stock and return to pot. Add chicken and vegetables, bring to a boil and add rice. Return to a boil, cover and cook together 20 minutes over a slow fire. Drain water from peas and add to rice mixture.

Serve in the casserole in which it has been cooked and decorate with sweet red peppers.

Oriental Chicken

Makes 8 servings

1	**egg white**
¼	**cup cornstarch**
2	**tablespoons soy sauce**
4	**tablespoons vegetable oil**
2	**whole chicken breasts, skinned, boned and sliced 1/8-inch thick**
4	**cups water**
2	**tablespoons sesame oil**
4	**slices fresh ginger, finely minced**
3	**cloves garlic, crushed**
1	**8-ounce can straw mushrooms, peeled and well drained**
½	**cup bamboo shoots, drained**
¼	**cup chicken stock**
1	**green pepper, seeded and thinly sliced**
3	**tablespoons Dijon mustard**
2	**green onions, chopped**

Combine egg white, corn starch, soy sauce and 1 tablespoon vegetable oil in a large bowl; blend well. Add chicken pieces, stir gently to coat evenly. Refrigerate for 1 hour.

Combine water and remaining 3 tablespoons vegetable oil in a large saucepan. Bring to a boil over high heat; reduce heat and simmer 5 minutes. Add chicken, stir gently. As soon as chicken has lost its pink color, remove from pan, drain on paper towels and set aside. Heat sesame oil in a wok over high heat. Add ginger and garlic and stir fry for 2 minutes. Reduce heat to medium. Add mushrooms, bamboo shoots, chicken stock, green pepper and Dijon mustard. Sauté until green pepper is tender. Add chicken and stir quickly to blend. Heat chicken through and serve immediately with green onions sprinkled on top.

Accompany with Fried Rice.

Chicken Provençale

A low calorie dish fit for a King!
Serves 8 to 10

10	**chicken breasts, skinned and deboned**
2	**egg whites**
1	**cup bread crumbs**
½	**cup Herbes de Provence (available in specialty food stores)**

Sauce:

1	**tablespoon butter**
2	**cups sliced mushrooms**
1	**15-ounce can peeled tomatoes, chopped, with juice**
1	**cup dry white wine**

Preheat oven to 350 degrees.

Rinse chicken breasts and pat dry. Brush thoroughly with egg whites and coat with combined bread crumbs/Herbes mixture. Spray a large 14 x 9 x 2 inch deep baking dish with vegetable cooking spray. Place chicken pieces meaty side down in dish. Bake 15 minutes, turn chicken and bake for another 15 minutes.

Sauce: In a saucepan, sauté sliced mushrooms in butter, add chopped tomatoes, juice and dry white wine. Mix thoroughly and pour over chicken breasts. Bake another 15 minutes, or until tender.

Dish may be prepared a day ahead, refrigerated and baked the final 15 minutes just prior to serving.

Hungarian Chicken

Favorite chicken recipe of the Austro-Hungarian emperor!
Serves 4

3½	pound chicken, cut into serving pieces
4	tablespoons butter or margarine
½	cup minced onion
½	cup white wine
1	heaping tablespoon sweet Hungarian paprika
1	teaspoon fresh lemon juice
	salt and freshly ground pepper
⅔	cup crème fraîche* or sour cream

Melt 2 tablespoons butter in a large heavy-bottomed skillet over medium heat, and sauté chicken on both sides until golden brown. Remove chicken and keep warm. In same skillet, melt remaining butter over medium heat. Stir in onion, reduce heat, cover and cook 10 to 15 minutes until onion is limp and golden. Add wine and paprika, reduce heat, cover and simmer 10 minutes.

Return chicken to skillet with lemon juice, salt and pepper. Cover and simmer 45 to 50 minutes, or until chicken is tender. Slowly stir in crème fraîche or sour cream. Cover and simmer until thoroughly heated before serving.

*Crème fraîche: Mix 1 cup whipping cream with 1 tablespoon sour cream in a hot, clean jar. Let stand at room temperature 8 to 24 hours. Stir and refrigerate. Will thicken in refrigerator.

Louisiana Chicken

Serves 4 to 6

1	frying chicken
	salt and pepper to taste
	paprika
1½	sticks butter
½	pound fresh mushrooms, sliced
1	can artichoke hearts
3	tablespoons flour
2	cups chicken stock
1	can Golden Mushroom soup, undiluted
1	cup pimento-stuffed olives, sliced
6	tablespoons dry sherry
	parsley sprigs for garnish

Preheat oven to 350 degrees.

Cut chicken in serving pieces, season with salt, pepper and paprika. Sauté chicken in 1 stick of butter, cover and cook until brown and tender. Remove chicken and in the same pan, sauté mushrooms and artichokes in remaining butter. Add flour, gradually add chicken stock and soup, stir until blended. Add sliced olives and sherry and cook 5 minutes.

Place chicken in a casserole dish, cover with sauce and bake 10 minutes. Garnish with parsley sprigs before serving.

Roast Quail with Gravy

Serves 8

> **Cornbread Stuffing with Oysters**
> **and Pecans (Page 120)**
> ....
> 16 **cleaned quail, legs and wings intact**
> ....
> **salt and freshly ground pepper to taste**
> ....
> **flour for dusting**
> ....
> 2 **sticks butter**
> ....

Prepare stuffing and chill.

Preheat oven to 350 degrees.

Sprinkle birds with salt and pepper and dust lightly with flour. To stuff quail, spoon chilled dressing into the cavity of each bird (do not put hot stuffing into quail as it will spoil). Truss birds and place breast side up in a roasting pan. Put 1/2 tablespoon butter on each bird. Add enough water to the pan so that half the bird is submersed. Cover tightly and roast for 1 hour. If birds are not stuffed, bake only 1/2 hour. Baste birds every 15 minutes with pan juices. Smooth out any lumps of flour with back of spoon as you baste.

Remove birds to a second roasting pan and return them to the oven uncovered. Roast until skin is golden brown.

Pour pan juices in a saucepan and reheat. Whisk in additional flour to thicken, if desired. Pour into a saucepan and serve with quail.

Rabbit Jambalaya

8 to 10 servings

> 2 **young rabbits, cleaned and dressed**
> ....
> 1 **pint milk, to marinate rabbits**
> ....
> 2 **tablespoons crushed peppercorns**
> ....
> 3 **bay leaves**
> ....
> 1 **tablespoon oil**
> ....
> 1 **large onion, finely chopped**
> ....
> 1 **cup diced salt pork**
> ....
> 1 **cup chopped celery**
> ....
> 1 **cup chopped green onions**
> ....
> 3 **cloves garlic, finely chopped**
> ....
> 1 **large green pepper, diced**
> ....
> 1 **cup flour**
> ....
> **salt and pepper to taste**
> ....
> 1 to 2 **tablespoons oil if needed**
> ....
> 1 **cup diced chicken giblets**
> ....
> **hot water as needed**
> ....
> 1 **teaspoon cayenne pepper**
> ....
> ½ **teaspoon salt or to taste**
> ....
> 2 **dozen oysters and liquid**
> ....
> 2 **cups uncooked rice**
> ....

Disjoint rabbits and place in a large bowl. Prepare a marinade of enough milk to cover rabbits, add crushed peppercorns and bay leaves. Marinate rabbits overnight in refrigerator.

In a large pot, slowly fry onion in oil until slightly brown. Remove from pot. Add pork, fry and remove from pot. Add green onions, garlic and green pepper and cook until tender, about 5 to 10 minutes. Dust rabbits in flour with salt and pepper to taste. Sear in pork fat, adding oil if needed. Remove rabbits from pot. Return pork and vegetables to pot and add giblets. When giblets are cooked, return rabbits to pot, add sufficient hot water to cover and bring to a boil. Season with cayenne pepper and salt. Cover and simmer slowly until meat falls from bones. Remove and discard bones. Add rice and oysters with liquid, cover and cook slowly over low heat, stirring frequently, until rice is cooked.

Doves Edward

Fried grits is a wonderful accompaniment for this dish.
Serves 8 to 10

2	sticks butter, no substitute
4	ribs celery, chopped
5	medium onions, chopped
1	chopped clove garlic
4	chopped green onions
½	bunch parsley, chopped
1	cup sliced fresh mushrooms
14 to 16 doves	
½	teaspoon salt
¼	teaspoon cayenne pepper
1	teaspoon coarsely cracked black pepper
2	slices bacon
1	can consommé
1	bay leaf
2	tablespoons flour

In a heavy pot melt butter, add celery, onions, green onions, garlic, parsley and mushrooms. While this simmers, salt and pepper doves thoroughly. Stuff each dove with small pieces of uncooked bacon. When vegetables are tender, place doves in pot with consommé and bay leaf. Cover and cook over low heat for 1¾ hours. Remove cover and add flour to thicken sauce if necessary.

Optional: Small oysters may be added in the last 10 minutes.

Absolutely Crisp Roast Duckling

Absolutely delicious!
Serves 4

3	tablespoons butter
4½ to 5 pound duckling	
	salt
	garlic salt
	coarse ground black pepper
	paprika
1	large carrot
2	large stalks celery
1	large onion
4	large cloves garlic

Preheat oven to 425 degrees.

Use a heavy 4-quart roasting pan with a tight-fitting cover. Put 3 tablespoons butter in pan and rub throughout.

Generously sprinkle duckling inside and out with salt, garlic salt, pepper and paprika. Be especially generous with pepper. Rub seasonings well into inside bones of duckling.

Cut carrot, celery and onion into medium size pieces, slice garlic thinly, and sprinkle vegetables in, on and around duckling. Place bird breast side down on butter in the pan. Pour in about 2 inches of water and cover pan tightly. Roast 2½ to 3 hours, depending on size of duckling. Let bird cool completely.

Discard liquid, fat and vegetables. Quarter duckling and place skin side up on a flat pan. Roast 35 to 45 minutes until crisp. Keep checking, sometimes it takes a bit longer. Serve with Orange Sauce.

If you put the quartered duckling in the refrigerator, it must be brought back to room temperature before crisping.

Orange Sauce:

8	ounces top quality orange marmalade with lots of rind
8	ounces orange juice
1	tablespoon Worcestershire sauce

Bring marmalade and orange juice to a boil, simmer a few minutes, then add Worcestershire sauce.

This sauce has no fat and is very tasty and thick. If a thicker sauce is desired, add a bit of cornstarch, or simmer longer to evaporate some of the liquid.

Frog Legs Provençale

Serves 4

8 to 12 pairs frog legs, 2 to 3 per serving
    milk
    salt and pepper to taste
    flour
2   tablespoons butter
1   tablespoon olive oil
½   cup chopped onions
½   cup finely chopped green onion tops
1   clove garlic, crushed
1   green pepper, thickly sliced
1   large tomato peeled, seeded and chopped, reserve juice
1   small bay leaf
⅛   teaspoon thyme
½   cup dry white wine
    toast points
1   sliced lemon
    sprigs of parsley for garnish

Soak frog legs in milk to cover for 1 hour. Pat dry with paper towels and rub with salt and pepper. Dredge each frog leg in flour until lightly coated.

Heat butter and olive oil in a heavy bottomed skillet until foam subsides, then sauté frog legs until golden brown on each side. As they are done, remove from skillet and keep warm while preparing sauce.

In the same pan, sauté chopped onions, green onion tops and garlic until transparent. Add green pepper, tomato with its juice, bay leaf and thyme. Cook slowly for 10 minutes, stirring frequently. Add wine and cook over medium heat another 5 to 10 minutes.

Return frog legs to skillet coating them with sauce and heating thoroughly. Remove bay leaf. Serve over toast points with sauce, lemon slices and parsley garnish.

Stuffed Cornish Game Hens au Grand Marnier

Serves 4

4   game hens, giblets removed and chopped
    salt and pepper to taste
4   tablespoons butter
1   package wild rice dressing mix
1   cup chopped fresh mushrooms
2   ounces Grand Marnier liqueur
2   ounces fresh orange juice

Season hens, including cavity, with salt and pepper. Place 1/2 tablespoon butter in each cavity.

Preheat oven to 375 degrees.

Prepare rice according to package directions, but cook only until soft. Add mushrooms and chopped giblets to rice while cooking. Stuff hens with rice mixture and place pieces of butter over hen breasts. Bake 1½ to 2 hours. Baking pan may be covered for the first hour. After 30 minutes mix Grand Marnier and orange juice and baste hens. Continue basting occasionally with pan juices until hens are done.

Clementine Hunter (American, born 1885)
FISHING
oil on board
Gift of Dr. and Mrs. Robert F. Ryan.

Flounder Veronique

Serves 4

1½	pounds flounder fillets
3	tablespoons butter
	salt and lime juice to taste
2	teaspoons fresh parsley
¼	teaspoon tarragon
1	clove garlic, minced
1	cup dry white wine
1½	tablespoons flour
2	tablespoons orange juice
¼	pound seedless green grapes

Melt 1 tablespoon butter in a large skillet and arrange fillets in it. Sprinkle with salt, lime juice, parsley, tarragon and garlic. Add wine and simmer for 10 to 15 minutes until fish flakes easily and looks milky white rather than transparent. Carefully remove fish from skillet and arrange in a warm baking dish that can come to the table. In the skillet, melt remaining butter and blend in flour stirring until smooth. Add orange juice, seedless grapes and cook, stirring mixture until it thickens. Add more wine if necessary. Pour sauce over fillets and serve.

Fillets and Wild Rice

Serves 6

2	pounds fresh trout fillets
1	teaspoon salt
¼	teaspoon pepper
3	slices bacon, chopped
1	cup fresh mushrooms, chopped
¼	cup minced onion
¼	cup minced celery
2	cups cooked wild rice
½	teaspoon melted butter
	Mushroom-Walnut Sauce

Preheat oven to 350 degrees.

Cut fillets into serving-size portions and season with salt and pepper. In a skillet, cook bacon until lightly browned. Add mushrooms, onion and celery and cook until tender. Stir in cooked rice and salt. Place fish in a well-greased baking pan. Spoon rice mixture on top of fish portions. Drizzle melted butter over rice. Cover and bake 20 minutes or until fish flakes easily when tested with a fork. Serve with Mushroom-Walnut Sauce.

Mushroom-Walnut Sauce

Yields: 2½ cups

3	tablespoons butter
1	tablespoon minced onion
1	cup sliced mushrooms
3	tablespoons flour
½	teaspoon dry mustard
½	teaspoon salt
¼	teaspoon thyme
2	cups half and half
¼	cup toasted walnuts

In a saucepan, melt 3 tablespoons butter. Add onion and mushrooms. Cook until tender. Stir in flour, dry mustard, salt and thyme. Gradually stir in half and half. Cook over medium heat until thickened, stirring constantly. Stir in toasted walnuts. Spoon sauce over fish and wild rice.

Fish à la Basque

A Spanish dish which brings raves!
Makes 4 to 6 servings

5	pound fish (red fish preferred)
	lemon juice
	salt
½	cup salad oil
1	clove garlic, finely chopped
1	large onion, finely chopped
1	tomato, chopped
2	red or green sweet peppers, seeded and julienned
2	bay leaves
1	teaspoon salt
½	teaspoon oregano
¼	teaspoon thyme
	approximately 8 almonds
1	cup white wine
1	tablespoon brandy
1	bunch parsley
2	tablespoons plain bread crumbs
2	lemons, sliced

Preheat oven to 400 degrees.

Wash the fish inside and out with lemon juice. Salt inside and out. Make 2 or 3 diagonal cuts in both flanks. Oil a large baking dish and place fish in it. Brush the upper side of the fish with oil and bake for 10 minutes. Reserve 1/4 cup oil for the sauce. Baste with more oil and bake an additional 5 minutes.

Meanwhile prepare the sauce. In 1/4 cup of oil, sauté garlic, onions, tomato and sweet peppers until soft. Add bay leaves and salt, cover and simmer on low flame 10 minutes. Remove from fire and cool slightly. Remove bay leaves. Place sauce in a blender with a little more salt, oregano, thyme and almonds, to form a paste. If there is not enough liquid, use some of the wine to which you have added 1 tablespoon of brandy. When the paste is made, add remainder of the wine, stir and paint fish with sauce. Finish baking fish in a 300 degree oven until fish flakes easily (about 1 hour in all).

Reserve a sprig of parsley to put in fish's mouth. Chop remaining parsley and mix with bread crumbs. Sprinkle on top of fish and return to the oven for 5 minutes. When ready to serve, baste fish with some of the sauce from baking pan. Place 2 or 3 slices of lemon in each of the upper diagonal cuts in the fish's flanks.

Baked Fish with Artichokes and Cheese

Just divine!
Serves 6

6	medium trout or catfish fillets
	juice of 1 lemon
	salt and pepper to taste
2	tablespoons chopped fresh parsley
1	14-ounce can artichoke hearts, drained and mashed
1	pint mayonnaise
2	4-ounce packages grated Mozzarella cheese
3	tablespoons grated Parmesan cheese

Preheat oven to 350 degrees.

Wash and dry fillets, lay flat in an 8½ x 12-inch baking dish. Pour lemon juice over fish, season and add parsley. Layer artichokes, mayonnaise, Mozzarella and Parmesan cheese over the fish. Bake 30 to 45 minutes or until fish flakes easily with a fork.

Fish Casserole

Serves 4

2	large skinless trout or catfish fillets
1½	cups dry white wine
¼	cup chopped onions
1	package frozen chopped broccoli
1	10¾-ounce can celery soup, undiluted
1	dozen medium shrimp, cooked, peeled and deveined

Poach fish with onions in 1 cup of wine until white and firm. Remove fish from liquid and set aside.

Boil broccoli until tender. Drain and mix with half of condensed soup. Pour vegetable/soup mixture into a greased 9 x 13-inch baking dish and place fish over it in a single layer. Mix remaining soup with half cup of wine and pour over fish. Place shrimp on top and broil 8 to 10 minutes.

Broiled Trout Florentine

Serves 4

Florentine

1	**10-ounce package frozen spinach**
¼	**cup sour cream**
2	**tablespoons grated Parmesan cheese**

Cook frozen spinach according to package directions. Drain. Combine with sour cream and cheese. Put spinach mixture in bottom of shallow baking dish and keep warm.

Preheat broiler.

1½	**pounds trout fillets**
2	**tablespoons butter, melted**
3	**tablespoons Italian bread crumbs**
3	**tablespoons grated Parmesan cheese**
½	**teaspoon mixed Fine Herbs**
¼	**teaspoon salt**
¼	**teaspoon garlic, minced**
¼	**teaspoon pepper**
¼	**cup sour cream**

Arrange fish in buttered broiling pan and brush with melted butter. Combine bread crumbs, cheese, herbs, salt, garlic and pepper. Sprinkle 2 teaspoons of mixture over fillets. Broil 4 to 6 inches from heat for 5 minutes. Turn fish, brush with remaining butter and sprinkle 2 more teaspoons of mixture over fillets. Broil 7 minutes. Spread sour cream over fish, sprinkle remaining bread crumb mixture and broil 2 to 3 minutes longer. Arrange fish on top of spinach mixture. Serve.

Redfish Robert

Serves 6

1	**large or 2 to 3 small redfish**
	salt and pepper
3	**tablespoons margarine or butter**
½	**teaspoon oregano**
1	**large onion, chopped**
1	**teaspoon garlic flakes**
1	**cup white wine**
3	**tablespoons minced parsley**
	lemon slices for garnish

Preheat oven to 325 degrees.

Line a baking dish with foil and place fish in it. Make 3 slits in fish. Salt, pepper and dot fish with butter. Sprinkle oregano, onions and garlic over fish. Pour in wine. Bake 30 to 40 minutes depending on size of fish, basting occasionally until fish is flaky and done. Top with parsley and garnish with lemon slices.

Redfish Delta

Sauce is delicious over any fish.
Makes 8 to 10 servings

8	pound redfish, cut into fillets
½	cup cooking oil
5	onions, chopped
1	bunch green onions, chopped
4	celery ribs, chopped
1	cup sliced fresh mushrooms
1	6-ounce can tomato paste
2	cups fish stock (page 206)
2	cups dry Burgundy wine
	juice of 1 large lemon
½	cup grated Parmesan cheese
2	bay leaves
1	tablespoon Worcestershire sauce
	dash of sugar
	hot pepper sauce to taste
	salt and pepper to taste
1 to 2	tablespoons bread crumbs
½	cup chopped parsley
	lemon slices

Sauce:

In a heavy pot sauté onions, green onions, celery and mushrooms in cooking oil until soft. Add tomato paste and mix well. Remove from heat and spoon off excess oil. Add fish stock, wine, lemon juice, cheese, bay leaves, Worcestershire, sugar, hot pepper sauce, salt and pepper and cook over low heat for 2 hours. Stir sauce frequently to prevent sticking. Add 1 or 2 tablespoons of bread crumbs to thicken sauce, if necessary. Cool. Remove bay leaves. *Sauce may be prepared ahead and refrigerated or frozen for later use.*

Preheat oven to 350 degrees.

Salt and pepper fish fillets and arrange in a baking pan. Pour sauce over fish, sprinkle with parsley and place thin lemon slices on top. Bake for 45 minutes or until fish flakes easily with a fork.

Poached Salmon with Cucumber Sauce

An elegant treat to impress your guests!
Serves 4 to 6

6	pound salmon*
2	quarts water
2	cups dry white wine
1	cup sliced onions
1	carrot, sliced
1	tablespoon salt
8	crushed peppercorns
½	lemon, sliced
½	teaspoon tarragon

Wash and dry fresh salmon and wrap in cheesecloth. Bring remaining ingredients to a boil and simmer covered for 20 minutes, cool slightly. Place salmon on a fish rack and lower into the liquid. Simmer 1 hour or until fish flakes easily. Remove fish from liquid, unwrap and carefully remove skin. Refrigerate.

Serve on a platter with cucumber sauce.

**Red fish may be substituted for the salmon.*

Cucumber Sauce

3	cups peeled, seeded and chopped cucumbers
⅓	cup chopped green onion
1¼	teaspoons lemon juice
1½	cups sour cream
1	teaspoon yellow mustard
3	tablespoons mayonnaise
1	tablespoon Worcestershire sauce
	salt and pepper to taste
	dash of garlic powder

Combine all ingredients and season to taste.

New Orleans Crabmeat

For a special party.
Serves 8

½   stick butter
2 or 3 green onions, finely chopped
2   tablespoons finely chopped parsley
1½ tablespoons flour
½   pint half and half
¼   pound Gruyére cheese, grated
3   tablespoons sherry
    salt and cayenne pepper to taste
    Tabasco to taste
1   pound fresh lump crabmeat, picked over
1   14-ounce package frozen artichoke hearts, cooked and drained
    dried bread crumbs for topping
⅛   stick or less of butter

Preheat oven to 350 degrees.

Melt butter in a 3-quart saucepan. Add green onions and parsley, sauté until limp. Add flour, blend over low heat, stirring constantly, for 1 minute, add half and half and stir well. Add cheese, stirring until melted. Add sherry, salt, cayenne pepper and Tabasco. Remove from heat and fold in crabmeat.

Place artichoke hearts in the bottom of a buttered 3-quart casserole. Pour crab mixture over artichokes, sprinkle with bread crumbs, dot with butter and bake 30 to 40 minutes.

Seafood Stuffed Eggplant

A favorite New Orleans dish.
Serves 4

2   large eggplants
    boiling water
1   cup lump crabmeat
1   stick butter
1   cup raw shrimp, peeled, deveined and chopped
5   tablespoons chopped green onions
2   cloves garlic, chopped
3   teaspoons chopped parsley
    salt and pepper to taste
¼   cup French bread crumbs
4   tablespoons freshly grated Romano cheese

Cut eggplants lengthwise. Cook in boiling water to cover until tender. When cool scoop out and chop or mash pulp. Keep skins intact for stuffing.

Preheat oven to 350 degrees.

Remove any shells or cartilage from crabmeat. In a skillet, sauté shrimp, green onions, garlic and parsley in butter. Season with salt and pepper. Cook about 10 minutes, add eggplant pulp and crabmeat, stir together and cook 5 minutes. Spoon mixture into eggplant shells. Sprinkle with bread crumbs and grated cheese. Bake 15 to 20 minutes or until brown.

Crabmeat Elegante

Serves 8 to 10

2	medium onions, finely chopped
2	cloves garlic, crushed
1	tablespoon oil
2	pounds fresh lump crabmeat
¼	teaspoon white pepper
70	Ritz crackers, crumbled
2	cups whipping cream
1½	sticks butter, melted

Preheat oven to 350 degrees.

Sauté onions and garlic in oil until transparent, add crabmeat, pepper and half of cracker crumbs. Put into a 4½-quart casserole and pour whipping cream over mixture. Sprinkle with remaining cracker crumbs and pour melted butter over top. Bake 20 minutes.

Mardi Gras Crabmeat Casserole

An easy dish to prepare for your guests after a Mardi Gras parade!

Serves 4 to 6

1	pound lump crabmeat, picked over
6	strips bacon
1	teaspoon dry mustard
1	tablespoon chopped parsley
½	teaspoon paprika
½	teaspoon celery salt
½	cup bottled chili sauce
1	teaspoon tarragon vinegar
6	drops Tabasco or to taste
1	cup mayonnaise

Preheat oven to 400 degrees.

Place crabmeat in a casserole and set aside. Fry bacon until crisp, crumble and reserve.

Blend together mustard, parsley, paprika and celery salt. Add chili sauce, vinegar, Tabasco and mix well. Blend in mayonnaise. Spread mixture over crabmeat and bake 20 minutes or until bubbly. Sprinkle crumbled bacon on top and serve.

Crabmeat Mornay

Serves 8 to 10

1	stick butter
1	cup chopped green onions
½	cup chopped parsley
2	rounded tablespoons flour
1	pint half and half
½	pound Swiss cheese, grated
1	pound lump crabmeat
2	tablespoons dry sherry
	salt and pepper to taste

Pick over crabmeat and set aside.

In a saucepan melt butter and sauté onions and parsley until onions are transparent. Add flour and half and half, stir until smooth. Add Swiss cheese. Fold in crabmeat, salt, pepper and sherry.

Heat and serve. Recipe may also be served as an hors d'oeuvre. Heat and place in a chafing dish. Serve with toast points.

Shrimp and Oyster Stew

Serves 6

2	tablespoons oil
3	tablespoons flour
1	small onion, minced
½	green pepper, chopped
1	16-ounce can tomatoes
1	8-ounce can tomato sauce
1	pound raw shrimp, peeled and deveined
1	tablespoon parsley
¼	teaspoon cayenne pepper sauce
	salt and pepper to taste
	water as needed
2	dozen oysters with their liquid
2	cups cooked rice

Heat oil in a Dutch oven, add flour and brown well. Add onions, green pepper and cook until soft. Add tomatoes and tomato sauce, sauté well. Simmer covered for 20 minutes. Add shrimp, all seasonings, oyster liquid and a little water if needed. Simmer 15 minutes or until shrimp are almost cooked. Before serving add oysters and heat until edges of oysters curl.

Serve over rice.

Seafood Paella

Serves 8

1	large onion, chopped
1	clove garlic, chopped
1	stick butter, melted
1½	cups raw rice
½	teaspoon cumin
½	teaspoon oregano
½	teaspoon ground mace
1	bay leaf
1	teaspoon salt
¼	teaspoon pepper
1	cup crabmeat
½	pound raw shrimp, peeled
3	cups boiling water
1	cup sliced mushrooms
1	can (4-ounces) clams and liquid
½	cup sliced stuffed green olives

Sauté onions and garlic in butter until soft. Add rice and brown well, stirring constantly. Add seasonings, crabmeat, shrimp and water. Cover and bring to a boil; reduce heat and simmer 30 minutes. Add mushrooms, clams with liquid and olives. Toss lightly, cover and cook 15 more minutes. Remove bay leaf before serving.

Shrimp Hallie

Serves 4

1	stick unsalted butter
4	small green onions, chopped
1	cup sliced fresh mushrooms
4	dashes Tabasco
1	teaspoon Worcestershire sauce
1	tablespoon capers
½	cup chopped ripe olives
2	small cloves garlic, pressed
1	unpeeled lemon, sliced thin
1	cup dry vermouth
2	pounds raw shrimp, peeled, deveined and butterflied with tail shell left intact
⅓	cup fresh lemon juice
	fresh parsley for garnish
1	cup rice, cooked

In a large frying pan sauté onions and mushrooms in butter until onions are transparent. While stirring, add sauces, capers, olives, garlic and lemon slices. Add vermouth and bring to a bubble. Reduce heat to low and add shrimp. Pour lemon juice over shrimp and cook until pink, about 4 minutes, stirring occasionally. Serve over rice. Garnish with fresh parsley.

Leftover juice and rice may be heated the next day in a double boiler. When hot, add a pint of fresh oysters, stirring to allow them to heat through.

Shrimp à la Creole

Serves 6~

4	pounds raw shrimp, peeled and deveined (reserve heads and shells)
2	cups water
1	tablespoon liquid crab boil
¾	cup salad oil
4	heaping tablespoons flour
1	bunch green onions, chopped OR 1 large onion, chopped
2 or 3	cloves garlic, minced
	salt, black and cayenne peppers to taste
1	6-ounce can tomato paste
4	green peppers, minced
3	bay leaves
	pinch of thyme
¼	teaspoon sugar
1	kitchen spoon dry sherry or dry vermouth (optional)
1½	cups rice, cooked

Boil shrimp heads and shells in water with crab boil for 5 minutes. Strain, and reserve liquid.

In a heavy skillet, heat oil, add flour, cook over low heat to make roux. Stir constantly until brown. Add onions and garlic and cook until slightly brown. Add shrimp, salt, black and cayenne peppers. Stir shrimp in roux mixture until each shrimp is coated and none of the roux sticks to the skillet. Add tomato paste and green peppers. Stir continuously for 5 minutes over moderate heat. When tomato paste adheres to shrimp, add 1 cup of the warm reserved shrimp stock. Add bay leaf, thyme and sugar. Reduce heat and cook 15 minutes more, stirring well. Add sherry or vermouth, if desired, or add as much as desired of the remaining warm shrimp stock. Remove bay leaves before serving.

Serve over cooked rice.

Sizzling Shrimp

Serves 6

1½ cups salad oil
1   tablespoon salt
½   cup ketchup
1   teaspoon paprika
3   tablespoons minced onion
1   chopped green pepper
1   tablespoon lemon juice
1   teaspoon parsley
1   tablespoon hot pepper sauce
3   pounds raw shrimp

Combine oil, salt, ketchup, paprika, onion, green pepper, lemon juice, parsley and hot pepper sauce in a large non-metal dish.

Peel and devein shrimp, leaving tails intact. Place shrimp in sauce and marinate at least 2 hours in the refrigerator.

Remove shrimp from marinade, arrange on skewers and place on barbeque pit. Baste with marinade while cooking.

Suggested accompaniment: Oriental Rice (page 122)

Devil's Island Shrimp

A simple and delicious treat for family or guest!
Makes 4 servings

1   stick butter
3   tablespoons minced onion
½   teaspoon dry mustard
     salt and pepper to taste
1   pound raw shrimp, peeled, deveined and chopped*
1   pound fresh mushrooms, sliced
6   tablespoons flour
1¼   cups milk
1   tablespoon sherry
1   cup Italian bread crumbs

Preheat oven to 350 degrees.

Sauté onion in butter until transparent. Add mustard, salt and pepper, shrimp, mushrooms and flour, stirring constantly. Add milk and bring mixture to a boil. Remove from heat and add sherry. Pour into a greased 9 x 12-inch casserole, cover with breadcrumbs and bake uncovered for 30 minutes.

To serve as an appetizer, double recipe and place in a chafing dish. Serve with toasted rounds.

**1 pound cooked, peeled crawfish tails may be substituted for shrimp.*

Shrimp and Rice Casserole

Serves 8

4	tablespoons butter
2	ribs celery, chopped
2	small green peppers, chopped
1	medium onion, chopped
1	clove garlic, chopped
½	cup tomato sauce
½	cup dry white wine
4	pounds raw shrimp, peeled and deveined
½	teaspoon red pepper, or to taste
	salt to taste
2	cups cooked rice, cooked dry not moist
½	cup heavy cream, more if needed
¾	cup grated Cheddar cheese
¼	cup grated Parmesan cheese

Sauté celery, green pepper, onion and garlic in butter until clear and transparent. Add tomato sauce and wine, then simmer 5 to 10 minutes. Add shrimp, salt and pepper, cook until shrimp are just tender and plump, approximately 5 minutes. If mixture is too dry add a little more wine or water.

Gently toss shrimp mixture with hot cooked rice and cream. Combine grated cheeses. Stir 1/2 cup of combined cheeses into the shrimp and rice. Place shrimp/rice mixture in a casserole and top with the remaining grated cheeses. *Casserole may be made to this point and refrigerated until ready to bake.*

Preheat oven to 350 degrees.

Cover casserole with foil and bake 30 minutes. Remove foil and bake an additional 15 minutes until cheese has melted and mixture is bubbly and brown.

Serve casserole garnished with plum tomatoes and sprigs of watercress.

Shrimp, Sausage and Chicken Jambalaya

Serves 15

1	3-pound fryer
1	pound hot smoked sausage, thinly sliced
3	tablespoons olive oil
⅔	cup chopped green pepper
2	cloves garlic, minced
¾	cup chopped fresh parsley
1	cup chopped celery
1	cup chopped onions
2	16-ounce cans tomatoes
2	cups chicken broth
1	cup chopped green onions
1	6-ounce can tomato paste
1½	teaspoons thyme
2	bay leaves
2	teaspoons oregano
1	teaspoon chili powder
1	teaspoon salt
½	teaspoon cayenne pepper
1	teaspoon black pepper
1	teaspoon garlic powder
2	cups long grain rice, washed and rinsed 3 times
3	pounds raw shrimp, peeled and deveined

In a large pot, cover chicken with water and boil until tender, about 1 hour. Reserve stock. Discard skin and bones, cut meat into small pieces and set aside.

In a heavy 4-quart pot, sauté sausage; remove with slotted spoon and drain on paper towels. Pour off drippings, add oil to pot and sauté green pepper, garlic, parsley, celery and onions 5 minutes. Chop tomatoes and reserve liquid. Add tomatoes with liquid, broth and green onions. Stir in tomato paste, spices and seasonings. Stir in rice. Add sausage and chicken, cover and cook 30 to 45 minutes over low heat, stirring occasionally. After most of the liquid has been absorbed by the rice, add shrimp and cook until shrimp are pink, 5 to 10 minutes.

May be made ahead and reheated before serving. Freezes well.

Serve with tossed salad and hot French bread.

Shrimp and Crabmeat

Serves 6 to 8

6	tablespoons butter
3	pounds raw shrimp, peeled and deveined
6	tablespoons chopped green onions
	salt and pepper to taste
⅓	cup Sherry
2	tablespoons butter
2	tablespoons flour
8	ounces half and half
1	pound fresh crabmeat, picked over
	Tabasco to taste
¾	pound fresh mushrooms, sliced
4	cups cooked rice

Melt 3 tablespoons of butter, add shrimp, green onions, salt and pepper to taste and cook 1 minute. Add Sherry, bring to a boil and cook 15 seconds longer. Set aside.

Melt remaining butter, add flour and cook a few minutes. Add half and half and cook until thickened. Add shrimp, crabmeat, Tabasco and cook 5 to 15 minutes.

Sauté mushrooms in butter for a few minutes and stir into cooked rice. Serve seafood mixture over rice.

Shrimp de Jonge

Serves 6

4	cups cooked shrimp
1½	sticks, plus 2 tablespoons butter
⅔	cup hot milk
1¼	cups fine bread crumbs
⅓	cup chopped parsley
1	clove garlic, minced
1½	teaspoons salt
⅛	teaspoon pepper
¼	cup grated Parmesan cheese

Preheat oven to 350 degrees.

Sauté shrimp in 1/2 stick butter until very lightly browned. Divide into 6 individual casseroles. Pour milk over crumbs and mix. Let stand until thick. Add parsley, 1 stick softened butter, garlic, salt and pepper and mix well. Spread over shrimp in casserole, dividing mixture evenly. Sprinkle with cheese and dot with 2 tablespoons butter. Bake for 20 minutes.

Spicy Crawfish

Serves 6 to 8

2	tablespoons olive oil
1	onion, chopped
3	cloves, garlic, minced
1	2-pound can good Italian plum tomatoes
2	tablespoons dried tarragon or 4 tablespoons fresh tarragon
	salt to taste
1	cup cream
2	pounds cooked, peeled crawfish tails
6	drops Tabasco
4	cups cooked rice

Sauté onions and garlic in olive oil. Drain tomatoes and add to onions; cover pot and cook over low heat for 20 minutes. Add tarragon, salt and stir. Remove mixture from fire, purée in a food processor and return to saucepan.

Add cream crawfish tails and Tabasco and cook 15 minutes over moderate heat. Serve over rice.

Lack-Aqua Shrimp
(Shrimp boiled without water)

Serves 6

3	pounds unpeeled raw shrimp with heads
1	garlic clove
1	lemon, sliced
1	onion, sliced
2	celery tops
¼	cup fresh parsley
10	peppercorns
2	bay leaves
⅛	teaspoon thyme
1 to 2 tablespoons liquid crab boil	
1 to 2 tablespoons salt	

Wash shrimp, drain and place on bottom of a large heavy pot. Add remaining ingredients, stir into shrimp and place pot on stove. Cover and cook for 12 minutes on medium to high heat. Lift cover once and stir for more even cooking. Taste, and if desired, add additional salt. After cooking, allow to stand covered for a few additional minutes.

Shrimp cooked this way have a better texture, more flavor and produce an excellent stock for sauces.

Imperial Scampi

Serves 4

2	pounds raw shrimp, peeled and deveined
3	tablespoons vegetable oil
4	tablespoons grated Parmesan cheese
2	tablespoons chopped fresh parsley
3	cloves garlic, chopped
4	tablespoons lemon juice
2	tablespoons Worcestershire sauce
¼	cup dry white wine
	salt and pepper to taste

Combine shrimp and all ingredients in a shallow bowl. Marinate several hours in the refrigerator. Remove shrimp from marinade and place in a shallow baking pan. Broil 15 to 20 minutes, turning once. Pour sauce over shrimp and serve with rice.

Asparagus Shrimp Casserole

A great luncheon dish.
Serves 8

1	pound cooked fresh asparagus spears, (enough to cover casserole bottom)
2	cups grated American cheese
1	cup freshly grated Parmesan cheese
3	pounds cooked shrimp, peeled and deveined
3	eggs, well beaten
1	cup Sauterne wine
1	tablespoon Worcestershire sauce
1	teaspoon hot pepper sauce
1½	teaspoons salt
1	cup fresh mushrooms, sliced
1	can cream of mushroom soup, undiluted
¾	cup bread crumbs
½	stick butter

Preheat oven to 350 degrees.

In a greased 9 x 13½-inch casserole, place a layer of asparagus and cover them with half of the American and Parmesan cheeses. Add a layer of boiled shrimp, the rest of the American cheese and top with remaining Parmesan cheese.

To eggs, add wine, Worcestershire sauce, hot sauce and salt. Pour this mixture over layered ingredients in casserole. Add mushrooms and pour mushroom soup over mixture. Cover with bread crumbs and dot generously with butter. Bake 30 minutes or until bubbly.

Except for bread crumb and butter topping, casserole may be made a day in advance. Green beans may be substituted for asparagus. Does not freeze well.

Crawfish Etouffée

So good you will want to prepare extra for the freezer.
Serves 8

2	sticks butter
¼	cup flour
1	cup chopped onions
1	cup chopped green onions
¾	cup chopped celery
2	cloves garlic, chopped
½	cup chopped green pepper
1	bay leaf
½	teaspoon thyme
1	cup seafood stock (page 206)
1	cup dry white wine
1	cup tomato sauce
1	tablespoon Worcestershire sauce
2	pounds cooked, peeled crawfish tails*
⅓	cup chopped parsley
	salt, pepper and Tabasco to taste
2	cups rice, cooked

In a large Dutch oven, melt 1 stick of butter and stir in flour. Continue stirring until flour browns and makes a dark roux.

In a separate pan melt remaining stick of butter and sauté onions, green onions, celery, garlic and green pepper until soft and translucent, about 10 minutes. Add vegetables to roux along with bay leaf, thyme, seafood stock, white wine, tomato sauce and Worcestershire sauce. Bring to a boil, reduce heat and simmer uncovered for 45 minutes, stirring occasionally. Add crawfish tails and chopped parsley. Season with salt, pepper and Tabasco. Stir mixture until well blended. Cover and refrigerate until ready to serve. Thoroughly reheat and serve over cooked rice.

Dish is better if made at least 1 day in advance. Freezes well.

*Shrimp may be substituted for crawfish.

Crawfish Pie

Serves 6

	pastry crust (page 168)
1	pound cooked, peeled crawfish tails
½	teaspoon Creole seasoning
2	tablespoons butter
½	cup chopped onion
½	cup chopped green pepper
¼	cup chopped celery
2	cloves garlic, chopped
1	cup fresh mushrooms, sliced
1	10½-ounce can cream of mushroom soup, undiluted
¼	cup minced parsley

Prepare a 9-inch pastry crust. Refrigerate.

Preheat oven to 350 degrees.

Season crawfish and set aside. Sauté chopped onions, pepper, celery, garlic and mushrooms over medium heat in butter until wilted. Add cream of mushroom soup, parsley and heat 2 minutes on high. Add crawfish tails and pour into prepared crust. Bake for 30 minutes. Let cool slightly before serving.

David Bates (American, born 1952)
GRASSY LAKE *1982*
oil on canvas
Museum Purchase through P. R. Norman Purchase Fund and
Gift of Mr. and Mrs. Claude C. Albritton, III. © David Bates.

Oysters Bayou Lafourche

Serves 6 to 8

1	stick butter
½	cup chopped onions
2	ribs celery, chopped
¼	teaspoon finely chopped garlic
¼	cup chopped fresh parsley
½	pound fresh mushrooms, sliced
1	tablespoon flour
1	8-ounce can tomato sauce
3	tablespoons Worcestershire sauce
1½	teaspoons salt
¼	teaspoon cayenne pepper
4	dozen oysters, drained
½	cup seasoned bread crumbs

In a skillet, melt 1/2 stick butter, add onions, celery, garlic, parsley, mushrooms and sauté for 5 minutes.

In a large skillet make a roux by mixing remaining butter with flour and cooking over low heat, stirring constantly, for about 20 minutes or until brown. Add cooked vegetables to roux, add tomato sauce, Worcestershire sauce, salt, cayenne pepper and oysters. Heat until edges of oysters curl.

Preheat oven to 350 degrees.

Divide mixture into 8 large ramekins, sprinkle seasoned breadcrumbs on top and bake 15 minutes.

Mixture may be put in a casserole and baked about 20 minutes, or until bubbly. Serve over cooked rice.

Scalloped Oysters and Pecans

Serves 4 to 6

1	cup unsalted cracker crumbs
1	cup soft bread crumbs
1	quart oysters, well drained and chopped, or left whole if desired
1	cup pecan halves
1½	sticks butter, melted
½	cup chopped green onions
2	tablespoons Worcestershire sauce
	Tabasco to taste
	paprika for dusting

Preheat oven to 425 degrees.

Sprinkle cracker and bread crumbs on bottom of a 9 x 13-inch baking dish. Spread oysters evenly over crumbs and top with pecans.

Sauté green onions in 2 tablespoons of butter, mix with remaining butter, Worcestershire sauce and Tabasco, and pour over oyster-pecan mixture. Dust with paprika and bake 10 to 15 minutes until thoroughly warmed, but not browned. Serve immediately.

New Orleans Oyster Bake I

Serves 8 to 10

⅓ **cup oil**
⅓ **cup flour**
1 **stick butter**
½ **cup chopped onions**
1 **clove garlic, minced**
½ **cup chopped green pepper**
3 **tablespoons chopped celery**
2 **teaspoons lemon juice**
2 **teaspoons Worcestershire sauce**
2 **teaspoons salt**
1 **tablespoon ketchup**
  Tabasco to taste
1 **cup sliced fresh mushrooms**
4 **dozen oysters, drained and water reserved**
¼ to ½ **cup seasoned bread crumbs**

Preheat oven to 350 degrees.

Heat oil, stir in flour and cook slowly for 20 minutes until it forms a dark brown roux, stirring constantly.

In another pan melt 4 tablespoons of butter and sauté onions, garlic, green pepper and celery 5 to 10 minutes, add to roux. Add remaining butter, lemon juice, Worcestershire, salt, ketchup, Tabasco and mushrooms and simmer for 15 minutes. Add oysters and cook for 10 minutes. (Gravy should be thick). Place mixture in a 3½-quart casserole, top with bread crumbs and bake 15 minutes or until bubbly.

New Orleans Artichoke-Oyster Bake II

When fresh artichokes are in season, their addition to New Orleans Oyster Bake I makes a delicious New Orleans dish.

4 **artichokes**
  boiling water
  ingredients for New Orleans Oyster Bake I

Boil artichokes until leaves pull easily from heart. Remove from water, drain and cool. Remove leaves and scrape meat from leaves. Clean and trim hearts and cut into small pieces.

Preheat oven to 350 degrees.

Prepare a roux. Sauté onions, garlic, green pepper and celery in 4 tablespoons of butter until translucent—about 5 to 10 minutes. Add to roux. Add remaining butter, lemon juice, Worcestershire sauce, salt, ketchup, Tabasco, artichoke meat, sliced mushrooms and continue stirring for 15 minutes.

Cook oysters in separate pan until edges curl. In individual ramekins place small pieces of artichoke hearts and 4 or 5 oysters. Cover with oyster sauce and bread crumbs. Bake until bubbly. If baked in a casserole, mix artichoke hearts and oysters with sauce, top with crumbs and bake.

May also be used as a dip. Add oysters with their water and eliminate breadcrumbs.

Oyster Stew

Our Friday night special.
Serves 6 to 8

7	tablespoons butter
1	medium onion, chopped
1	small green pepper, chopped
½	bunch green onions, chopped
¼	cup flour
1½	cups milk
1	cup whipping cream
½	bay leaf
¼	teaspoon thyme
¼	teaspoon cayenne pepper
½	teaspoon celery salt
1	quart oysters
2	cups cooked rice

Sauté onion, green pepper and green onions in 3 tablespoons butter over low heat until vegetables are tender, about 5 minutes.

Melt the remaining 4 tablespoons of butter, blend in flour stirring constantly to prevent burning. Add milk and cream, stirring constantly until smooth, to make a béchamel sauce. Add bay leaf, thyme, cayenne pepper and celery salt and simmer 20 minutes.

Purée vegetables in a food processor or blender and add to the béchamel sauce. Add oysters and simmer briefly, about 5 minutes, or until edges of the oysters begin to curl. Remove bay leaf prior to serving over cooked rice.

Oven Barbecued Shrimp

This informal dish is a New Orleans favorite—easy to prepare, messy to eat, but yummy!
Serves 4 to 6

4	pounds large raw shrimp, unpeeled
1½	sticks butter
3	tablespoons olive oil
⅓	cup Worcestershire sauce
½	teaspoon paprika
1	teaspoon rosemary
½	teaspoon oregano
1	teaspoon salt
½	teaspoon cayenne pepper
3	teaspoons garlic salt
3	teaspoons garlic powder
1	teaspoon thyme
½	teaspoon celery salt
	lots of fresh ground black pepper (approximately 2 tablespoons)
1	loaf French bread

Place shrimp in a large pan in a single layer. Melt butter, add remaining ingredients except fresh pepper, and pour over shrimp. Grind pepper over shrimp. Cover and marinate 4 to 24 hours in the refrigerator, turning shrimp occasionally.

Preheat oven to 350 degrees.

Bake shrimp in marinade, uncovered, 30 minutes or more, depending on size of shrimp. Turn them once while baking. Serve in a large bowl with marinade. Cut French bread into serving pieces to be dipped into marinade and eaten along with shrimp.

Wood "Pops" Whitesell (American, 1875-1964)
PEP AND PEPPERS
gelatin silver print
13½ x 16½"
Collection of New Orleans Museum of Art.

Stuffed Mirlitons

A delicate vegetable pear found in the South.
Serves 10 to 12

10 to 12 medium-sized mirlitons*
6   tablespoons butter
¼   pound ham, chopped
1   cup finely chopped onions
4   cloves garlic, minced
2   tablespoons chopped fresh parsley
½   teaspoon thyme
2   pounds cooked shrimp, peeled,
        deveined and chopped
½   teaspoon Worcestershire sauce
¼   teaspoon Tabasco
        salt and pepper to taste
1½   cups French bread crumbs

Boil mirlitons until tender, but do not overcook. Drain and set aside.

Preheat oven to 350 degrees.

In a sauce pan melt 4 tablespoons of butter and sauté ham with onions until slightly brown. Add garlic, parsley, thyme and sauté until onions are well browned.

Slice mirlitons in half lengthwise. Discard seeds and scrape out pulp, taking care not to cut shell. Add pulp to onion mixture, along with chopped shrimp and cook over low heat until thoroughly warmed. Add Worcestershire sauce and Tabasco. (Taste before adding salt and pepper as ham may make mixture salty enough.) Remove from heat. Add 1¼ cups bread crumbs and mix well. Spoon into mirliton shells. Sprinkle remaining bread crumbs over top and dot with butter. Bake 20 minutes.

May be prepared in advance and refrigerated. Freezes well.

*5 or 6 medium eggplants may be used instead of mirlitons.

Creole Okra and Lima Beans

Great with Southern style chicken.
Serves 6 to 8

2   cups chopped okra, fresh* or frozen
1½   cups lima beans, fresh or frozen
2   tablespoons butter
½   cup chopped onion
1   cup diced celery
½   cup chopped green pepper
2½   cups cooked tomatoes
2   8-ounce cans tomato sauce
1   tablespoon sugar
1   cup water
¼   teaspoon pepper
½   teaspoon basil
½   teaspoon oregano
¼   teaspoon cayenne pepper sauce

*Fresh okra should be cooked in 1 to 2 tablespoons of oil until ropey texture is gone, about 25 minutes.

Cook lima beans for 20 minutes in a large pot of water.

In a deep pot or Dutch oven, sauté onions, celery and green pepper in butter until tender. Add tomatoes, tomato sauce, sugar, water and seasonings. Bring to a boil, cover and simmer about 1 hour. Add okra and lima beans, return to a boil, cover and simmer 20 minutes.

May be made a week in advance then reheated. Freezes well. Serve as a meatless entrée with rice and a green salad.

Turnip Casserole

Serves 8

12	medium turnips, cleaned and peeled
1/2	pound bacon
1/2	stick butter
3	green onions, chopped
2	medium onions, chopped
2	cloves garlic, chopped
2	egg yolks, beaten
1	small can evaporated milk
1/2	cup Italian bread crumbs
2	teaspoons sugar, or to taste

Preheat oven to 350 degrees.

Boil, drain and mash turnips. In a small skillet cook bacon. Remove bacon, crumble and reserve. Drain grease from skillet and add butter. Sauté chopped green onions, onions and garlic until translucent.

In a bowl combine egg yolks, milk, bread crumbs, turnips, sugar and bacon. Add onion/garlic mixture and blend thoroughly. Put in a greased baking dish and bake 30 minutes.

Southern Turnip Greens

Makes a delicious accompaniment to pork roast, sweet potatoes and corn bread.
Serves 4

1	bunch turnips with tops
1/2	pound pickled pork cut into 3/4 inch strips
1	cup chopped onions
1	teaspoon minced garlic
1/2	teaspoon freshly ground black pepper
1/2	teaspoon sugar

Cut tops from turnips and strip leaves from the stems. Wash leaves thoroughly to remove all dirt, (several changes of cold water may be necessary). Place leaves in a heavy 4-quart pot with sufficient water to cover. Cook, stirring frequently until greens are limp, about 10 minutes. Drain greens in a colander. In the same pot, brown the pickled pork. When meat has been rendered, add greens, onions, garlic, ground pepper and sugar. Peel and quarter turnips and add to the above ingredients with about 1½ cups of water. Cover pot and bring to a boil. Lower heat and simmer 20 to 30 minutes or until turnips can be easily pierced with a fork.

This dish may be prepared a few days in advance.

Squash and Carrot Casserole

Serves 12

4	cups cooked fresh yellow squash
1	cup grated carrots
1	cup finely chopped onions
1	2-ounce jar pimiento strips
1	10-ounce can undiluted cream of chicken soup
	dash of Tabasco
½	pint sour cream
1	stick butter
1	package cornbread dressing mix
¼	teaspoon Creole seasoning (optional)

Preheat oven to 350 degrees.

Mash squash and mix with carrots, onions, pimiento, soup, Tabasco and sour cream. In a separate pan melt butter and toss with dressing mix and Creole seasoning. Butter a 9 x 13-inch casserole and spread a layer of crumb mixture on the bottom. Add vegetable mixture and top with remaining crumb mixture. Bake 30 minutes.

Yellow Squash Stuffed with Shrimp

Serves 10

5	large yellow squash
	salt, black and cayenne pepper to taste
2	pounds raw shrimp, peeled and deveined
5	tablespoons butter
2	cloves garlic, minced
½	cup bread crumbs
⅓	cup chopped fresh parsley
3	tablespoons Parmesan cheese

Preheat oven to 325 degrees.

Parboil the squash and cut in half lengthwise. Carefully scoop out the seeds with a spoon. Season the inside of the squash with salt, black and cayenne pepper.

Sauté shrimp in a pan with butter and garlic over medium heat for 3 to 5 minutes until just cooked. Spoon shrimp mixture into the squash shells, sprinkle with bread crumbs, parsley and Parmesan cheese. Place on a buttered baking sheet and bake 30 minutes or until tops are golden.

White Squash, Ham and Shrimp Casserole

No one will know it's squash unless you tell!
Serves 6

6	medium white squash
½	stick butter
1	large onion, chopped
2	cloves garlic, chopped
2	pounds raw shrimp*, peeled and deveined
1	cup cubed, cooked ham
1	teaspoon chopped parsley
1	egg, slightly beaten
1	cup plain bread crumbs
	salt and pepper to taste
1	cup grated Parmesan cheese

Peel squash, remove seeds and cut into chunks. Parboil until slightly tender. Drain all but a little water from squash, mash and set aside.

Preheat oven to 350 degrees.

In a large skillet melt butter and sauté onion and garlic until translucent. Stir in squash and cook over low heat about 10 minutes. Add shrimp and ham and continue cooking until shrimp turn pink. Remove from heat. Add chopped parsley, stir in egg and cook 10 minutes. Season to taste with salt and pepper. Add 1/2 to 3/4 cup bread crumbs to thicken. Place mixture in a casserole and sprinkle remaining bread crumbs and Parmesan cheese on top. Bake uncovered 15 to 20 minutes until thoroughly heated.

*Crabmeat may be used instead of shrimp.

Tomato Casserole

Serves 6 to 8

2	16-ounce cans tomato sauce
¾	cup brown sugar
⅓	teaspoon salt
3	cups bread cubes (not toasted)
1	stick butter

Preheat oven to 350 degrees.

Mix tomato sauce, brown sugar and salt. Put in a baking dish and place bread cubes on top. Melt butter and pour over bread. Bake approximately 30 minutes or until bread is brown and toasted.

Sweet and Sour Stuffed Cabbage

Try this with your black-eyed peas and rice for a New Year's Day supper.

Serves 6 to 8

1	large cabbage, water to cover
1	pound ground beef
¼	cup water
1	egg
2	cloves garlic, chopped
2	tablespoons grated onion
¼	cup parsley flakes
¼	cup Parmesan cheese
	salt and pepper to taste
½	cup bread crumbs

Core cabbage and boil in water in a large pot for approximately 15 minutes. Remove from pot and let cool. Remove leaves without breaking them. Set aside.

Mix ground meat, water, egg, garlic, onion, parsley flakes, Parmesan cheese, salt, pepper, bread crumbs and blend together until very fine. Put a tablespoon of meat mixture on a cabbage leaf. Fold sides so the meat mixture is enclosed, secure with a toothpick. Repeat until all of the meat mixture is used.

Sauce:

¼	cup oil
2	cups chopped onions
2	15-ounce cans tomato sauce
¼	cup sugar
¼	cup vinegar
¼	cup water

In a large saucepan sauté chopped onions in oil until translucent. Add the tomato sauce and cook 10 minutes. Combine sugar and vinegar with water and blend into tomato sauce.

Place cabbage rolls and leftover leaves in a partially covered saucepan, to allow some steam to escape. Add tomato/onion sauce and cook 30 minutes or until done.

Spicy Carrots

Serves 4 to 6

1	pound fresh carrots, peeled
½	stick butter
½	cup brown sugar
1	small can frozen orange juice concentrate
¼	teaspoon cinnamon

Cut peeled carrots into 2 to 3-inch pieces and steam just until tender.

In a saucepan, combine butter, brown sugar, orange juice and cinnamon. Cook on low heat 5 minutes. Add carrots and cook an additional 5 minutes before serving.

Tarragon Carrots

Serves 6

2	tablespoons butter
3	tablespoons flour
2	cups milk
¾	teaspoon dried tarragon
2	tablespoons parsley
1	teaspoon sugar
	salt, pepper and garlic powder to taste
1	pound carrots, peeled and sliced

Make a cream sauce by melting butter, stir in flour and gradually add milk, stirring constantly. Cook until smooth. Add tarragon, parsley, sugar, seasoning and cook 3 to 5 minutes. Steam carrots and fold into sauce.

Cajun Style Cabbage

Serves 6

1	medium cabbage
2	tablespoons bacon or ham drippings
1	pound Tasso, andouille, smoked sausage, or ham, thinly sliced
¾	teaspoon salt
¼	teaspoon cayenne pepper
	sprinkling of black pepper
1¼	cups water

Select a cabbage with lots of green leaves on the outside. Rinse thoroughly. Slice off stem and trim off 8 or 10 outer leaves. Cut the rest of the head in quarters for easier handling. Trim out the core and slice cabbage quarters into thin shreds.

In a pot large enough to hold all the cabbage, put the bacon drippings and smoked meat of your choice. Bring the pot to medium hot and lightly sauté the meat. Add the water, bring to a boil, then lower heat and simmer 45 minutes or until meat is almost tender.

Shred the green outer leaves and drop into the pot. Cook uncovered for 10 minutes, taking care that cabbage does not stick to bottom of pot. Season with salt and pepper. (If using hot smoked sausage reduce amount of salt and pepper.) Add remaining cabbage and cook uncovered for a few minutes. Add more water if necessary, and continue stirring frequently for about 30 minutes. Do not cover pot or overcook.

Creamed Cabbage

A tasty dish, easy to prepare for a crowd.
Serves 10

1	medium cabbage, quartered
1	stick butter
¼	cup flour
1	cup milk
	salt and pepper to taste
¾	pound Cheddar cheese, grated

Preheat oven to 350 degrees.

Boil cabbage until tender and drain. In a saucepan melt butter and add flour, stirring constantly until smooth. Add milk, blend and cook until mixture is thickened. Add salt and pepper to taste.

Break cabbage leaves in bite-size pieces. Butter a casserole and layer cabbage, sauce and cheese, topping with cheese. Bake 30 minutes.

Artichoke Casserole

Be prepared for seconds.
Serves 8 to 10

1	large onion, chopped
1	teaspoon chopped fresh garlic
3	tablespoons olive oil
4	14-ounce cans artichoke hearts, drained and quartered
1	cup grated sharp Cheddar cheese
½	cup grated Romano cheese
3	drops Tabasco
1	cup seasoned bread crumbs
	butter for topping

Preheat oven to 300 degrees.

Sauté chopped onion and garlic in olive oil until translucent. Add artichoke hearts, cook over low heat, stirring, for about 5 minutes. Add grated cheeses and Tabasco, stirring while continuing to cook over low heat. Add bread crumbs and mix well. Place in a greased 2-quart baking dish, lightly sprinkle with additional bread crumbs and dot with butter. Bake approximately 30 minutes or until bubbly.

Recommend making at least 1 day ahead of time. Refrigerate and bake just prior to serving.

Stuffed Grape Leaves

Something different to try out on your guests.
Serves 10

1	jar grape leaves
1½	pounds lean ground beef
1	egg, beaten
1	cup finely chopped onions
½	cup partially cooked long grain rice
1	tablespoon chopped fresh parsley
1	tablespoon chopped fresh mint leaves OR 2 teaspoons dried crushed mint leaves
2	tablespoons olive oil
½	cup Zante currants
½	cup pine nuts, chopped
	small amount of water
	salt and pepper to taste
1½	cups undiluted beef broth
½	cup water

Rinse grape leaves very well and soak in a bowl of clear water while preparing stuffing mixture.

Mix ground beef and egg. Add onion, rice, parsley, mint, olive oil, currants, pine nuts and just enough water to mix well. Season to taste with salt and pepper.

Drain grape leaves and pat dry. Place shiny side of grape leaf down. Put a spoonful of meat mixture on rough side of leaf and roll folding ends of grape leaf inside as you roll it to help seal in filling. Place roll, folded side down, in a heavy saucepan, making more than one layer of rolls if necessary. Pour beef broth and water over the stuffed leaves. Cover and simmer 50 minutes.

Creole Green Beans and Tomatoes

A Creole delight!
Serves 4

1½	pounds fresh string beans
1	tablespoon bacon drippings
1	medium onion, chopped
2	small cloves garlic, chopped fine
½	green pepper, sliced thin
1	14-ounce can peeled tomatoes, drained and chopped, reserve juice
½	teaspoon sugar
⅛	teaspoon thyme
1	small bay leaf
2	dashes hot pepper sauce
	salt and pepper to taste

Wash green beans, snap off ends and remove any strings. Drain and set aside.

In a 3-quart saucepan, sauté onion, garlic and green pepper in bacon drippings over medium heat, until soft and translucent. Add tomatoes and their juice, along with sugar and other seasonings. Cover saucepan and simmer on low heat for 10 to 15 minutes. Add green beans, stir well and cook just until beans are tender, but still crisp. (A small amount of water may be added if necessary. However, cooking the beans in the tomato juice without added water, retains all the natural flavor of the ingredients.) Taste to correct seasoning. Remove bay leaf before serving.

Creole Stewed Corn

Serves 8

6	tablespoons butter
1	cup chopped onions
½	cup minced green pepper
3	whole cloves garlic
1	tablespoon flour
1	4-ounce can tomato sauce
4	cups fresh corn cut from cob (approximately 6 to 8 ears)
¼	cup water
1	teaspoon salt
½	teaspoon white pepper
¼	teaspoon hot pepper sauce
½	teaspoon sugar
2	tablespoons chopped parsley

Melt butter over low heat, stir in onions, green pepper and garlic. Sauté over medium heat until onions and pepper are transparent and soft. Remove garlic cloves. Stir in flour until smooth. Stir in tomato sauce, corn and water. Cook over medium heat, stirring often, for 10 minutes or until corn is tender. Add seasonings and sugar. Cover and simmer an additional 10 minutes. Stir in parsley.

Serve over hot buttered rice with roasted chicken or breaded veal.

Fresh Creamed Corn

An old fashioned favorite!
Serves 6

6	ears of corn
3	slices bacon
2	green onions, finely chopped
½	cup evaporated milk
	salt and pepper to taste
	pinch of sugar
½	cup milk
2	teaspoons flour

Cut kernels from ears of corn. Scrape cob with a spoon to obtain juice.

Cook bacon until crisp, remove from pan and set aside. Stir onions into hot bacon drippings, cook 5 minutes. Add evaporated milk, salt, pepper, sugar, corn and corn juice. Cook 10 minutes, uncovered, over medium heat, stirring constantly.

In a separate bowl gradually mix milk and flour stirring until a smooth paste is formed. Add to corn mixture and cook over medium heat, stirring until thickened. Top with crumbled bacon and serve.

Eggplant Fritters

Serves 4

1	eggplant
2	eggs
4	tablespoons self-rising flour
2	teaspoons baking powder
	vegetable oil for frying
	confectioners sugar or grated Parmesan cheese

Boil eggplant, drain and set aside to cool, then peel and mash. In a large bowl beat eggs, mix in flour, baking powder and mashed eggplant. Blend thoroughly. Drop by spoonfuls into hot oil in a large, black-iron skillet. Do not overcrowd. When edges of fritters are turning brown, turn to brown the other side.

Drain fritters on paper towels. Serve hot, sprinkled with confectioners sugar or grated Parmesan cheese as desired.

Eugene J. Bellocq (American, 1873-1949)
GIRLS PLAYING CARDS, STORYVILLE
gelatin silver print
8¹³⁄₁₆ x 6¾"
Collection of New Orleans Museum of Art.

Green Bean Casserole

This is a great vegetable to serve in a chafing dish for a buffet.
Serves 6 to 8

1½ pounds fresh cooked green beans, OR 2 10-ounce packages frozen French-cut green beans
4 tablespoons butter
1 cup sliced fresh mushrooms
2 tablespoons flour
½ pint sour cream
  salt and pepper to taste
½ teaspoon sugar
½ teaspoon Worcestershire sauce
1 tablespoon grated onion
½ pound Gruyère cheese, grated

Preheat oven to 350 degrees.

If using frozen green beans, cook according to package directions and drain.

Sauté mushrooms in 2 tablespoons of butter. Place beans and mushrooms in a buttered 2½-quart casserole.

In a small 1-quart saucepan, melt 2 tablespoons butter, add flour and blend in sour cream. Add salt, pepper, sugar, Worcestershire sauce and grated onion. Stir well, add to casserole and blend with green beans and mushrooms. Sprinkle grated cheese over mixture and bake until cheese is melted. Serve at once.

Hungarian Potato Casserole

Serves 4 to 6

2 pounds white potatoes, peeled
2 medium onions, chopped
2 tomatoes, peeled, seeded and roughly chopped
1 teaspoon Hungarian paprika
1 to 2 cans beef bouillon
  salt to taste

Cut potatoes into thick slices. Combine potatoes, onions, tomatoes and paprika in a casserole. Pour in bouillon to just barely cover potato mixture. Bake uncovered 45 minutes to 1 hour or until potato can be broken with a fork.

Large Lima Beans with Shrimp

Serves 6 to 8

1 pound large dried lima beans
4 quarts water
2 medium onions, chopped
1 stalk celery, chopped
¼ teaspoon thyme
2 teaspoons minced garlic
2 bay leaves
4 tablespoons butter
2 pounds raw shrimp, peeled and deveined
¼ tablespoon parsley
  salt and pepper to taste

Wash beans, drain and place in a 6 or 8-quart pot, add water, onions, celery, thyme, garlic and bay leaves. Cover and cook over medium heat approximately 2 hours or until liquid is creamy.

Sauté shrimp in butter, stirring until shrimp have turned pink. Add shrimp to beans and cook 1/2 hour longer. Add parsley, lower heat and cook uncovered 20 minutes. Salt and pepper to taste. Serve over cooked rice.

Broccoli Casserole

Curry makes this dish unique.
Serves 6 to 8

5 10-ounce packages frozen chopped broccoli
¾ cup mayonnaise
  dash of curry powder
1 tablespoon lemon juice
1 small box Ritz cheese crackers
½ stick butter or margarine

Cook broccoli according to package directions, drain well in a collander. Place broccoli in a mixing bowl, add mayonnaise, curry powder, lemon juice and mix well. Place in a casserole. *At this point, dish may be sealed with aluminum foil and frozen.*

Preheat oven to 350 degrees.

Crumble cheese crackers and sprinkle crumbs over broccoli, dot with butter and bake 1 hour.

Black-eyed Peas

A must for your New Year's Day meal along with cabbage and pork.

Serves 6

1	pound dried black-eyed peas
1	onion, diced
1	clove garlic, minced
5	cups water
1	teaspoon salt
1	teaspoon Worcestershire sauce
¼	teaspoon Tabasco
2	bay leaves

Wash and pick over peas. In a large soup pot or Dutch oven place all ingredients and bring to a boil, stirring frequently to prevent sticking. Reduce heat to low and simmer for several hours, stirring occasionally, until beans are tender. Remove bay leaves and serve.

Left over ham and ham bone or smoked sausage may be added for flavoring. May be served over cooked rice if desired.

Brabant Potatoes

Serves 6 to 8

4	Idaho potatoes
1	cup oil, or to cover potatoes
	salt to taste
	garlic powder to taste

Peel potatoes and cut into small cubes. Rinse in cold water and drain. Boil in water until partially tender. Drain in collander. Fry in deep fat until golden brown and crispy. Remove and drain on paper towel. Sprinkle with salt and garlic powder.

Reheat left over potatoes in butter, sprinkle with parsley.

Candied Orange Shells Stuffed with Sweet Potatoes

Wonderful for a Thanksgiving dinner.

Serves 12

4	cups sugar
2	cups water
6	large navel oranges cut in half crosswise
4	large baked sweet potatoes
1	stick butter, softened
¼	cup Grand Marnier liqueur
1	tablespoon Angostura bitters
1	teaspoon allspice
1	teaspoon cinnamon
	grated and toasted meat of 1 coconut (approximately 2 cups)

Make a simple syrup by dissolving sugar in the water in a saucepan and boiling 5 minutes. Set aside.

Working over a bowl, loosen the orange pulp with a sharp knife. Scoop out pulp and discard seeds and fibrous membrane. Reserve pulp and place orange shells, cut side up, in a Dutch oven. Pour in syrup, add pulp, cover and simmer 45 minutes. Remove oranges and strain syrup. Discard pulp. Reduce syrup by half or until very thick.

Preheat oven to 350 degrees.

Mash potatoes, beat in butter, liqueur, bitters, allspice and cinnamon. Sweeten to taste with strained syrup and add all but 1/2 cup coconut.

Fill a pastry bag with potato mixture and pipe into orange shells. Sprinkle remaining coconut on top. Place on a buttered baking sheet and reheat in oven 15 minutes or until warmed through. Broil until tops are brown. Serve immediately.

Louisiana Praline Yams

Serves 8 to 10

3   cups cooked yams
½   cup sugar
2   eggs, beaten
½   teaspoon salt
½   cup milk
¼   teaspoon vanilla

Preheat oven to 350 degrees.

Mix above ingredients in food processor or electric mixer and pour into a buttered casserole. (If food processor is used, you might use only 1/4 cup milk in yam mixture.)

Topping:

1   cup brown sugar
½   cup flour
1   cup chopped pecans
½   stick butter

Mix above ingredients until crumbly and place on top of yam mixture. Bake uncovered 20 to 25 minutes.

Cheesy Zucchini

Serves 6

3   medium zucchini
¾   stick butter, melted
2   cloves garlic, finely chopped
1   cup grated Parmesan cheese

Slice off zucchini ends and cut into halves. Steam until fork tender. Remove from fire, cool slightly and cut into spears. Place in a buttered, shallow baking dish. Combine melted butter and chopped garlic, pour over zucchini. Sprinkle on enough Parmesan cheese to cover zucchini. Place under broiler until bubbly.

Courgettes Farcies aux Amandes (Zucchini stuffed with almonds and cheese)

Different and unusually delicious!
Serves 8

4   zucchini (each about 8 x 2 inches)
¾   cup minced onions
2   tablespoons cooking oil
¾   cup ground almonds
¾   cup heavy cream or evaporated milk
¾   cup French bread crumbs
½   cup grated Gruyère cheese
2   large eggs
½   teaspoon salt
¼   teaspoon pepper
    pinch of powdered cloves
4   tablespoons melted butter
    paprika

Blanch zucchini in boiling water until fork tender. Cut each in half lengthwise and hollow out core with a spoon to form a boat. Salt boats lightly and drain upside down on paper towels. Chop zucchini pulp, squeeze out water in a strainer and reserve for stuffing.

Sauté onions in oil over low heat, covered, until transparent. Stir in reserved zucchini and sauté until tender and golden brown. Remove from heat and add almonds and cream. Stir in 1/2 cup bread crumbs. Blend in 1/4 cup cheese and the eggs. Mixture should hold its shape in a spoon, but if it is too soft, add more bread crumbs. Blend in salt, pepper and cloves.

Arrange zucchini halves skin side down in a long rectangular, buttered dish. Fill zucchini boats with stuffing. *Recipe may be prepared to this point, refrigerated and baked the next day.*

Preheat oven to 350 degrees.

When ready to bake, top zucchini boats with remaining cheese and bread crumbs that have been mixed together. Drizzle 4 tablespoons melted butter over them and sprinkle with paprika. Bake about 10 minutes or until slightly brown on top. Do not over cook.

Baked Cushaw

Cushaw is a Cajun squash resembling a giant zucchini. It tastes like a combination of squash and pumpkin.

Serves 4 to 6

2	pounds cushaw
1	cup water
1	teaspoon salt
8	tablespoons butter (1 stick)
¼	teaspoon cloves
¼	teaspoon mace
½	teaspoon allspice
¼	teaspoon pepper
	dash of cayenne pepper
¼	cup plus 1 teaspoon sugar
1	tablespoon vanilla

Preheat oven to 400 degrees.

Peel and seed cushaw and cut into small pieces. In a large saucepan boil cushaw with salt. Cook about 20 to 25 minutes until tender. Drain off water and mash cushaw. Add 7 tablespoons butter, cloves, mace, allspice, pepper, cayenne and 1/4 cup sugar to cushaw and mix well. Cook over medium heat 10 minutes, stirring constantly.

Remove from heat, stir in vanilla and transfer to a 3-quart casserole. Dot with remaining butter and sprinkle sugar over top. Bake uncovered in the oven 15 to 20 minutes, or until a browned crust forms on the top.

Baked Apricots

Serves 16 to 18

6	cans (16 ounces each) apricots
1	16-ounce box light brown sugar
2	sticks butter
1	medium box Ritz crackers

Preheat oven to 300 degrees.

Drain apricots, and pat with paper towels to remove all liquid. Place the apricot halves in a buttered 13 x 9 x 2-inch pan. Sprinkle with brown sugar and cracker crumbs; dot with butter. Repeat layering until all ingredients are used. Bake for 1 hour or until the top is crusty.

Serve as a side dish with turkey, meat or ham.

Baked Pumpkin

Serves 6 to 8

4	cups pumpkin
1	stick butter
¼	cup sugar
½	cup milk
2	eggs, lightly beaten
½	teaspoon nutmeg
½	teaspoon cinnamon
½	teaspoon allspice
⅛	teaspoon salt
1	tablespoon vanilla

Preheat oven to 350 degrees.

Wash peeled pumpkin and cut into small pieces. Boil until tender and drain. Mash pulp well and blend in all other ingredients. Place mixture in an uncovered baking dish and bake 40 minutes.

Hot Fruit Compote

Serves 6 to 8

1	17-ounce can peaches
1	17-ounce can apricots
1	17-ounce can pears
1	17-ounce can sliced pineapple
1	medium banana, sliced
1	package macaroon cookies
⅓	cup butter
1	cup light brown sugar
1	teaspoon sherry

Preheat oven to 400 degrees.

Drain canned fruit. Place in a large casserole with banana and add macaroons. Blend butter, brown sugar and sherry and spoon over fruit. Add juices from fruit. Bake uncovered 30 minutes. Serve hot.

Basic Bulgur

It has a nutty flavor.
Serves 4 to 5

1   cup bulgur (cracked wheat, available at natural or specialty food stores and some supermarkets)
2   cups chicken broth
½   teaspoon salt
⅛   teaspoon pepper, or to taste
1   teaspoon basil
1   teaspoon oil

Wash and drain bulgur twice. In a large pot bring to a boil chicken broth, salt, pepper, basil and oil. Add bulgur and return to a boil. Lower fire, cover and cook 10 to 15 minutes until tender.

Freezes well.

Bulgur Pilaf

This is an ideal stuffing for roast lamb, pork or chicken, or it may be served as a side dish.
Serves 6 to 8

3   cups chicken broth
4   bay leaves
½   teaspoon allspice
4   whole cardamom seeds
¼   teaspoon ground ginger
¼   teaspoon ground cinnamon
¼   teaspoon dried thyme
½   stick unsalted butter
2   medium onions, minced
2   cups medium bulgur (cracked wheat, available in natural or specialty food shops and some supermarkets)
⅓   cup currants or small raisins
¼   cup dry pine nuts or pecans, toasted until golden

Cook chicken broth, bay leaves and spices in a 4½ to 6-quart covered saucepan. Bring to a boil and simmer 5 minutes. Strain and bring back to a simmer.

In a large skillet melt butter. Add onions and stir over medium heat until golden. Add bulgur and cook about 3 to 4 minutes until mixture is slightly dry. Add to simmering broth, cover and cook over very low heat for 25 minutes. Add currants, cover 2 minutes. Just before serving stir in toasted pine nuts or pecans.

Cornbread Stuffing with Oysters and Pecans

Yield: 8 to 10 cups

2   cups chopped onions
1   bunch green onions, chopped
3   cloves garlic, minced
1   cup rendered chicken fat or butter
3   cups chopped celery
6   cups crumbled corn bread
2   pints oysters with their liquid
¾   cup rich chicken stock
¼   cup chopped parsley
3   tablespoons sage
2   tablespoons paprika
2   teaspoons white pepper
     salt to taste
4   eggs
1   cup chopped pecans

In a skillet over low heat, sauté onions, green onions and garlic in chicken fat or butter until soft and translucent, but not brown. Add celery and sauté another minute.

Stir in the cornbread so that it absorbs all of the fat. Chop large oysters in halves or quarters. Stir in chicken stock, oysters and their liquid. Add herbs and seasonings. Cool.

Mix in eggs, one at a time, stirring after each addition. Stir in pecans. Place in refrigerator until ready to stuff poultry or bake.

Oyster dressing should never be left in uncooked poultry overnight.

To use as a side dish, bake uncovered in a buttered casserole at 350 degrees for 45 minutes.

Cajun Rice Dressing

A favorite of Louisiana rice aficionados.
Serves 10 to 12

2	cups raw rice
4	cups boiling water
6	tablespoons cooking oil
2	medium onions, chopped
4	ribs celery, chopped
¾	pound chicken livers
½	cup chopped fresh parsley
1½	teaspoons salt
1	teaspoon pepper
2	pints oysters
1½	cups gravy (page 205)
	paprika for garnish

Cook rice in boiling water until tender and fluffy. Drain and set aside.

Heat 3 tablespoons of oil in a 6-quart Dutch oven and sauté onions and celery over medium heat until tender and translucent, stirring occasionally. Remove from pot. In same pot, add remaining oil and partially cook chicken livers until slightly browned. Remove from pot and cut in pieces that are not too fine.

Combine onions, celery and livers with the cooked rice. Add chopped parsley and season with salt and pepper to taste. Lightly toss mixture so that seasoning and livers will be evenly distributed through the cooked, dry rice. Place in a 3-quart casserole. *Can be frozen at this point, covered with aluminum foil and thawed completely before baking.*

Preheat oven to 400 degrees.

Poach oysters in their own liquid until edges are lightly curled. Add oysters and liquid to rice casserole and stir thoroughly. Large oysters may be cut into smaller pieces. *If rice mixture seems dry, add about 1½ cups cooked gravy.* Sprinkle top with paprika. Bake 30 minutes until hot and bubbling.

Cook rice or noodles in chicken broth with a teaspoon of butter or oil for added flavor.

Green and Golden Rice Ring Mold with Shrimp Sauce

Delicious and a colorful presentation.
Serves 8 to 10

1⅓	cups raw rice
3	cups chicken broth
½	teaspoon salt
½	cup chopped green pepper
½	cup chopped green onions
⅓	cup pimiento

Preheat oven to 250 degrees.

Combine rice, broth and salt, heat to boiling. Stir in green pepper and onions. Cover, reduce heat and simmer about 15 minutes until tender and liquid is absorbed. Remove from heat, add pimiento and toss lightly. Pack in a 6-cup buttered ring mold. Let stand in a pan of hot water in the oven until serving time, approximately 1 hour. Unmold onto serving platter.

If rice is cooked ahead of time, reheat in a colander then pack into buttered ring mold.

Shrimp Sauce:

1	10-ounce can cream of shrimp soup, undiluted
1	cup light cream
2	bay leaves
2	tablespoons lemon juice
⅛	teaspoon pepper
6	drops Tabasco
4	pounds shrimp, cooked, peeled and deveined OR 1 pound lump crabmeat

In a medium saucepan, combine soup, cream and bay leaves. Bring to a boil stirring constantly. Lower heat, add remaining ingredients and simmer until thoroughly heated. Discard bay leaves. Place in a casserole and serve alongside molded rice ring.

Orange Pilaf

Light and simple to prepare, makes an excellent accompaniment to chicken.
Serves 4 to 5

2	tablespoons butter
¼	cup sliced celery
1	tablespoon finely chopped onion
1	tablespoon of orange zest
1	tablespoon chopped parsley
½	teaspoon salt
⅛	teaspoon pepper
2	cups water
2	chicken bouillon cubes
1	cup raw rice

Melt butter in a saucepan, add celery and onion and sauté over low heat for about 10 minutes or until tender. Stir in orange zest, parsley, salt, pepper, bouillon cubes and water. Bring to a boil over high heat and add rice. Reduce heat, cover and simmer for about 15 minutes or until liquid is absorbed.

If desired garnish pilaf with orange sections.

Oriental Rice Casserole

Serves 6 to 8

1	stick butter
1	cup raw rice
1	6-ounce can water chestnuts, drained and sliced
1	pound fresh mushrooms, sliced
1	10½-ounce can onion soup
¾	cup water

Preheat oven to 300 degrees.

In a large skillet melt butter, add rice, water chestnuts and mushrooms. Cook for 10 minutes over low heat until rice is golden brown. Add onion soup and water. Mix well, pour into covered casserole. Bake about 1 hour and 10 minutes, or until firm.

Rice and Cheese Casserole

Spicy and simple, with a South-of-the-border flavor.
Serves 10 to 12

3	cups sour cream
¾	pound Monterrey Jack cheese, cubed
2	cans green chilies, chopped
	salt and pepper to taste
3	cups cooked white rice
1	cup grated Cheddar cheese

Preheat oven to 350 degrees.

Mix sour cream and Monterrey Jack cheese cubes. Drain and chop chilies, add to cheese mixture. Add salt and pepper to taste. Combine mixture with rice and top with Cheddar cheese. Place in a 2½-quart casserole and bake uncovered for 30 minutes.

3 medium chicken breasts, boiled, skinned, deboned and sliced in strips may be added to rice mixture before topping with grated Cheddar cheese. Dish may be made in advance. Freezes well.

New Orleans Oyster Dressing

Serves 10

2	long loaves stale French bread (buy bread 2 or 3 days before making dressing)
2	sticks butter
3	cups finely chopped onions
4	cloves garlic, finely chopped
3	cups finely chopped celery
6	dozen oysters
¾	teaspoon salt
1	teaspoon Worcestershire sauce

Preheat oven to 350 degrees.

Break French bread into pieces, toast in oven and then crumble. Sauté onions, garlic and celery in butter until tender. Add bread crumbs and mix well. Stir in 1 cup oyster water, oysters, salt and Worcestershire sauce. Cook on a low fire for 10 minutes, stirring frequently. Add more water if necessary. Remove from heat and place in a 4 quart casserole. Bake 30 minutes.

As seafood stuffing should be removed before refrigerating, this dressing is usually cooked in a casserole, rather than stuffed in a turkey.

Shrimp Fried Rice

Now a universal dish.
Serves 6

1   cup raw rice
1½ cups chicken broth
¼   cup butter
1   egg, slightly beaten
1   pound cooked shrimp, peeled and deveined
1   teaspoon salt
¼   teaspoon pepper
1½ tablespoons soy sauce
¼   cup chopped green onions

Wash rice in cold water and drain. Bring chicken broth to a boil, add rice, lower heat and cook 15 to 20 minutes. Remove from heat.

Melt butter in a skillet until bubbly and hot, but do not allow it to brown. Add the egg, which will puff up. As egg begins to cook, break into pieces. Add remaining ingredients, blend well and continue cooking about 10 minutes. Combine with warm rice.

This dish can be made in advance and heated in a double boiler.

Spinach Rice Casserole

Serves 8 to 10

3½ cups water
2   cups long grain rice
2   teaspoons salt
1   10-ounce box frozen chopped spinach
½   stick butter or margarine
2   stalks celery, chopped
4   green onions, chopped
1   small green pepper, chopped (optional)
1   clove garlic, finely chopped
     salt and pepper to taste
1   teaspoon chopped parsley

Place water, rice and salt in a 1½ or 2-quart saucepan and bring to a rapid boil, allow to boil for 1 minute. Reduce to very low heat and cover with a tight-fitting lid. Cook approximately 15 to 20 minutes or until all water is absorbed.

Cook frozen spinach and drain. Sauté remaining ingredients in butter for 5 minutes. Add spinach and heat mixture thoroughly. Salt and pepper to taste. Toss with cooked rice and garnish with parsley.

May be served in a vegetable dish, or molded. Excellent with any baked or broiled fish, fowl or meat.

Clarence John Laughlin (American, 1905-1985)
POSSESSED BY THE PAST
13⁷/₁₀ x 10"
Collection of New Orleans Museum of Art.
©Historic New Orleans Collection

Crawfish Pasta

Delicate, delicious crawfish sauce!
Serves 10 to 12

3	tablespoons butter
½	cup chopped green pepper
½	cup chopped onion
2	pounds cooked and peeled crawfish tails
1½	teaspoons salt
¼	teaspoon pepper
¼	teaspoon mace
1½	cans tomato soup, undiluted
1	pint half and half
¾	cup sherry
1	pound fresh angel hair pasta
3	quarts water
1	tablespoon oil
1	teaspoon salt

Heat butter in a skillet and sauté green pepper and onion about 5 minutes. Add crawfish tails, salt, pepper, mace, soup, half and half and sherry. Heat until warm.

In a large pot bring water, oil and salt to a boil. Add pasta and cook 1 minute. Drain and mix with crawfish sauce.

Sauce may be prepared 1 day in advance and reheated thoroughly before serving over pasta or rice. Freezes well.

Fettucini Carbonara

Serves 8 to 10

1½	sticks butter
2	cups sliced fresh mushrooms
2	cups ham, chopped
1½	pounds raw shrimp, peeled, deveined and chopped
4	cups chopped zucchini
1	can artichoke hearts, drained
1	cup whipping cream
1	pound fresh fettucini
¾	cup freshly grated Parmesan cheese
½	cup chopped parsley
	salt and pepper to taste

In a large skillet sauté mushrooms, ham, shrimp and zucchini in 1/2 stick butter for 5 minutes. Add artichoke hearts, cream and 1 stick of butter cut into small pieces. Bring ingredients to a boil and simmer 3 minutes.

Cook fettucini until "al dente," drain. Add pasta to skillet, along with cheese, parsley, salt and pepper to taste. Toss the mixture with wooden forks. Serve on a heated platter.

Pasta Florentine

Everyone will enjoy this dish with an Italian flair.
Serves 8 to 10

2	10-ounce packages frozen, chopped spinach
½	cup chopped onion
8	ounces uncooked spaghetti
½	cup grated Parmesan cheese
1	4-ounce jar chopped pimientos
8	tablespoons softened butter
2	eggs, slightly beaten
3	cups sliced fresh mushrooms
1	16-ounce jar meatless spaghetti sauce
8	ounces shredded mozzarella

Cook frozen spinach according to package directions, adding the chopped onion. Drain well. Purée spinach and onion.

Preheat oven to 375 degrees.

Cook spaghetti according to package directions, drain. In a large bowl combine spinach mixture, spaghetti, cheese, pimientos, 4 tablespoons of butter and eggs. Mix well and place in a greased 13 x 9½-inch oblong casserole.

In a saucepan sauté mushrooms in remaining butter for 5 minutes. Combine with spaghetti sauce and pour over mixture. Cover with aluminum foil and bake 25 minutes. Remove foil, sprinkle mozzarella cheese over top and bake 5 minutes longer or until cheese is melted.

Pasta Ittati (Frutta di Mare)

Serves 6 to 8

1	stick butter
¼	cup virgin olive oil
½	cup minced green onions
8	ounces sliced fresh mushrooms
4	tablespoons chopped fresh basil
1	pint oysters
1	pound cooked and peeled crawfish tails
½	teaspoon salt
¼	teaspoon ground cayenne pepper
1	cup half and half, or more to reach desired consistency
1	cup grated Parmesan cheese

Melt butter with oil and cook green onions and mushrooms 10 minutes or until just tender. Add basil.

In a medium saucepan heat oysters until edges curl, drain and add crawfish. Combine cooked vegetables with crawfish and oysters. Add salt and pepper, then slowly add half and half. Place all ingredients in a double boiler and heat, stirring occasionally, until hot.

May be prepared a day ahead and reheated before pouring over freshly cooked pasta.

Pasta:

4	quarts boiling water
1	tablespoon salt
1	chicken bouillon cube
1	tablespoon oil
1	pound fresh green or white fettucini

Place pasta in boiling water with salt, bouillon cube and oil. Boil for 5 minutes or until "al dente." Remove from stove immediately, drain in a colander and sprinkle with cold water.

Place pasta in a large serving bowl, toss with hot seafood sauce and sprinkle with freshly grated Parmesan cheese. Serve with extra cheese at the table.

Pasta Pie

Serves 8 to 10

2	tablespoons olive oil
½	pound Italian sausage, sliced thin
½	pound boiled ham, chopped
1	cup sliced fresh mushrooms
¼	pound pepperoni, chopped
1	cup freshly grated Parmesan cheese
1	cup freshly grated mozzarella cheese
6	eggs, lightly beaten
3	tablespoons freshly chopped Italian parsley
8	lasagna strips
	boiling water
1	teaspoon salt
1	tablespoon vegetable oil
	watercress and cherry tomatoes for garnish

Preheat oven to 350 degrees.

In a skillet, heat oil and sauté sausage, ham, mushrooms and pepperoni until lightly browned, about 5 minutes. In a mixing bowl, combine cheeses, beaten eggs and parsley, set aside.

Add salt and oil to boiling water and cook lasagna strips about 10 minutes. Drain and lay strips on paper towels, pat dry. Butter a 9 x 3-inch round baking dish and arrange 4 lasagna strips, placing end of first strip in center of dish, up the side, with an overhang. Repeat procedure with other 3 strips, slightly overlapping each strip to cover baking dish with lasagna strips.

Fill the lasagna 'crust' with half the meat/mushroom filling and bring overlapping ends of lasagna in to cover filling. Add remaining half of filling and cover with 4 remaining strips of lasagna. Cover with foil and bake 45 minutes. Remove from oven and allow to cool for 30 minutes. Invert pie onto serving dish, garnish with sprigs of watercress and cherry tomatoes.

Cut into pie-shape wedges to serve.

Bordelaise Shrimp Spaghetti

Serves 8

½	pound butter
8	ounces olive oil
1	cup minced shallots
½	cup minced garlic
5	pounds raw shrimp, peeled and deveined
1½	cups oyster water
1	tablespoon Tabasco
	salt and pepper to taste
1	cup minced parsley
1	pound No. 2 spaghetti, cooked
½	cup freshly grated Parmesan cheese
½	cup freshly grated Romano cheese

Using a large black skillet, melt butter, add olive oil, bring to a simmer. Add shallots, sauté over medium heat for 5 minutes. Add shrimp and continue cooking for an additional 5 minutes. Remove skillet from fire, add oyster water, Tabasco, salt and pepper while stirring. Set mixture aside to marinate for one hour.

When ready to serve, reheat slowly. After mixture simmers for a few minutes, add parsley and remove to a serving dish. Place spaghetti on individual plates; spoon on generous amounts of shrimp mixture, sprinkle with cheeses and serve.

Noodle Pudding

A delicious side dish with chicken or turkey.
Serves 8 to 10

1	12-ounce package noodles
1	tablespoon oil
2	eggs
½	cup sugar
3	tablespoons ground cinnamon
1	apple, peeled and chopped
1	cup raisins
¼	pound butter

Topping:

¼	cup sugar
1	tablespoon cinnamon

Preheat oven to 375 degrees.

Cook noodles following package directions. Drain and pour cold water over noodles, drain again. Pour into a well-oiled baking dish. Add beaten eggs, sugar, cinnamon, apples, raisins and butter. Sprinkle sugar-cinnamon mixture on top and bake 45 minutes or until firm.

Stuffed Tufoli

Just add tossed salad, garlic bread and enjoy!
Serves 10

1	box tufoli
1	tablespoon salt
1	tablespoon oil
3	pounds cooked shrimp, peeled, deveined and chopped
1	cup ricotta cheese
2	hard boiled eggs, peeled and chopped
3	tablespoons grated Romano cheese
2	tablespoons chopped parsley
2	tablespoons sweet basil

Place tufoli in boiling water with salt and oil. Boil until tender, drain and rinse with cold water until pliable. Set aside.

Preheat oven to 350 degrees.

Combine shrimp, ricotta cheese, eggs, Romano cheese, parsley and sweet basil, mixing thoroughly. Stuff tufoli with mixture and place in a well-greased baking dish.

Cream Sauce:

3	tablespoons butter
3	tablespoons flour
1	pint half and half
	dash of nutmeg
¼	cup of sherry
1	8-ounce package mozarella cheese
½	cup grated Parmesan cheese

In a saucepan over low heat, melt butter, add flour, stirring until smooth. Gradually stir in half and half and continue stirring until thickened. Add nutmeg and sherry. Pour cream sauce over stuffed tufoli. Lay strips of mozzarella cheese on top, sprinkle with Parmesan cheese. Bake 20 minutes or until bubbly.

Elisabeth Louise Vigée Lebrun (French, 1775-1842)
PORTRAIT OF MARIE ANTOINETTE, QUEEN OF FRANCE *1788*
oil on canvas
Gift of the Women's Volunteer Committee
in honor of the 75th Anniversary of the Museum.

IV. Tea At The Museum

Apple Bread

Yield: 2 loaves

4	cups diced fresh apples
1½	cups sugar
¾	teaspoon cinnamon
¾	cup vegetable oil
2	teaspoons vanilla extract
2	eggs, beaten
3	cups unsifted flour
2	teaspoons baking powder
2	teaspoons baking soda
2	teaspoons cinnamon
½	teaspoon salt
1	cup chopped pecans
1	cup raisins

Preheat oven to 350 degrees. Grease two 9 x 5 x 3 inch bread pans.

Combine apples, sugar and cinnamon in mixing bowl. Mix well and let stand about 30 to 35 minutes until juice is drawn from the apples.

Combine oil, vanilla, eggs and add to prepared apples. Combine flour, baking powder, soda, cinnamon, salt and mix well into apple mixture. Stir in raisins and chopped pecans.

Pour into prepared pans. (Mixture will be thick.) Bake for approximately 45 minutes, or until a straw inserted in the center comes out clean.

Apricot Nut Bread

Yield: 1 loaf

2½	cups flour
1	cup sugar
3½	teaspoons baking powder
4	teaspoons grated orange peel
3	tablespoons salad oil
½	cup milk
¾	cup orange juice
1	egg, slightly beaten
1	cup finely chopped pecans
1	cup finely chopped dried apricots

Preheat oven to 350 degrees.

Grease a 9 x 5 x 3 inch pan. In a large bowl combine all ingredients and mix until well blended. Pour into pan and bake 55 to 60 minutes. Cool 10 minutes in pan.

If baked ahead, pour 3 tablespoons melted butter over top, wrap in foil and heat before serving.

Apple Muffins

Yield: 15 muffins

1   egg, beaten
¼   cup shortening, melted
½   cup sugar
2½ cups finely chopped, peeled and cored apples
2   cups all-purpose flour
1   tablespoon, plus 1 teaspoon baking powder
½   teaspoon salt
½   teaspoon ground cinnamon
⅛   teaspoon ground nutmeg
1   cup milk
1   tablespoon sugar
½   teaspoon ground cinnamon

Preheat oven to 375 degrees.

Grease 15 medium size muffin tins. Set aside.

Combine egg, shortening, 1/2 cup sugar, stir well. Add apples, mixing well.

Combine flour, baking powder, salt, cinnamon, nutmeg. Add to egg/apple mixture alternately with milk, beginning and ending with flour mixture. Stir just until moistened. Spoon into muffin tins, until two-thirds full. Mix the tablespoon of sugar and 1/2 teaspoon cinnamon and sprinkle over muffins. Bake 20 to 55 minutes.

Herbed Casserole Bread

Yield: 1 round loaf

2   cups warm water (105 to 115 degrees)
2   packages active dry yeast
2   tablespoon sugar
2   teaspoon salt
2   tablespoons soft butter or margarine
½   cup plus 1 tablespoon grated Parmesan cheese
1½ tablespoons dried oregano leaves
4¼ cups sifted all-purpose flour

Sprinkle yeast over water in large bowl of an electric mixer. Let stand a few minutes; stir to dissolve yeast. Add sugar, salt, butter, 1/2 cup cheese, oregano and 3 cups flour. Beat at low speed until blended. At medium speed, beat until smooth, 2 minutes. Scrap down bowl and beaters. With wooden spoon gradually beat in remainder of flour. Cover with waxed paper and a towel.

Let rise in a warm place free from drafts about 45 minutes or until light and bubbly and more than double in bulk. Lightly grease a 1½ or 2-quart casserole and set aside.

Preheat oven to 375 degrees.

With wooden spoon, stir down batter. Beat vigorously 1/2 minute or about 25 strokes. Turn into casserole. Sprinkle top of batter evenly with 1 tablespoon Parmesan cheese. Bake 55 minutes or until nicely browned. Turn out onto a wire rack. Let cool, or serve slightly warm, in wedges.

Banana Blueberry Bread

Great with coffee or as a sweet afternoon snack.
Yield: 1 loaf

⅓	cup shortening
½	cup sugar
2	eggs
1¾	cups flour
1	teaspoon baking powder
½	teaspoon baking soda
½	teaspoon salt
1	cup well ripened, mashed bananas
½	cup blueberries, fresh or canned

Preheat oven to 350 degrees.

Cream together shortening and sugar. Add eggs and beat well. Sift together dry ingredients and add to creamed mixture alternately with bananas, blending well after each addition. Carefully stir in blueberries. (If using canned blueberries, be sure they are well drained.)

Pour into a well greased and floured 9 x 5 x 3 inch loaf pan and bake 40 to 45 minutes. Remove from pan immediately to cool on rack.

Freezes well.

Corn Bread

Try this with Southern turnip greens.
Yield: 16 1-inch squares

1	egg
1	teaspoon baking powder
1	teaspoon baking soda
1	tablespoon flour
1	teaspoon salt
1	tablespoon sugar
1	cup buttermilk
1	cup cornmeal
	grated onion (optional)
	cayenne pepper (optional)
	milk, if needed

Preheat oven to 400 degrees.

Mix the egg, baking powder, soda, flour, salt and sugar together in a bowl. Stir in buttermilk and cornmeal. If mixture seems too thick, add a small amount of milk. Blend in onion and cayenne pepper if desired. Spoon into a greased 8-inch square baking dish and bake 20 minutes.

Olive Nut Appetizer Bread

Yield: 1 round loaf

1	**cup milk**
3	**tablespoons sugar**
2	**tablespoons margarine**
2	**teaspoons salt**
1	**cup water**
2	**packages active dry yeast**
4½	**cups flour**
2	**cups shredded cheese**
¾	**cup thinly sliced green olives**
¾	**cup chopped walnuts**

Scald milk, stir in sugar, margarine and salt. Cool to lukewarm. Dissolve yeast in water, add milk mixture. Stir in flour until well blended, about 2 minutes, then add remaining ingredients. (The batter will be fairly stiff.) Cover with a towel and let rise in a warm place until more than doubled in bulk.

Preheat oven to 350 degrees.

Stir batter down and beat vigorously for ½ minute. Shape into a roll 16 to 18 inches long. Put into a well greased bundt pan, making sure the free ends are sealed together.

Bake 50 minutes. Turn onto wire rack to cool.

Orange Cranberry Bread

This is a favorite.
Yield: 1 loaf

2	**cups all-purpose flour**
1	**cup sugar**
1½	**teaspoons baking powder**
1	**teaspoon salt**
½	**teaspoon baking soda**
¼	**cup shortening**
1½	**teaspoons zest of orange**
¾	**cup orange juice**
1	**well beaten egg**
1	**cup chopped fresh cranberries**
¾	**cup chopped pecans**

Preheat oven to 350 degrees.

Sift together dry ingredients; cut in shortening. Combine orange zest, juice and egg and add to flour/shortening mixture. Fold in berries and nuts.

Pour into a well greased and floured 9½ x 5 x 3 inch pan and bake for 60 minutes. Remove from pan and cool on rack.

Freezes well.

Egyptian Bread
"Ti"—pronounced "Tea"

This is an ancient recipe from King Tut's time, given to us by an archaeologist.

Yield: 2 loaves

1½ cups lukewarm water and 2 cakes compressed yeast OR

2 cups lukewarm water and 2 packages dry yeast

2 tablespoons oil

⅓ cup molasses

2 teaspoons salt

2 tablespoons sesame seeds (optional)

5 to 6 cups unsifted whole wheat flour or half wheat, half white

Measure lukewarm water into medium-size mixing bowl. Add yeast, crumbling the cake, or sprinkling the dry form over the water. Allow to stand until dissolved, about 5 minutes, while preparing the other ingredients.

Measure oil into wet measuring cup and add molasses to fill cup to 1/3 mark. (This allows oil and molasses to be poured out of cup without waste.) Add oil and molasses to yeast and water mixture. Add salt and, if desired, sesame seeds. Add half of flour and stir well with a wooden spoon. Knead in more flour until a workable dough which no longer sticks to the bowl is obtained.

Form dough into a ball, return to bowl, cover with plastic wrap and put in a warm place to rise until doubled in bulk, about 2 hours.

Remove plastic cover and punch down dough. Sprinkle on a little more flour if dough is sticky. Divide in half to form 2 round loaves and place on a well greased baking sheet. Cover with plastic wrap and put in warm place 50 minutes or until doubled in bulk.

Preheat oven to 375 degrees.

Remove plastic wrap and bake 30 to 35 minutes. Remove from baking sheet immediately and place on a rack to cool for 30 minutes before serving.

Spread with herb butter. Serve with ground lamb, chopped onion, and a green salad.

Holiday Yeast Bread

Makes a wonderful Christmas gift.
Yield: 2 loaves

Dough:

5 to 7 cups flour

⅓ cup sugar

1 teaspoon salt

1 package dry yeast

1¼ cups milk

1 stick butter

3 eggs

Nut Filling:

Mix together:

1 cup chopped pecans

¼ cup sugar

1 teaspoon cinnamon

2 tablespoons butter

Cheese-onion Filling:

Mix together:

1½ cups grated Cheddar cheese

½ cup finely chopped onion

½ teaspoon paprika

In a large bowl thoroughly mix 2 cups flour, sugar, salt, yeast and set aside.

Heat milk and butter to 130 degrees (butter does not need to melt completely.) Gradually add warm milk and butter to flour mixture and beat 2 minutes with an electric mixer at medium speed. Add eggs and 1/2 cup flour and beat at high speed for 2 minutes. Stir in enough flour to make a stiff dough. Knead 8 to 10 minutes until smooth and elastic. Place in a greased bowl, cover with a towel and let rise in a warm place about 1 hour until doubled in size.

Punch down dough and divide in half. On a floured surface roll each half to an 18 x 10-inch rectangle. Spread with desired filling. Starting at long side, roll and place seam side down in a crescent shape on a greased cookie sheet. With a knife, cut 1/2 inch deep gashes about 1 inch apart. Cover with linen towel, let rise 45 minutes or until doubled in bulk.

Preheat oven to 350 degrees.

When nut filling is used, glaze bread with melted butter. Bake 50 minutes or until brown and crusted.

When cheese-onion filling is used, sprinkle bread with paprika before baking.

Breads are best if eaten the same day baked.

Spinach Bread

Serves 8

2	10-ounce boxes chopped spinach
1	8-ounce package cream cheese
1	6-ounce tube Jalapeño cheese
¼	teaspoon Creole seasoning
1	loaf French bread
2	cups shredded mozzarella cheese

Preheat oven to 325 degrees.

Cook spinach according to package directions. Do not add salt. Drain spinach and pat dry to remove all liquid.

Melt cream cheese and Jalapeño cheese. Blend into spinach, along with seasoning. Split French bread loaf in half lengthwise, lay open face on a cookie sheet and spread with spinach/cheese mixture. Cover with shredded mozzarella and bake 10 minutes or until cheese melts. Slice and serve.

Orange Pecan Muffins

Yield: 36 miniatures

2	cups sugar
½	cup orange juice
½	cup butter
2	cups flour, sifted
1	teaspoon baking soda
1	teaspoon salt
¾	cup sour cream
2	teaspoons grated orange rind
½	cup chopped pecans

Preheat oven to 375 degrees.

Mix 1 cup of sugar and the orange juice. Set aside for dipping muffins after they are baked.

Cream butter and remaining sugar. Combine flour, baking soda and salt. Add sour cream, alternating with the dry ingredients. Fold in orange rind and pecans. Pour into well greased miniature muffin tins and bake 15 minutes. While still warm, dip in sugar and orange juice mixture.

Sweet Potato Muffins

Yield: 24 muffins or 1 loaf

¼	pound butter
1¼	cups sugar
1¼	cups cooked sweet potatoes, mashed
2	eggs
1½	cups all purpose flour
2	teaspoons baking powder
1	teaspoon cinnamon
¼	teaspoon nutmeg
¼	teaspoon salt
1	cup milk
½	cup chopped pecans
½	cup chopped raisins

Preheat oven to 350 degrees.

Cream butter, sugar and sweet potatoes until smooth. Add eggs and beat.

Sift flour, baking powder, cinnamon, nutmeg and salt together. Add to batter, alternating with milk, beating lightly. Fold in pecans and raisins. Pour into greased muffin tins and bake 25 minutes, or until done. May also be baked in a greased 9½ x 5½ x 2 inch deep loaf pan for 1 hour and 10 minutes, or until done.

Pumpkin Bread

A fireside treat with tea.
Yield: 2 loaves

⅔   cup shortening
2⅔   cups sugar
4   eggs
2   cups cooked, mashed pumpkin
⅔   cup water
3 to 3½ cups flour
2   teaspoons baking soda
½   teaspoon baking powder
1½   teaspoons salt
1   teaspoon cinnamon
½   teaspoon nutmeg
1   cup chopped walnuts
⅔   cup raisins

Preheat oven to 350 degrees.

Cream shortening and sugar, add eggs, pumpkin, water and mix well. Blend in dry ingredients, stir in nuts and raisins. Pour into two greased and floured 9 x 5 x 3 inch pans. Bake 60 to 70 minutes or until a tester comes out clean. Remove from pans and cool on racks.

May be made in advance. Freezes well.

Reuben-Wich

A great filler after a Mardi Gras parade.
Yield: 1 loaf

3¼   cups flour
1   tablespoon sugar
1   teaspoon salt
1   package rapid rise yeast
1   cup hot water (120 degrees)
1   tablespoon softened butter
¼   cup Thousand Islands dressing
6   ounces thinly sliced corned beef
¼   pound thinly sliced Swiss cheese
1   8-ounce can sauerkraut,
      rinsed and drained
1   egg white, lightly beaten
1   tablespoon caraway seeds

Set aside 1 cup of flour. In a large bowl, mix remaining flour with sugar, salt and yeast. Stir in hot water and butter. Add enough of the reserved flour to make a soft dough. Knead 4 minutes. Roll dough on a floured board into a 14 x 10-inch rectangle, and place it on a greased baking sheet.

Spread dressing down middle third of dough, top with layers of corned beef, cheese and sauerkraut. Cut dough from outer edge into layered section, at 1 inch intervals. Cover filling by braiding alternating slices at an angle until completed. Cover with cloth, and let rise over a pan of hot water about 15 to 30 minutes.

Preheat oven to 400 degrees.

Brush loaf with egg white and sprinkle with caraway seeds. Bake 25 minutes.

Loaf slices may be used as a main dish for a light lunch or supper.

Zesty Lemon Bread

Yield: 2 loaves

2	sticks sweet butter
1½	cups sugar
4	eggs, separated
⅔	cup fresh lemon juice
2	tablespoons lemon zest
3	cups cake flour
4	teaspoons baking powder
1	cup milk
	pinch of salt
1	cup chopped pecans
¼	cup water

Preheat oven to 350 degrees.

Butter two 9 x 5 x 3-inch loaf pans with 3 table-spoons of the butter.

In a mixing bowl cream remaining butter and 1 cup sugar. Beat in egg yolks one at a time, stir in 1/3 cup lemon juice and lemon zest.

Combine cake flour and baking powder. Add one third of flour mixture to the butter/sugar mixture. Add half of the milk and another one third of the flour, then add remaining milk and flour. Do not over mix.

In a separate bowl combine egg whites and salt and beat until stiff but not dry. Gently fold egg whites and pecans into batter. Pour batter into prepared pans. Place on middle rack of oven and bake 45 to 50 minutes or until a straw inserted in center of loaf comes out clean.

Cool bread slightly, remove from pans and cool thoroughly on a rack. In a small saucepan, combine remaining sugar, lemon juice and the water. Boil for 2 minutes. Drizzle this lemon syrup over tops of cooled loaves. Do not wrap loaves until topping is completely set.

Zucchini Nut Bread

Yield: 2 loaves

3	eggs
1	cup oil
3	cups sugar
3	teaspoons vanilla
2	cups grated raw zucchini
4	cups flour
3	teaspoons cinnamon
¼	teaspoon baking powder
1	teaspoon baking soda
½	cup chopped nuts

Preheat oven to 325 degrees.

Grease and flour two 8 x 5-inch loaf pans.

In a large mixing bowl, beat eggs until foamy. Add oil, sugar, vanilla and zucchini.

In another bowl, stir together flour, cinnamon, baking powder and soda. Add to egg mixture, combining well. Stir in nuts. Pour into prepared pans and bake 55 to 60 minutes. Cool in pan.

Freezes well.

Basic Croissants

Worth your time and effort—a real treat.
Yield: 24

¾	**cup milk, scalded**
¼	**cup sugar**
1	**teaspoon salt**
2	**packs dry yeast**
	pinch of ginger
½	**cup water (105-115 degrees)**
1	**egg, beaten**
3⅓	**cups unbleached all-purpose flour, sifted**
¾	**cup unsalted butter, well chilled**
¾	**cup margarine, well chilled**

Egg wash: 1 egg beaten with 1 tablespoon water

Scald milk, add sugar and salt then cool. Dissolve yeast in water with ginger, add to milk then stir in egg.

Reserve 1/3 cup flour. Gradually beat in enough of the remaining flour to make a soft dough. Knead until smooth and elastic. Shape into a square, wrap loosely in waxed paper, place in a large plastic bag (do not close) and refrigerate to rise, 1 to 2 hours.

Cut well-chilled butter and margarine into 1/2 inch pieces, work into remaining 1/3 cup flour, working quickly so butter and margarine remain firm. Form into a 5-inch square, wrap in plastic and refrigerate for at least 1 hour.

To fold dough:

Remove dough from refrigerator and roll out to a 12-inch circle, then into a 4-leaf clover design by cutting part way through the dough in four spots and then roll dough up and down and crosswise. Put chilled butter mixture in center, catch each corner of the clover and fold dough over butter mixture to enclose it. Do not stretch dough. Seal dough on top. Dust with flour, then roll out to a 16 x 8-inch rectangle, keeping sides even. If butter breaks through, dust with flour. Fold bottom 1/3 of the rectangle up and the top 1/3 down over this. Turn 90 degrees so the open edge faces your right. Roll out again to another 16 x 8-inch rectangle and fold again as before. Put 2 thumb prints in the dough to signify that you have rolled it twice. Wrap in waxed paper and refrigerate 1 to 2 hours in a plastic bag. After refrigeration, roll out and fold two more times as before. Wrap in waxed paper again and refrigerate overnight. If during the folding process the butter starts to soften and run,

immediately wrap dough in plastic and freeze 10 to 15 minutes. The butter pieces must remain layered throughout dough to ensure flaky pastry.

To shape croissants:

Pat dough into a rough rectangle. Cut in half lengthwise through the center, then crosswise into thirds, forming 6 equal pieces. Return 5 pieces to refrigerator. Roll remaining piece out on well-floured surface into a 5½ x 14-inch rectangle. Using pastry cutter or long sharp knife, divide dough in half crosswise to form two 5½ x 7-inch pieces. Cut each piece diagonally to form a total of four triangles. Taking one triangle at a time, gently roll across shortest side until dough measures 7 inches across. Then gently roll from the longest side to point until dough measures 8 inches across. Holding point of triangle with one hand, loosely roll dough up from wide base to point with other hand. Transfer croissant tip side down to an ungreased rimmed baking sheet. Curve both ends slightly down and in towards center forming a crescent. Repeat process with remaining refrigerated dough. Brush croissants with egg-wash mixture. Set aside uncovered in a warm area (70 to 75 degrees) and let rise until doubled in volume, about 1 to 2 hours. Reglaze once with egg-wash during rising.

To bake:

Preheat oven to 375 degrees. Reglaze croissants with egg-wash. Bake on center rack until puffed and golden brown, about 10 to 15 minutes. Let cool on rack at least 10 minutes before serving.

Croissants can be cooled completely, wrapped airtight and frozen. Reheat unthawed croissants in 375-degree oven for 10 minutes.

Schnecken

A deliciously different coffee roll!
Yield: 6 to 7 dozen

Dough:

4	**packages dry yeast**
½	**cup water (110 to 120 degrees)**
5 to 6 cups flour	
1½	**cups butter**
½	**cup sugar**
1	**teaspoon salt**
½	**cup cold milk**
1	**cup sour cream**
2	**teaspoons lemon juice**
1	**teaspoon vanilla**
3	**eggs, beaten**

Topping:

¾	**cup soft butter**
1	**cup brown sugar**
1½	**tablespoons white corn syrup**
1	**cup chopped pecans**

Filling:

1½	**cups white granulated sugar**
3	**teaspoons ground cinnamon**
½	**cup finely chopped pecans**

Egg Wash:

1	**egg white mixed with**
1	**tablespoon water**

Dough should be made a day ahead, covered and refrigerated.

In a large bowl soften yeast in warm water. Mix 2½ cups flour and the butter, using a pastry blender. Add sugar, salt, milk, sour cream, lemon juice and vanilla to the yeast mixture. Stir in eggs. Combine yeast mixture with the flour/butter mixture, adding more flour as needed, approximately 3 cups, to make dough pliable. Knead on floured table for 5 minutes until smooth and elastic (dough will be sticky). Place dough in a buttered bowl, cover with a towel and place in the refrigerator overnight to rise.

For topping, cream butter, sugar and syrup until smooth. Butter 2 inch muffin tins. Put 1/2 teaspoon of mixture into each muffin pan, place in oven and melt. Remove from oven and put a few pieces of chopped pecans in each tin.

Filling: Combine sugar and cinnamon in a small bowl. Divide dough into 4 portions, return 3 portions to the refrigerator. Roll out dough on a heavily floured board to prevent sticking, and form a 12 x 17-inch rectangle. Sprinkle with 1/4 of the filling and pecans. Roll tightly jelly-roll style from long side. Seal side and ends with egg white wash. Refrigerate 10 minutes or longer. Cut in 1/2 inch rolls and place in prepared muffin tins. Cover and let rise 25 minutes.

Preheat oven to 375 degrees.

Bake rolls 20 minutes. Immediately after baking, remove muffins from tins and using a knife spread syrup and pecans remaining in tins on top of each muffin. Repeat directions for next 3 portions of dough.

Strawberry Bread

Yield: 2 loaves

3	**cups flour**
1	**teaspoon cinnamon**
1	**teaspoon salt**
1	**teaspoon baking soda**
2	**cups sugar**
2	**10-ounce packages frozen strawberries, drained**
1½	**cups cooking oil**
4	**eggs, well beaten**
¾	**cup chopped pecans**

Preheat oven to 350 degrees.

Mix dry ingredients. Make a hole in the center and pour in drained strawberries, oil, eggs and pecans. Mix thoroughly. Pour into 2 greased and floured loaf pans and bake 1 hour.

Serve with Strawberry Spread.

Strawberry Spread

8	**ounces cream cheese**
½	**cup juice from strawberries**

Mix cream cheese and strawberry juice until blended. Serve on thinly sliced strawberry bread.

Georgia O'Keeffe (American, 1887-1986)
MY BACKYARD *1937*
oil on canvas
Museum Purchase through City of New Orleans Capital Funds.

Bananas Foster

A fitting conclusion to any meal, but especially delightful at the end of a Sunday brunch.

Makes 6 to 8 servings

4	bananas, peeled
8	ounces rum
3	ounces banana liqueur
½	stick unsalted butter
4	tablespoons dark brown sugar
1	teaspoon cinnamon
	vanilla ice cream

Remove ends from bananas and slice in half lengthwise, set aside. Combine rum and banana liqueur, set aside.

In a flat chafing dish, melt butter and stir in brown sugar. When sugar is dissolved, add combined liqueurs and continue heating. Add banana halves, cook until soft but not mushy. Add cinnamon. Remove 1 tablespoon of liquid from chafing dish. Ignite liquid in spoon and carefully transfer flame to liquid in chafing dish.

Serve while still burning over vanilla ice cream.

Blueberry Clafouti

Serves 8 to 10

2½	cups fresh blueberries, sweetened to taste
3	drops almond extract
1	cup flour
1	cup sugar
½	teaspoon salt
2	teaspoons baking powder
¾	cup milk
1	stick butter, melted
	vanilla ice cream

Preheat oven to 350 degrees.

Sprinkle almond extract over sweetened blueberries and set aside.

Sift dry ingredients into a 2½-quart souffle dish in which the clafouti is to be baked. Add milk and mix well. Pour melted butter over dough and place blueberries on top. Bake for 1 hour and 15 minutes or until dough rises through the blueberries and the top is brown.

Serve warm with vanilla ice cream.

Bread Pudding
with Whiskey Sauce

Serves 12

4   **cups white bread ends and scraps, broken into small pieces**

2   **cups sugar**

4   **eggs**

2   **cups milk**

½   **tablespoon cinnamon**

1   **tablespoon pure vanilla extract**

½   **teaspoon salt**

1½   **sticks butter, melted**

       raisins (optional)

Preheat oven to 350 degrees.

Place bread and sugar into a very large mixing bowl. In a blender combine the eggs, milk, cinnamon, vanilla extract, salt and blend until foamy. Pour over bread and sugar mixture and let stand at room temperature 2 hours or until the bread has softened and absorbed some of the liquid. Add melted butter and mix well. Add raisins if desired.

Bake 25 to 30 minutes in a 9 x 13 x 2 inch cake pan. Serve with whiskey sauce.

Whiskey Sauce:

1   **stick butter**

1   **cup sugar**

1   **egg, beaten**

¼   **cup bourbon**

In top of a double boiler, melt butter and sugar. Add egg gradually, stirring with a wire whisk. Cool slightly and add bourbon. If serving immediately, pour sauce over warm pudding. If not, warm sauce slightly before serving.

Extra sauce may be kept in refrigerator up to one week. To reuse soften with one tablespoon of water and heat.

Charlotte Russe

Old fashioned and elegant!
Serves 10

2   **eggs**

2   **cups milk**

1   **cup sugar**

1   **teaspoon vanilla**

1   **envelope unflavored gelatin, dissolved in ½ cup cold water**

½   **cup whipping cream, whipped**

10   **lady fingers**

2   **tablespoons sherry**

Beat eggs well, stir in milk and sugar. Cook in top of a double boiler until mixture coats spoon. Add vanilla. Remove from heat, add dissolved gelatin and cool in refrigerator.

When mixture is completely cool, fold in whipped cream. Line a clear serving bowl with halved lady fingers. Sprinkle them with 2 tablespoons sherry and cover cake layer with custard mixture. Chill in refrigerator for several hours.

May be served garnished with cherries and slivers of chocolate.

Dessert may be prepared one day in advance, but cannot be frozen.

If eggs are cold, place in warm water for about 5 minutes to bring to room temperature.

Floating Island

An old fashioned custard, wonderfully light and fluffy!
Serves 10

Custard:

1	quart half and half
6	egg yolks
6	scant tablespoons flour
6	tablespoons sugar
1	tablespoon vanilla
	nutmeg

Scald half and half in a saucepan. In the top of a double boiler, beat yolks until light yellow, whisk in flour and sugar. Slowly add the scalded half and half, stirring constantly until smooth. Cook in double boiler, stirring constantly until mixture is slightly thickened, about 25 minutes. Do not allow mixture to boil. Blend in vanilla. Pour into a serving dish and refrigerate.

Islands:

6	egg whites
¼	teaspoon cream of tartar
4	tablespoons sugar
2	cups milk

Beat egg whites with cream of tartar until stiff peaks form. Slowly add sugar while beating constantly.

In a large skillet heat milk and simmer. While simmering, spoon in heaping tablespoons of egg whites. Let cook about 2 minutes. Using a slotted spoon, turn and cook an additional 2 minutes. Remove, drain on waxed paper and cool. To serve; float islands on top of chilled custard and sprinkle with nutmeg.

Lemon Mold

A quick, easy, delicious dessert.
Serves 10

2	8-ounce packages cream cheese
4	3-ounce boxes lemon gelatin dissolved in 2 cups boiling water
1½	pints whipping cream
	fresh raspberries or strawberries

Soften cream cheese on low fire. Remove from heat, add lemon gelatin and process in a blender until smooth.

After mixture cools, whip cream and fold into mixture. Pour into a 2-quart mold and chill overnight.

Unmold and garnish with strawberries or raspberries around edge of mold. Raspberry sauce, page 175, may be used instead of fresh fruit.

Raspberry Delight

Serves 8

½   cup flour
2   tablespoons brown sugar
½   cup chopped pecans
½   cup melted butter
4   ounces cream cheese
½   cup confectioners sugar
½   teaspoon vanilla
1   2-ounce envelope whipped topping
2   cups raspberries*, rinsed
½   cup water
½   cup sugar
2   tablespoons cornstarch

Preheat oven to 350 degrees.

Mix flour, brown sugar, pecans and melted butter. Spread in an 8-inch square pan and bake 10 to 15 minutes. Cool completely.

Cream the cheese and sugar. Add vanilla and whipped topping which has been prepared according to package directions. Spread over the cooled crust.

In a 1½-quart saucepan over low heat, cook 1 cup of raspberries, water, sugar and cornstarch, stirring until thickened. Remove from heat and add remaining berries. Cool completely, then spread over cheese mixture. Chill 12 hours before serving.

Other berries may be substituted.

Spanish Flan

A perfect dessert to complete any meal.
Serves 10

1   cup sugar
1   13-ounce can evaporated milk
1   14-ounce can condensed milk
1   can homogenized milk, measured in empty condensed milk can
4   whole eggs at room temperature
1   tablespoon vanilla

Topping: (optional)

1   cup sliced toasted almonds
½   pint whipping cream, whipped

Preheat oven to 350 degrees.

Cook sugar in a heavy skillet over medium heat, stirring constantly. When mixture is melted, turning brown and beginning to smoke, quickly pour it into a 2½-quart glass baking dish, or 10 individual custard cups.

In a blender, thoroughly blend milks, eggs and vanilla. Pour into caramel-coated dish or cups and place in a pan of hot water sufficiently deep to cover one-half of container. Bake 50 to 60 minutes, or until knife inserted in center comes out clean. Remove from hot water, cool to room temperature and refrigerate. (Flan should never remain unrefrigerated for a long period of time. It may be frozen and defrosted in the refrigerator.)

Unmold onto a flanged plate, or individual serving dishes just prior to serving. Top with sliced almonds and whipped cream if desired.

Strawberry Meringues Chantilly

Impress your guests!
Serves 8

1   **quart fresh strawberries, rinsed, stems removed, and sweetened with sugar if desired**

Meringue Shells:

2   **egg whites at room temperature**
1   **teaspoon vanilla**
½   **teaspoon cream of tartar**
¼   **teaspoon almond extract**
    dash of salt (optional)
1   **cup granulated sugar**

Cream:

1   **cup whipping cream**
2   **tablespoons sifted confectioners sugar**
2   **tablespoons brandy**

Preheat oven to 300 degrees.

Cover baking sheets with parchment paper or brown paper bag. Draw 8, 3-inch diameter circles, spaced 2 inches apart.

Beat egg whites, vanilla, cream of tartar, almond extract and salt until soft peaks form. Gradually add sugar, beating to stiff peaks. Place 1/3 cup mixture on each circle, using back of spoon to shape into shells. Bake 35 to 40 minutes until light beige colored. Cool and peel off paper. If not used immediately, wrap meringues in waxed paper and store in a cool dry place.

Whip cream until soft peaks form, then beat in sugar and brandy until stiff. Fill meringue shells with sliced strawberries and top with cream.

The volume of beaten egg whites is increased when eggs are at room temperature.

White Chocolate Mousse

Serves 6

6   **ounces white chocolate**
1½   **cups whipping cream, well chilled**
¼   **cup confectioners sugar**
8   **egg whites, room temperature**
1   **teaspoon cream of tartar**
¼   **cup granulated sugar**
3   **tablespoons whipping cream**

Slowly melt chocolate in top of a double boiler over low heat. When melted, remove from heat. Cool.

Whip 1½ cups whipping cream until soft peaks form. Add confectioners sugar and whip again until stiff. Whip egg whites in a bowl with the cream of tartar, gradually adding granulated sugar until stiff peaks form.

Add whipped cream to cooled chocolate and fold in gently. Fold egg whites into chocolate cream mixture. Chill 4 hours or more before serving.

Serve with Raspberry Sauce (page 175) and shaved semi-sweet chocolate.

Zitronencreme Fein (Lemon Cream)

Light and refreshing!
Serves 12

3	eggs, separated
1⅓	cups sugar
1	envelope unflavored gelatin
½	cup cold water
½	cup fresh lemon juice
¼	cup fresh orange juice
1	teaspoon grated lemon zest
1	teaspoon grated orange zest
1½	cups heavy cream, whipped

Beat egg yolks, add sugar and beat until thick and lemon colored. Soften gelatin in cold water, place in a double boiler, dissolve over hot water, then slowly stir into egg mixture. Add lemon, orange juices and zest, mixing well. Pour mixture into a large bowl and chill until it begins to thicken, and resembles unbeaten egg whites.

Beat egg whites until stiff peaks form, and fold into custard mixture. Gently fold in whipped cream. Pour into a glass serving dish or individual ramekins and chill until set.

May be made one day in advance, or frozen.

Orange Glazed Pecans

Yield: 3 cups

2	cups light brown sugar
½	cup heavy cream
1	tablespoon vinegar
	zest of 3 oranges
1	pound pecan halves

Combine sugar and cream in a large saucepan. Cook mixture to boiling stage, stirring constantly, until soft ball will form in a cup of cold water. Remove from heat, stir in vinegar and orange zest. Add pecans and stir until they are well coated. Spread mixture on a large platter to cool. When thoroughly cooled, separate into individual pecans.

Date-Nut Pudding

Serves 8

1	cup dates
1	cup nuts (pecans)
2	tablespoons flour
1	cup sugar
1	cup milk
2	eggs
1	teaspoon baking powder
	grated nutmeg

Flour dates and nuts, mix together with sugar, milk, eggs and baking powder. Steam in a double boiler 40 minutes. Sprinkle with grated nutmeg before serving.

Serve with Lemon Sauce.

Lemon Sauce

2	teaspoons cornstarch
½	cup sugar
	pinch salt
	pinch nutmeg
1	cup water
2	egg yolks, beaten
2	tablespoons butter
2	tablespoons lemon juice
½	teaspoon grated lemon peel

Mix cornstarch, sugar, salt and nutmeg; gradually stir in water. Cook over low heat, stirring constantly, until thick and clear. Stir small amount of hot mixture into egg yolks, then return to hot mixture. Cook 1 minute. Remove from heat and add butter, lemon juice and grated lemon peel; stir.

Rich and delicious.

Baked Alaska

At supper dances after Mardi Gras balls, a New Orleans custom is for waiters to come dancing out with flaming Baked Alaska to the tune of "When the Saints Go Marching In."

Serves 8

1½ **cups sifted cake flour**
½ **teaspoon baking powder**
¼ **teaspoon salt**
5 **large eggs, separated**
1½ **cups sugar**
½ **cup cold water**
1 **teaspoon vanilla**
¾ **teaspoon cream of tartar**

For Meringue:
6 **egg whites**
1 **teaspoon cream of tartar**
6 **tablespoons sugar**
1 **gallon vanilla ice cream (in block form)**
1 **cup brandy**

Preheat oven to 325 degrees.

Prepare cake: On wax paper sift together flour, baking powder and salt. In a large bowl beat egg yolks until they begin to thicken and are lemon-colored. Gradually beat in sugar until mixture is very thick and ivory colored. Add water and vanilla and beat to blend. Gradually fold in flour mixture.

With clean beaters in a medium bowl, beat egg whites with 3/4 teaspoon cream of tartar until they hold stiff straight peaks when beater is slowly withdrawn. Gradually fold into egg yolk mixture. Turn into an ungreased 9 x 12-inch loaf pan. Bake 1 hour, or until surface springs back when lightly touched with finger.

After cake cools, loosen with a small spatula and cut in half lengthwise. Invert one half cut cake on a 9 x 12-inch flat baking pan. Cut ice cream block in half lengthwise and mold on top of cake. Place other cake half on ice cream. Layer remaining ice cream on top, smoothing sides to make an even finish. Place cake in freezer while preparing meringue.

Beat 6 egg whites with cream of tartar and sugar until stiff. Ice cake with one inch layer of meringue, covering it completely and return to freezer.

When ready to serve, bake in a preheated 450 degree oven 6 to 8 minutes or until meringue is lightly browned.

Warm brandy in a small saucepan, carefully pour over cake and ignite. Slice and serve.

Delicious served with chocolate sauce.

Chocolate Sauce

Yield: 2 cups

4 **ounces (4 squares) unsweetened chocolate**
2 **tablespoons butter**
1 **cup sugar**
⅛ **teaspoon salt**
1 **cup light cream**
1 **teaspoon vanilla extract**

Put chocolate and butter in a double boiler over hot, not boiling, water. Stir frequently until chocolate melts. Stir in sugar and salt, then gradually add cream, stirring until smooth.

Remove top pot and place over low heat, stirring constantly until sauce thickens slightly. Remove from heat and stir in vanilla.

Will keep three weeks in the refrigerator. Reheat in a double boiler over hot water. If too stiff, stir in a little cream or milk.

Fresh Coconut Cake

A real treat for cake lovers!
Serves 12 to 15

1   fresh coconut

Puncture fresh coconut, drain milk, and set aside. Place coconut in a pan and bake at 350 degrees until shell begins to crack, about 45 minutes. Cool, then tap with a hammer to break shell. Pry out meat with a knife and grate.

Cake Batter:

2   sticks butter

2   cups sugar

4   eggs, separated

2⅔ cups all-purpose flour

⅛   teaspoon salt

4   teaspoons baking powder

½   cup milk

½   cup coconut milk

1   teaspoon vanilla

Preheat oven to 375 degrees.

Grease and flour three 8-inch cake pans.

Cream butter and sugar well. Add egg yolks and beat until creamy. Sift flour, salt and baking powder together. Add to butter-sugar mixture, alternating with the milk, then add vanilla. Beat egg whites until stiff and fold into mixture. Pour into cake pans and bake 25 minutes or until done.

Coconut Filling:

1   egg yolk

1   cup milk or part coconut milk

1   cup sugar

1   tablespoon cornstarch

1   teaspoon vanilla

½   cup grated fresh coconut meat

Mix together all ingredients except grated coconut and cook in a double boiler over low heat, stirring until thickened. Cool filling and stir in grated coconut. Spread filling on top of cooled cake layers.

Fluffy White Icing:

2   egg whites, unbeaten

1½ cups light corn syrup
**   dash of salt**

1   teaspoon vanilla

½   cup grated fresh coconut meat

Combine egg whites, corn syrup and salt in top of double boiler, beating with rotary beater until mixed. Place over boiling water. Cook for 7 minutes, beating constantly, until it stands in stiff peaks. Remove from boiling water, add vanilla and beat until thick enough to spread over cooled cake. Sprinkle remaining grated coconut on top of iced cake.

Pumpkin Pound Cake

Serves 10 to 12

3   cups sifted all-purpose flour

½   teaspoon salt

2   teaspoons baking powder

¼   teaspoon soda

2   teaspoons cinnamon

1   teaspoon nutmeg

1   teaspoon allspice

1   cup salad oil

3   cups sugar

3   eggs

1   16-ounce can pumpkin

1   cup chopped pecans

Preheat oven to 350 degrees.

Sift all dry ingredients together twice.

In a mixer blend salad oil and sugar thoroughly. Add eggs one at a time, beating well after each addition. Add pumpkin and mix thoroughly. Turn mixer to lowest speed and blend in sifted dry ingredients. Stir in chopped pecans. Pour batter into a greased and floured 10-inch tube pan and bake 1 hour.

May be baked in two 9½ x 5-inch loaf pans.

Good topped with whipped cream.

Doberge Cake

Everyone's favorite!
Serves 12 to 14

Cake Layers:

2   frozen Genoise cakes (page 160)
Frozen cake cuts easier with serrated knife.

Make a cardboard base the same diameter as cake, on which to place the first layer. Split each cake into 3 or 4 thin layers.

Pastry Cream Filling:

6   egg yolks, room temperature
½   cup sugar
2   cups hot milk
½   cup flour, unsifted
½   teaspoon salt
1½ to 2 tablespoons butter, softened
1   tablespoon vanilla extract

In a 2½-quart heavy saucepan gradually beat sugar into egg yolks using a wire whisk. While beating, heat milk in another pan. Do not boil milk. Beat egg yolks until they are pale yellow, thick, and form a ribbon when beaters are lifted. Combine flour and salt and beat into eggs until completely blended. Beat in hot milk in a thin stream.

Place saucepan over moderate heat. Stir constantly with wire whisk, taking care to include the entire bottom of pan. As mixture thickens it will get lumpy. Beat vigorously to a smooth texture. Be sure to cook it thick enough as it can be thinned later with milk or cream if necessary.

Remove from heat. Beat in butter, then vanilla. If scorched, pass through a fine sieve into a clean bowl. To prevent crusting, cover immediately with a rounded sheet of waxed paper placed directly on top of the cream or put a smooth layer of butter on top of cream. Refrigerate to cool.

Will keep several days under refrigeration, or may be frozen. If cream becomes watery, just mix well to reconstitute.

Spread custard filling on top of each layer while stacking layers. Ice cake with chocolate frosting or fondant icing

Doberge Cake (Frostings)

Chocolate Frosting:

4½   ounces semi-sweet chocolate
½   cup butter
3   cups sifted confectioners sugar
⅓   cup milk
2   egg whites, unbeaten
1   teaspoon vanilla

Melt chocolate and butter together over very low heat. Add sugar, then milk, egg white and vanilla, stirring until well blended. Place in a bowl of ice water and beat with rotary beater until of spreading consistency.

Fondant Icing:

2   ounces semi-sweet chocolate, melted
⅓   cup water
2   tablespoons corn syrup
1   pound confectioners sugar
1   teaspoon vanilla extract

Bring 1/3 cup water and corn syrup to a boil. Sift sugar into a large bowl, add hot syrup mixture and stir to dissolve. Add chocolate and vanilla, stir until smooth.

Fondant icing will be more "runny" than other frostings. Place the cake on a rack with waxed paper underneath. Pour icing over top and sides, using a spatula to pick up drippings and completely coat sides.

Chocolate Dome

Elegant appearance, delicious taste!
Serves 12

Cake:

6	eggs, separated
1	cup sugar
½	cup all-purpose flour
½	cup cocoa

Filling:

1	pint whipping cream
½	cup cocoa
½	cup sugar

Frosting:

	red currant jelly
1	tablespoon kirsch (cherry liqueur)
8	ounces semisweet chocolate
2	tablespoons vegetable oil

Preheat oven to 350 degrees.

Line a 3-quart round ovenproof glass bowl with foil and butter well.

Cake:

Beat yolks in a large glass bowl until pale yellow. Gradually add 3/4 cup sugar, beating constantly until mixture looks white and forms a ribbon when dropped from beaters.

In another bowl beat egg whites until stiff peaks form. Gradually add remaining sugar, 1 tablespoon at a time, and continue beating until very stiff. Pour yolk mixture into whites. Sift dry ingredients together and then sift evenly over top of mixture. Gently fold all ingredients together. Pour into prepared bowl and bake 15 minutes. Reduce oven to 325 degrees and continue baking until cake springs back when lightly touched, about 30 to 35 minutes. Cool in pan on a rack for 15 minutes. Carefully invert onto plate and peel off foil (cake will have shrunk).

Filling:

Whip cream until soft peaks form. Combine cocoa and sugar and blend into whipped cream.

Cut a 1-inch lid off top of cake and carefully hollow out cake, leaving a 1½-inch shell. Break scooped out cake into small pieces and let cool completely.

Reserve half of whipped cream for decoration. Spread some whipped cream over bottom of shell and top with cake pieces. Continue layering whipped cream and cake pieces until shell is completely re-filled and cake is dome shaped. Replace lid.

Frosting:

Melt currant jelly in a small saucepan over low heat, stirring continuously until smooth and spreadable. Remove from fire and add kirsch. Cover cake with jelly glaze, making sure it covers seam where lid was replaced.

Heat chocolate and oil in a double boiler over hot water until melted. Slowly pour chocolate over entire cake, making sure not to miss any spots. Chill until frosting hardens.

If necessary, beat reserved cream until stiff enough to fill a pastry tube, and use to decorate cake. Refrigerate overnight.

Will stay moist in refrigerator for several days or can be frozen. To serve, let stand at room temperature for 1 hour before slicing.

New York Deli Cheesecake

An original New York favorite.
Serves 16

1 pound ricotta cheese
2 cups sour cream
2 8-ounce packages cream cheese
1½ cups sugar
½ cup butter, melted
3 extra large eggs
3 tablespoons flour
3 tablespoons cornstarch
5 teaspoons vanilla
5 teaspoons fresh lemon juice

Preheat oven to 350 degrees.

Have all ingredients at room temperature. Combine ricotta cheese and sour cream in a large food processor. Slowly add cream cheese, sugar and butter. Add eggs, flour, cornstarch, vanilla and lemon juice and blend to a smooth consistency. Pour mixture into a 10-inch springform pan. Bake 1 hour on middle rack of oven. Turn heat off and leave cake in oven with door closed for one more hour. Cool on rack.

Note: Using a food processor will assure a smooth, velvety-textured cake.

Chocolate Cheesecake

Essentially chocolate!
Serves 12

2 cups chocolate cookie crumbs
⅓ cup butter, melted
3 8-ounce packages cream cheese
3 eggs
1 cup sugar
12 ounces chocolate chips, melted
1 teaspoon vanilla
1 cup sour cream
1 cup whipping cream, whipped
12 chocolate leaves*
½ cup chocolate chips

Combine chocolate cookie crumbs and melted butter. Pat on bottom and up one-third of the sides of a 9 inch springform pan. Refrigerate until ready to use.

Preheat oven to 350 degrees.

Beat cream cheese, add eggs one at a time, blending well after each addition. Add sugar and continue to beat while adding melted chocolate, vanilla and sour cream. Mix well. Pour into prepared pan and bake 1 hour. Cool, then refrigerate. *May be frozen at this point.*

Remove side of springform pan. Cover top and sides with whipped cream. Circle top edges of cake with chocolate leaves.

*Chocolate leaves:

4 ounces (½ cup) semi-sweet chocolate chips
½ teaspoon vegetable shortening

Wash and pat dry 12 rose or camellia leaves. Melt chocolate and shortening over low heat in a non-stick pan. Using small brush, cover undersides of leaves with chocolate. Place in freezer 4 to 5 minutes. Carefully peel leaf away from chocolate and store in freezer until ready to use.

Chocolate Chip Cheesecake

Serves 12

1¾ cups chocolate wafer crumbs
¾ stick butter, melted
18 ounces cream cheese
¾ cup sugar
3 eggs
6 ounces mini chocolate chips
1 pint sour cream
¼ cup sugar
1 teaspoon vanilla

Preheat oven to 350 degrees.

Line a 9½-inch springform pan with mixture of cookie crumbs and butter.

Mix cream cheese, 3/4 cup sugar and eggs with an electric mixer until smooth. Stir in mini chips. Pour into cookie crust-lined pan and bake 30 to 40 minutes. Let cool 10 to 15 minutes, then top with a mixture of sour cream, 1/4 cup sugar and vanilla. Bake 5 minutes to set topping.

Decorate with additional chocolate chips and refrigerate.

Seventh Heaven

Truly heavenly!
Serves 10 to 12

7 ounces butter
7 ounces semi-sweet chocolate
7 ounces sugar (1 cup less 2 tablespoons)
7 eggs, separated

Preheat oven to 325 degrees.

In a double boiler, melt butter and chocolate. Add sugar, blend and cool. Add egg yolks and beat until very thick, 10 to 15 minutes. Mixture should be so thick it will hold stiff peaks when the bowl is shaken.

Beat egg whites until stiff and fold into chocolate mixture. Spoon three-fourths of the batter into a greased springform pan. Bake 35 minutes. Cool thoroughly. Spoon remaining batter over cold cake and chill thoroughly before serving.

Chocolate Mousse Cake

A sinful experience for chocolate lovers!
Serves 24

Crust:
3 cups chocolate wafer crumbs
1 stick unsalted butter, melted

Combine crumbs and butter and press into bottom and three-fourths up the sides of a 10-inch springform pan. Refrigerate 30 minutes or chill in the freezer.

Filling:
1 pound semi-sweet chocolate
4 egg yolks
2 whole eggs
1 tablespoon liqueur, Kahlua or kirsch (optional)
3 cups whipping cream
6 tablespoons confectioners sugar
4 egg whites at room temperature

Soften chocolate in top of a double boiler over simmering water. Cool to lukewarm (95 degrees on candy thermometer). Add egg yolks and mix until thoroughly blended. Add whole eggs, mixing well. Add liqueur, if desired, and mix well.

Whip cream with confectioners sugar until soft peaks form. Beat egg whites until stiff, but not dry. Stir a little of the cream and egg whites into the chocolate mixture to lighten. Fold in remaining cream, then egg whites until completely incorporated. Turn into crust and chill at least 6 hours, preferably overnight.

Final Assembly:
2 cups whipping cream
confectioners sugar to taste
chocolate leaves (page 153)

Whip cream with sugar until quite stiff. Using a sharp knife, loosen crust on all sides and remove springform. Spread all but 3/4 cup whipped cream over top of the mousse. Pipe remaining cream into rosettes in center of cake. Arrange chocolate leaves in overlapping pattern around cream rosettes. Freeze and serve directly from freezer.

Cut cake into wedges with a thin, sharp knife.

Chocolate Sheet Cake

Your guests will rave!
Serves 15

2	cups flour
2	cups sugar
1	teaspoon baking soda
4	tablespoons cocoa
1	stick butter
1	cup water
½	cup shortening
2	eggs, beaten
½	cup buttermilk
1	teaspoon vanilla

Preheat oven to 350 degrees.

Sift flour, sugar and soda into a mixing bowl.

Mix together cocoa, butter, water and shortening in a saucepan and bring to a boil. Pour over flour/sugar mixture and stir well. Mix in eggs, buttermilk and vanilla. Pour into a well greased 11 x 13-inch cake pan and bake 25 minutes.

Icing:

Prepare 5 minutes before cake is finished baking.

1	stick butter
⅓	cup milk
4	tablespoons cocoa
1	box confectioners sugar
1	teaspoon vanilla
1	cup chopped pecans

Bring butter, milk and cocoa to a boil. Remove from heat and pour over sugar and vanilla, mixing well. Stir in pecans and spread mixture over cake while still hot. (Some of the icing will settle to the bottom of the pan, making the cake very moist.) After cake is cooled, cut in squares.

Chocolate Truffle Cake

A Grand Finale!
Serves 8 to 10

8	1-ounce squares semi-sweet chocolate
8	ounces unsalted butter, room temperature
1¼	cups sugar
6	large eggs at room temperature

Preheat oven to 350 degrees.

Butter a 9 x 1½-inch round cake pan. Line pan with parchment or waxed paper and butter it.

Melt chocolate in top of a double boiler over hot water. Add butter, stirring until melted and mixture is smooth. Whisk sugar in gradually until chocolate mixture is thick and smooth.

In a separate bowl beat eggs until foamy and whisk into chocolate mixture until well incorporated. Pour into prepared cake pan and place pan in a 14 x 11-inch baking dish. Add enough boiling water to come halfway up the sides of cake pan. Bake in center of the oven 1½ hours.

Remove cake pan from oven and cool 5 minutes. Invert onto a plate and remove the waxed paper. May be served with whipped cream topping or frosting.

Accompany with Raspberry Sauce, page 175.

Frosting:

1	teaspoon vegetable oil
6	ounces semi-sweet chocolate chips

In top of a double boiler over hot water, combine vegetable oil and chocolate chips, melt and blend well. Pour over cooled cake.

Very Rich Frosting:

12	ounces semi-sweet chocolate
1	cup heavy cream

Over low heat boil cream and chocolate together, stirring to blend. Refrigerate until spreadable and use to frost top and sides of cake.

New Orleans Fresh Apple Cake

Serves 12

2	cups sugar
3	cups flour, unsifted
1	teaspoon baking soda
1	teaspoon baking powder
1	teaspoon salt
3	teaspoons pumpkin spice
1	teaspoon ground cloves
1½	cups salad oil
3	eggs
2	teaspoons vanilla extract
3	cups peeled, chopped Granny Smith apples
1	cup chopped pecans
1	cup chopped dates, floured

Preheat oven to 325 degrees.

Mix first 7 ingredients in a large mixing bowl. Gradually add oil, eggs, vanilla, and using an electric mixer, beat until thoroughly blended. Stir in apples, nuts and dates until distributed throughout. (This makes a stiff dough.) Pour batter into a lightly greased and floured bundt pan. Bake 1½ hours. Cool on rack 15 to 20 minutes before removing from pan.

Great served with a glob of whipped cream on top!

Carolina Pound Cake

A family recipe handed down from generation to generation.

Serves 12

1	cup butter
½	cup solid white shortening
2½	cups sugar
5	eggs
3	cups cake flour
1	cup milk
1	teaspoon vanilla

Have all ingredients at room temperature. Cream butter, shortening and sugar well, add eggs, one at a time, beating well after each addition. Add flour and milk alternately. Add vanilla and beat 5 minutes. Pour into a large greased and floured tube pan or 2 loaf pans. Place in a cold oven. Heat oven to 325 degrees and bake 1½ to 1¾ hours.

John Gutmann (American, born 1905)
THE GAME, NEW ORLEANS
gelatin silver print
13 1/16 x 10 1/2"
Collection of New Orleans Museum of Art.

Carnival King Cake

The Carnival Season in New Orleans commences on January 6, or Twelfth Night, and concludes at Midnight of Mardi Gras (Fat Tuesday). The first seasonal King Cake is baked for Twelfth Night parties. An uncooked dry bean, but more recently a small plastic baby figure, is inserted at random into the baked cake. The lucky person who finds the pecan or bean in his/her slice of cake is "king or queen" for the evening's celebration. The traditional Carnival colors of purple, green and gold (yellow) are carried out in the tinted sugar on the cake.

Cake:

Yield: one 12-inch ring

½	cup warm water (110 to 115 degrees)
2	packages active dry yeast
½	cup plus 2 teaspoons sugar
3½ to 4½	cups flour, unsifted
1	teaspoon freshly grated nutmeg or ground nutmeg
2	teaspoons salt
1	teaspoon lemon zest
½	cup warm milk (110 to 115 degrees)
5	egg yolks
1	stick butter cut into slices and softened, plus 2 tablespoons butter, softened
1	egg slightly beaten with 1 tablespoon milk
1	teaspoon cinnamon

Pour the warm water into a small shallow bowl, and sprinkle yeast and 2 teaspoons sugar over it. Allow yeast and sugar to rest for 3 minutes then mix thoroughly. Set bowl in a warm place for 10 minutes, or until yeast bubbles up and mixture almost doubles in volume. Combine 3½ cups of flour, remaining sugar, nutmeg and salt, and sift into a large mixing bowl. Stir in lemon zest. Separate center of mixture to form a 'hole' and pour in yeast mixture and milk. Add egg yolks and using a wooden spoon slowly combine dry ingredients into the yeast/milk mixture. When mixture is smooth, beat in 8 tablespoons butter, 1 tablespoon at a time and continue to beat 2 minutes or until dough can be formed into a medium-soft ball.

Place ball of dough on a lightly floured surface and knead as for bread. During this kneading, add up to 1 cup more of flour, 1 tablespoon at a time sprinkled over the dough. When dough is no longer sticky, knead 10 minutes more or until smooth, shiny and elastic.

Using a pastry brush, coat the inside of a large bowl evenly with 1 tablespoon softened butter. Place dough ball in the bowl and rotate until the entire surface is buttered. Cover bowl with a moderately thick kitchen towel and place in a draft-free spot for about 1½ hours, or until the dough doubles in volume. Using a pastry brush, coat a large baking sheet with 1 tablespoon of butter and set aside.

Remove dough from bowl and place on lightly floured surface. Using your fist, punch dough down with a heavy blow. Sprinkle cinnamon over the top, pat and shape dough into a cylinder. Twist dough to form a curled cylinder and loop cylinder onto the buttered baking sheet, pinch ends together to complete the circle. Cover dough with towel and set it in draft-free spot for about 45 minutes until the circle of dough doubles in volume. *Preheat oven to 375 degrees.*

Brush top and sides of cake with egg wash and bake on middle rack of oven for 25 to 30 minutes, or until golden brown. Place cake on wire rack to cool to room temperature. At this time the dry bean or plastic baby may be pushed into the underside of cake.

Colored Sugars:

	Green, purple and yellow food-coloring pastes
12	tablespoons sugar

While cake is cooling, prepare colored sugars. Squeeze a dot of green paste onto the center of the palm of one hand. Sprinkle 2 tablespoons of sugar into hand over the paste and rub both palms together rather quickly until sugar is evenly colored green. More paste may be added if green is too light, and the sugar rubbed a few minutes more. Place the green sugar on a piece of waxed paper and repeat procedure to color 2 more tablespoons of sugar. Repeat procedure 4 more times to color 4 tablespoons in purple and yellow, taking care to wash your hands between each color. Set colored sugars aside.

Icing:

3	cups confectioners sugar
¼	cup fresh lemon juice, strained
3 to 6	tablespoons water

Combine sugar, lemon juice and 3 tablespoons of water in a deep bowl, stirring until smooth. If icing is too stiff beat in 1 tablespoon water at a time until spreadable. Place cooled cake on serving plate or piece of heavy cardboard, spread icing over top, using a small spatula and let it drizzle down the sides. Immediately sprinkle colored sugars in individual rows about 2 inches wide of green, purple and yellow.

Carrot Cake

Serves 12 to 15

2	**cups sugar**
1½	**cups vegetable oil**
4	**eggs**
3	**cups grated carrots**
2	**cups sifted all-purpose flour**
1	**teaspoon salt**
2	**teaspoons baking soda**
2	**teaspoons cinnamon**

Preheat oven to 300 degrees.

Grease and lightly flour three 9-inch round cake pans.

Cream sugar and oil. Beat in eggs, one at a time. Add carrots and dry ingredients and mix well. Divide mixture among prepared pans and bake 1 hour or less.

Cream Cheese Frosting:

1	**8-ounce package cream cheese**
1	**stick butter or margarine**
1	**box confectioners sugar**
1	**teaspoon vanilla**
1	**cup chopped pecans**

Heat cream cheese in top of a double boiler until soft. Add butter, sugar and vanilla. Mix well until creamy. Blend in pecans.

Spread frosting between and on top of cooled cake layers.

Pineapple Banana Cake

Serves 12 to 15

3	**cups all-purpose flour**
2	**cups sugar**
1	**teaspoon baking soda**
1	**teaspoon salt**
1	**teaspoon cinnamon**
3	**eggs**
1½	**cups safflower oil**
2	**teaspoons vanilla**
1	**8-ounce can crushed pineapple, undrained**
1	**cup chopped pecans**
2	**cups chopped bananas**
	Cream Cheese Frosting

Preheat oven to 350 degrees.

Sift together flour, sugar, baking soda, salt and cinnamon. Add eggs and oil, stirring until moistened. Do not beat. Fold in vanilla, pineapple, pecans and bananas. Grease and flour three 9-inch cake pans and divide batter between them. Bake approximately 30 minutes. Cool and frost with Cream Cheese Frosting.

Nut Cake

2	**cups sugar**
2	**sticks butter or margarine**
6	**eggs**
1	**12-ounce bag vanilla wafers, crushed**
½	**cup milk**
1	**cup grated coconut (fresh or canned)**
2	**cups chopped pecans**

Preheat oven to 350 degrees.

Cream sugar and butter. Add eggs, one at a time, beating well after each addition. Add vanilla wafers. Add milk and coconut, mixing well with each addition. Stir in chopped nuts.

Line bottom of a well-greased tube pan with waxed paper and pour in mixture. Bake 1 hour or until a wooden pick comes out clean. Let cake cool well before removing from pan.

Genoise Cake

Basic French Cake
Created in memory of Marie Antoinette—
"Let them eat cake!"
Serves 10 to 12

For two 7 or 8-inch cake pans or one 10 x 15-inch jelly roll pan:

5	eggs, separated
¾	cup sifted flour
	pinch of salt
¾	teaspoon vanilla
¾	cup sugar

For Chocolate Genoise cake:

substitute 5/8 cup sifted flour and add 1/8 cup cocoa

For two 9 or 10-inch cake pans or one 11 x 17-inch jelly roll pan:

6	eggs, separated
1	cup sifted flour
	pinch of salt
1	teaspoon vanilla
1	cup sugar

For Chocolate Genoise cake:

substitute 3/4 cup sifted flour and add 1/4 cup cocoa

Preheat oven to 400 degrees.

Separate eggs and allow them to come to room temperature. Grease pans with margarine and sprinkle with flour. Line with parchment or waxed paper.

Sift flour 3 times. Put egg yolks in a bowl and place in large pan filled with hot water. Beat 5 to 10 minutes over high heat until thick and very pale yellow. Add salt and vanilla. Remove pan from stove, keeping bowl in hot water.

Beat whites until soft peaks form. Add sugar gradually, beating until stiff peaks form. Remove bowl of yolks from hot water. Fold in beaten whites, then fold in flour a little at a time. (Batter is to be worked without stopping, as air beaten in makes cake rise.)

Pour batter into prepared cake pans and level. Bake 15 minutes on center rack until cake springs back to touch or pulls away from sides of pan. Invert cakes onto rack and remove from pans. Leave on rack to cool. Remove paper after cakes cool. Fill cooled layers as desired. *See Cake Fillings page 161.*

If using a jelly roll pan, brush bottom and sides of pan with oil, line with parchment or waxed paper, leaving an overhang, and oil paper. Pour in batter and bake 5 to 7 minutes. Turn out on waxed paper placed on top of a damp towel. Remove paper pan liner. Dust with confectioners sugar, roll up lengthwise and cool completely. Unroll and fill as desired.

Three Layer Cake

No one will know it is so easy to prepare!
Serves 8 to 10

Preheat oven to 400 degrees.

First layer:

1	stick butter
1	cup flour, sifted
½	cup nuts, finely chopped

Melt butter in an 11¾ x 7½ x 1¾-inch pan. Mix flour and nuts together, spread in pan and bake until slightly brown. Let cool completely.

Second layer:

1	large box instant chocolate pudding
1½	cups milk
½	pint whipping cream, whipped

Prepare pudding according to package directions. Fold in whipped cream and pour over first layer.

Third layer:

1	large box instant vanilla or chocolate pudding
1½	cups milk

Prepare pudding according to package directions and pour over second layer.

Topping:

½	cup whipping cream, whipped
	grated semi-sweet chocolate

Spread whipped cream on top of third layer and grate semi-sweet chocolate on top. Refrigerate before serving.

Dessert tastes best if made a day ahead.

Fillings for Cakes or Jelly Rolls

Simple Butter Cream

Yield: 3½ cups

2	**cups soft unsalted butter**
1⅓	**cups cooled simple syrup (page 180)**
1	**teaspoon vanilla extract**

Cream butter until fluffy. Gradually beat in syrup and vanilla.

Chocolate Butter Cream

4	**1-ounce squares semi-sweet chocolate**
2	**sticks unsalted butter**
½	**teaspoon vanilla extract**
2	**egg yolks**

Break up chocolate squares and place in top of double boiler over hot water on moderate heat. Cover until partially melted, uncover and stir until smooth. Remove from stove and set aside uncovered.

Cream butter until light and fluffy. Mix in vanilla and melted chocolate, add egg yolks, one at a time, beating well after each addition. Beat at high speed until mixture is smooth and color is light.

Lemon Cream

1	**cup sugar**
1	**tablespoon cornstarch**
3	**eggs, beaten**
	juice of 3 lemons
	zest of 2 lemons
2	**tablespoons unsalted butter**

Combine sugar and cornstarch, add eggs, lemon juice and zest. Cook in the top of a double boiler until very thick, stirring constantly. Add butter and cool.

Mocha Butter Cream

3	**sticks unsalted butter, softened**
1½	**cups sifted confectioners sugar**
2	**egg yolks, lightly beaten**
1	**tablespoon instant powdered coffee**
1	**teaspoon water**
2	**teaspoons vanilla extract**

Cream butter until light and fluffy, gradually add sugar, then egg yolks. Dissolve coffee in water, add vanilla and combine with butter/sugar mixture.

Crispy Almond Cookies

Yield: 7 dozen

8	**ounces almond paste**
8	**ounces granulated sugar**
3	**large egg whites**

Preheat oven to 300 degrees.

Mix all ingredients with an electric mixer or food processor until smooth. Drop batter by half-teaspoons 1 inch apart onto baking sheets lined with foil. Bake 25 to 30 minutes or until edges are golden. Let cookies cool and then gently peel them from foil. Store in airtight tin.

Almond Macaroons

Chewy and delicious!
Yield: 3 dozen

8	**ounces almond paste**
8	**ounces granulated sugar**
3	**medium egg whites**

Preheat oven to 300 degrees.

Mix all ingredients with an electric mixer or food processor until smooth. Drop batter by rounded tea-spoon 2 inches apart onto baking sheets lined with parchment paper. Bake 25 to 30 minutes or until edges are golden. Let macaroons cool on baking sheet then gently peel them from parchment paper. Store in an airtight tin.

Crispy Almond Cookies have the same ingredients but smaller size cookies make the difference.

Almond Delight

1	cup light brown sugar
1	stick butter, room temperature
1	teaspoon vanilla
1	egg
5	tablespoons all-purpose flour
½	teaspoon almond extract
½	cup chopped pecans
½	cup chopped almonds

Blend brown sugar and butter until smooth. Add vanilla, egg, flour and vanilla. Mix in pecans and almonds. Form into a log, wrap in foil. Chill overnight or freeze.

Cut into 1/2-inch thick slices and serve topped with sweetened whipped cream.

Anise Sugar Cookies

Yield: 4 dozens

1	stick softened butter or margarine
1	cup sugar
1	egg, unbeaten
2	cups sifted all-purpose flour
2	teaspoons baking powder
½	teaspoon salt
½	cup milk
1	teaspoon oil of anise (or to taste)
	butter and sugar for topping cookies

Preheat oven to 375 degrees.

Cream butter and sugar; beat in egg. Sift dry ingredients together. Add alternately with milk to sugar mixture; blend thoroughly and add oil of anise.

Drop by teaspoonfuls onto a lightly greased cookie sheet. For a sugary top, butter the bottom of a small glass, dip in sugar and use to lightly flatten each cookie. Bake 10 to 12 minutes. Remove from cookie sheet while still hot.

Chocolate Ice Box Cake

Serves 12 to 14

5	1-ounce squares unsweetened chocolate
1	cup milk
5	eggs, separated
1	cup sugar
3	packages lady fingers (2 or 3 dozen depending on size)
1	pint whipping cream, whipped

Melt chocolate with milk in top of a double boiler over medium heat until melted and slightly thickened. Cool.

Beat egg yolks with sugar until thick. Beat egg whites until stiff. Add melted chocolate mixture to beaten yolks and sugar and blend well. Fold in beaten egg whites with a wire whisk. Pour into a 9-inch springform pan that has been lined with lady fingers. Alternate layers of lady fingers and chocolate mixture, ending with chocolate. Top with whipped cream before serving.

Mincemeat Oatmeal Cookies

Yields 48 cookies

1 ¼   **cups all-purpose flour, sifted**
¾   **teaspoon soda**
½   **teaspoon salt**
½   **cup shortening**
1   **cup brown sugar, finely packed**
1   **egg**
1 ⅓   **cups mincemeat, ready-to-use, OR boxed mincemeat crumbled in 3/4 cup water and cooked 1 minute**
1 ½   **cups oatmeal, uncooked**

Preheat oven to 350 degrees.

Sift flour, soda and salt together.

In a large mixing bowl, cream shortening, gradually adding sugar and beat until fluffy. Beat in egg. Stir in mincemeat. Gradually add flour mixture and blend well. Fold in oatmeal to distribute evenly.

On a greased cookie sheet, drop mixture by teaspoonful about 2 inches apart. Bake 15 minutes. Allow cookies to cool before removing.

Old Fashion Lace Cookies

2   **sticks butter**
1   **cup brown sugar**
½   **cup white sugar**
1   **whole egg, plus 1 egg yolk**
2   **teaspoons vanilla extract**
1   **cup cake flour**
¾   **teaspoon salt**
½   **teaspoon baking soda**
2 ½   **cups uncooked oats**
3   **tablespoons milk**

Preheat oven to 350 degrees.

Cream butter well; add sugar and beat until well blended. Add eggs and continue beating. Add vanilla, flour, salt, soda, oats and milk. Beat rapidly for a few minutes.

Line a cookie sheet with wax paper. Drop mixture from a teaspoon onto cookie sheet. Bake 8 to 10 minutes or until light brown. Cool on a wire rack.

Artist's Palate Bayou Brownies

*Served in the Artist's Palate restaurant.
These are so delicious that the recipe has been
given to visitors from all over the world!*
Yield: 16

Preheat oven to 325 degrees.

Bottom layer:

1   box yellow cake mix (18.25 ounces)
1   cup pecans
1   stick butter, melted
1   egg, beaten

Mix the above ingredients together by hand. Press
into a greased 9 x 13-inch pan.

Top layer:

1   8-ounce package cream cheese
1   pound box confectioners sugar
2   eggs, beaten until fluffy

Mix the above ingredients with an electric mixer and
pour over the first layer. Bake in oven 40 to 50 minutes.
Cool and cut into squares.

Peanut Butter Yummies

Yummie!
Yield: 3 dozen

1 ¼   sticks butter, softened
1   cup peanut butter
1   cup graham cracker crumbs
2 ¼   cups confectioners sugar
1   6-ounce package chocolate chips
1   teaspoon oil

In a food processor blend softened butter, peanut
butter, graham cracker crumbs and sugar. Press firmly into the bottom of a 9 x 13-inch pan.

Melt chocolate chips and oil in top of a double
boiler over hot water. Pour over crumb mixture and
spread evenly. Refrigerate. When cool, cut into 1-inch
squares.

Cookies freeze well.

Brownies

Yield: 3 dozen

4   eggs
2   cups sugar
1   cup flour, sifted
1   cup melted butter
4   squares chocolate, melted
2   teaspoons vanilla
2   cups chopped pecans

Preheat oven to 350 degrees.

Lightly beat eggs, add sugar and beat well. Add flour,
melted butter and chocolate and blend well. Stir in
vanilla and chopped pecans. Pour mixture into a
greased 9 x 13-inch pan and bake approximately 25
minutes. Cool and refrigerate.

Chocolate Icing:

1   stick butter
4   tablespoons cocoa
6   tablespoons milk
1   teaspoon vanilla
1   box confectioners sugar

Melt butter in a saucepan, add cocoa and milk. Stir
until blended and bring to a boil. Add vanilla and
sugar and stir until well mixed.

This is a very rich, creamy frosting.

Cheesecake Squares

This recipe can be easily doubled for a crowd.
Yield: 4 dozen

Preheat oven to 350 degrees.

Crust:

1	cup flour
¼	cup light brown sugar, tightly packed
¾	cup finely chopped pecans
1	stick butter, melted

In a small bowl, mix flour, brown sugar and pecans. Pour melted butter over mixture and press into the bottom of a 13 x 9-inch baking dish. Bake 15 minutes, or until brown.

Filling:

16	ounces cream cheese, softened
1	cup sugar
1	teaspoon vanilla
3	eggs

In a food processor, blend cream cheese, sugar and vanilla. Add eggs and mix well. Pour into crust and bake 20 minutes.

Glaze:

2	cups sour cream
7	tablespoons sugar
1	teaspoon vanilla

In a food processor, mix sour cream, sugar and vanilla and pour over baked filling. Bake 5 minutes, or until firm on top. Refrigerate cheesecake until thoroughly cooled or overnight. Cut into squares for serving.

Frozen Chocolate Miniatures

A delicious chocolate treat.
Yield: 36 to 40 miniature pies

1 ¼	cups vanilla wafer crumbs
1	cup plus 3 tablespoons butter, softened
1	cup cocoa
2	cups confectioners sugar
4	eggs
½	teaspoon orange liqueur or Grand Marnier
2	teaspoons vanilla

Place 36 to 40 paper baking cups in miniature muffin pans. Combine vanilla wafer crumbs with 3 tablespoons butter. Mix well and press into the bottom and sides of the paper cups.

Beat remaining butter until creamy. Sift together cocoa and sugar, gradually add to butter, beating continuously. (Constant beating is the secret to this recipe's success.) Add eggs, one at a time, beating well after each addition. Beat in liqueur and vanilla. The mixture will resemble chocolate whipped cream. Spoon or pour chocolate mixture over crumbs in muffin cups. Freeze at least 2 hours or overnight.

Serve frozen, garnished with chocolate curls, if desired.

This recipe may also be made in a 9-inch pie pan. Peppermint extract may be substituted for the liqueur if you prefer.

Chocolate Cream Bars

You will not stop with just one!
Yield: 4 dozen

Crust:

1½	cups graham cracker crumbs
1	cup finely chopped pecans
½	cup unsalted butter
¼	cup granulated sugar
⅓	cup unsweetened cocoa
1	egg, beaten
1	teaspoon vanilla extract

Custard:

½	cup unsalted butter, softened
3	tablespoons powdered vanilla custard*
2	tablespoons milk
2	cups confectioners sugar

Topping:

4	ounces semi-sweet chocolate
1	teaspoon oil

Crust:

In a large bowl mix together graham crumbs and pecans and set aside. In a small saucepan, mix together butter, granulated sugar, cocoa, egg and vanilla. Cook and stir over low heat until mixture is well blended and the consistency of custard, about 3 to 5 minutes. Pour cocoa mixture into crumb mixture and blend thoroughly. Press into an ungreased 7½ x 12 x 2-inch oblong pan and place in freezer to firm while making next layer.

Butter Cream Custard:

In food processor, cream butter until fluffy, and blend in the custard powder. Blend in milk and slowly add confectioners sugar to creamed mixture. Carefully spread butter mixture evenly over chilled crumb layer and return pan to freezer until quite firm.

Topping:

In a small saucepan over very low heat, melt chocolate with oil, blending together. With a spatula spread a thin layer of chocolate over the chilled butter cream layer. Work quickly, and frost only a small section at a time, as the chocolate hardens rapidly when it touches the cold butter cream.

To serve cut into 1¼ to 1½ inch squares.

*Bird's English dessert mix, which may be found in gourmet stores, is preferred or vanilla custard pudding mix may be used.

These uncooked "cookies" are so delicious they may be eaten immediately. If any are left over, they may be kept in the refrigerator for 2 to 3 weeks or in the freezer for 3 months.

Fruit Cake Cookies

Perfect for Christmas giving.
Yield: 5 dozen

1	quart pecans, chopped
1	cup white raisins
2	8-ounce boxes dates, chopped
1	large bottle red maraschino cherries, chopped
1	pound candied pineapple, chopped
1	stick butter
1	cup brown sugar
4	eggs
3	tablespoons milk
3	cups all-purpose flour
3	teaspoons baking soda
1	teaspoon ground cloves
1	teaspoon ground cinnamon
1	teaspoon freshly ground nutmeg
1	cup whiskey

Place pecans, raisins, dates, cherries and pineapple in individual bowls and lightly dredge with flour. Set aside.

Preheat oven to 300 degrees.

Cream butter and sugar until lemon colored. Add eggs one at a time, beating after each addition. Add milk and blend.

Sift dry ingredients together and add to above mixture, alternating with whiskey. Stir in dredged pecans and fruits.

Drop mixture by full teaspoons onto a greased cookie sheet. Bake 20 minutes, or until firm. Cool one hour before storing in an airtight container.

German Cookies

Yield: 5 to 6 dozen

½	**pound butter, softened**
1	**cup sugar**
2	**teaspoons cinnamon**
2	**cups all-purpose flour**
1	**egg yolk**
1	**teaspoon vanilla**
1	**cup chopped pecans**

Preheat oven to 350 degrees.

Use a fork to cream together butter, sugar and cinnamon. Mix thoroughly, then add remaining ingredients, except pecans. Mix until uniform in color; dough will be crumbly. Spread dough on an ungreased 10 x 13-inch cookie sheet using fingertips and heel of your hand to press down evenly. Spread pecans over and into dough.

Bake 40 minutes in center of oven. Cookies must be timed exactly because they do not achieve a "done" appearance. Remove from oven and immediately cut into 1-inch squares.

Cookies may be kept in an airtight container for 4 to 5 weeks.

Tangy Lemon Squares

Yield: 4 dozen

2	**cups sifted flour**
½	**cup confectioners sugar**
¼	**teaspoon salt**
1	**cup chilled butter**
4	**beaten eggs**
2	**cups granulated sugar**
⅓	**cup fresh lemon juice**
1½	**teaspoons lemon zest**
¼	**cup flour**
1	**teaspoon baking powder**
	confectioners sugar for dusting

Preheat oven to 350 degrees.

In food processor blend flour, 1/2 cup confectioners sugar, salt and butter, pulsing on and off until mixture resembles coarse meal. Press mixture evenly into a 9 x 13 x 2-inch pan and bake 20 minutes or until lightly browned. Cool 10 to 15 minutes.

Put eggs in a food processor and slowly add granulated sugar, mixing well. Add lemon juice and zest. Sift together 1/4 cup flour and baking powder and blend into egg mixture. Spread mixture evenly over baked, slightly cooled crust and bake 25 minutes. Cool in the pan on a rack. Sprinkle with confectioners sugar. Refrigerate for several hours.

Remove from refrigerator and sprinkle on more confectioners sugar if desired. Cut into squares.

The squares will keep in an airtight tin for about 4 days or under refrigeration about 1½ weeks.

Old Fashioned Sugar Cookies

Yield: 5 to 6 dozen

3	cups flour
1¾	cups sugar
1	teaspoon baking powder
2	sticks butter, softened
1	egg
3	teaspoons vanilla extract
2	tablespoons milk
½	cup sugar for topping

Sift together flour, sugar and baking powder. Cream butter in a large mixing bowl and gradually add half of the flour mixture, until dough is stiff.

In another bowl, beat egg, add vanilla and milk. Add egg mixture to dough, and blend in remaining flour mixture. Roll into a ball in waxed paper and chill for 1 hour.

Preheat oven to 350 degrees.

Roll out dough on lightly floured board to 1/8-inch thickness and cut with a 2½-inch round cookie cutter. Place 2 inches apart on an ungreased cookie sheet. Sprinkle each cookie with sugar. Bake 10 to 15 minutes or until lightly brown.

Pastry Crust I

Yield: 2 crusts

2	cups unsifted flour
8	tablespoons unsalted butter, chilled and cut into bits
3	tablespoons shortening, chilled
	dash of salt
⅓	cup ice water

In a chilled bowl combine flour, butter, shortening and salt. With fingertips, rub flour and fats together until they look like flakes of coarse meal. A food processor may be used, pulsing on/off until mixture has consistency of coarse meal. Pour in water, toss mixture and form a ball. Divide into 2 separate balls and chill at least 3 hours. *Freezes well.*

Preheat oven to 425 degrees.

When ready to use, roll out dough on floured board and place in chilled quiche or pie pan and refrigerate while preparing your filling. Best results are obtained by keeping crust mixture chilled so sides will remain firm in pan during baking.

For pre-baked crust: Cover crust with sheet of foil and weight with rice or beans, and return to refrigerator to chill. Bake on middle rack of oven for 10 minutes. Remove foil, lower heat to 375 degrees and bake 5 more minutes.

Allow to cool before adding filling of your choice.

Pastry Crust II

Yield: 1 crust

½	cup butter
3	ounces cream cheese
1	cup flour

Using on/off motion, blend ingredients together in a food processor until a ball forms. Chill in plastic wrap until firm. Press chilled dough into pie pan.

If baked pie shell is needed, prick bottom and sides well with a fork. Bake until pastry is golden 10 to 12 minutes. Allow to cool before adding filling of your choice. If filling and crust are to be baked together, do not prick pastry. Pour in filling and bake as directed in pie recipe.

Apple Tart

Delicious and as beautiful as that served in any French restaurant!
Serves 6

Pastry:

1	cup flour
1	tablespoon sugar
1	stick unsalted butter
3	tablespoons ice water

Filling:

4	Granny Smith apples, peeled, cored, quartered and thinly sliced
¼	cup sugar
4	tablespoons unsalted butter
¼	cup apricot preserves

In a food processor combine flour, sugar and butter. Pulse on and off until mixture looks like flakes of coarse meal. Add ice water. Pulse on and off until mixture forms a ball.

Roll pastry dough onto a lightly floured board and form an 8 inch wide by 12-inch long strip. Fold bottom third up, then fold top third down. Rotate dough one-half turn counter-clockwise, roll dough to a 1/4-inch thick rectangle, and repeat, folding bottom third up and top third down. Wrap in wax paper, refrigerate 1 hour. When cold, roll dough to form a circle and place into a flan or quiche pan.

Preheat oven to 450 degrees.

Arrange apple slices on the dough-lined pan in a circle, finishing in the middle. Sprinkle sugar on top and dot with butter. Cook 40 minutes on lowest rack in oven. Remove from oven. Warm apricot preserves and using a pastry brush, spread on top of tart.

Best when eaten day baked, but can be cooked day before and warmed in oven before serving.

Chocolate Pecan Pie

Serves 6

4	tablespoons unsalted butter
1	ounce square semi-sweet chocolate
4	eggs, well beaten
1	cup brown sugar
¾	cup dark corn syrup
¼	teaspoon salt
1	tablespoon vanilla
1½	cups pecan pieces
9-inch unbaked pie shell (page 168)	

Preheat oven to 400 degrees.

Place chocolate and butter in top of double boiler over moderate heat. Cover until partially melted, then uncover and stir until completely melted. Remove from hot water and set aside to cool slightly.

To well beaten eggs, add sugar and syrup. Mix in salt and vanilla, then slowly stir in the chocolate and butter mixture. Add pecans, stir and pour into unbaked pie shell. Adjust rack one third up from the bottom of the oven. Bake 10 minutes, reduce heat to 325 degrees and bake 40 minutes more. Do not bake any longer, even if the filling seems soft. Filling hardens as it cools.

Southern Pecan Pie

This recipe has been passed down through generations!
Serves 6

3	eggs, well beaten
1	cup brown sugar
¾	cup dark corn syrup
¼	teaspoon salt
1	tablespoon vanilla
3	tablespoons melted butter
1½	cups pecan pieces
9-inch unbaked pie shell (page 168)	

Preheat oven to 400 degrees.

Thoroughly mix together eggs, sugar, syrup, salt, vanilla, butter and pecans. Pour into unbaked pie shell and bake 10 minutes. Reduce heat to 325 degrees and bake 35 to 40 minutes, or until knife inserted in center comes out clean.

Egg Nog Chiffon Pie

Serves 6 to 8

Crust:

1⅔	cups vanilla wafer crumbs
⅓	cup butter, melted

In a bowl combine vanilla wafer crumbs and butter, mix well and press firmly into the bottom and up sides of a 9 inch pie pan. Bake 10 minutes and cool.

Preheat oven to 350 degrees.

Filling:

1	envelope plain gelatin
2	tablespoons cold water
3	egg yolks
4½	tablespoons sugar
½	cup undiluted evaporated milk
¼	cup water
	pinch of salt
1	teaspoon nutmeg
3	tablespoons pale dry sherry
3	egg whites
4½	tablespoons sugar
1	9-inch graham cracker or chocolate crumb crust, baked and cooled

Topping:

1	cup whipping cream, whipped
6 to 8 tablespoons sliced almonds, toasted	

Soften gelatin in 2 tablespoons cold water and set aside. Beat together egg yolks, sugar, milk, water, salt and nutmeg. Cook in double boiler until mixture coats spoon, add gelatin, dissolving well. Chill slightly, add sherry and return to refrigerator.

Beat egg whites until soft peaks form, add remaining sugar slowly and beat until stiff. Fold egg whites into slightly gelled custard, spoon into crust and chill until firm. Top with whipped cream and toasted almonds.

New Orleans Own Chess Pie

This rich, heavy dessert would best be served with a light entrée.
Serves 6

Cream cheese pastry for an 8-inch pie:

1	cup flour
8	tablespoons very cold butter
1	3-ounce package cream cheese, well chilled

Cut butter and cream cheese into small pieces and add to flour in a food processor. Process until mixture leaves sides of the bowl and forms a ball. Wrap in wax paper and refrigerate until chilled or overnight.

Filling:

1	cup sugar
2	tablespoons butter, room temperature
1	tablespoon yellow corn meal
⅓	cup lemon juice
	grated rind of 2 lemons
3	large eggs

Preheat oven to 350 degrees.

Line an 8-inch pie pan with pastry, crimp edges and chill.

Put sugar, butter, corn meal, lemon juice, lemon rind and eggs into a bowl. Beat with a fork until well blended. Pour filling into prepared pie shell. Place pie in oven and bake 35 to 40 minutes.

Pie may be made in advance. Freezes well.

Orange Velvet Pie

Serves 6 to 8

Preheat oven to 375 degrees.

Chocolate Crumb Crust:

1⅓	**cups thin chocolate wafer crumbs**
3	**tablespoons softened butter**
2	**ounces semi-sweet chocolate squares, room temperature for garnish**

Combine wafer crumbs and butter and mix until crumbly. Press mixture firmly into buttered pie plate and bake for 8 minutes. Set aside to cool before filling.

Filling:

1	**tablespoon unflavored gelatin**
1	**cup cold water**
2	**egg yolks, slightly beaten**
½	**cup sugar**
	pinch of salt
1	**6-ounce can frozen orange juice**
2	**teaspoons lemon juice**
1	**cup whipping cream**
2	**egg whites**
¼	**cup sugar**

Soak gelatin in 1/4 cup cold water; set aside.

Combine remaining 3/4 cup cold water and egg yolks in top of a double boiler. Add sugar, salt and softened gelatin. Cook over boiling water, stirring until consistency of custard. Remove from heat and stir in orange concentrate and lemon juice. Refrigerate until cool and slightly thickened.

Whip 1/2 cup of the whipping cream until stiff peaks form. Beat egg whites until soft, add sugar and beat until stiff.

Remove slightly thickened custard mixture from refrigerator and fold into whipped cream. Fold in beaten egg whites. Pour filling into cooled crumb crust.

Whip remaining 1/2 cup of cream and spread over custard filling. To garnish, shave chocolate squares with vegetable parer to form curls. Return garnished pie to refrigerator. Remove from refrigerator about 20 minutes before serving.

Peanut Butter Pie

Easy, spectacular dessert from the freezer.
Serves 18 to 24
Yield: 3 9-inch pies

1	**can sweetened condensed milk**
2	**8-ounce packages cream cheese**
1	**cup peanut butter, plain or crunchy**
1	**pint whipping cream, whipped**
2	**cups confectioners sugar**
3	**9-inch vanilla wafer or butter pie crusts (page 170)**

With an electric mixer, mix condensed milk, cream cheese and peanut butter. Combine half of the whipped cream with the confectioners sugar and fold into the cream cheese mixture. Pour into 3 prepared crusts and freeze before icing. Ice with remaining whipped cream and return to freezer. Cut while still frozen.

Semi-sweet chocolate shavings may be sprinkled over the top before serving.

Pecan Mocha Torte

A very rich dessert, should be served sparingly!
Serves 10

8	**ounces butter**
2	**cups confectioners sugar**
2	**large egg yolks**
3	**teaspoons vanilla**
2	**tablespoons strong coffee**
1	**teaspoon almond extract**
4	**tablespoons tapioca, corn starch or matzo meal**
3	**cups coarsely chopped pecans, dry roasted in oven**
1	**cup whipping cream, whipped**

Beat butter in an electric mixer until creamy. Add 1 cup confectioners sugar and cream well. Add egg yolks, vanilla and remaining sugar, beating well after each addition. Add coffee, almond extract, tapioca, corn starch or matzo meal and continue beating well. Add cooled pecans. Put into a 9-inch square pan, slip pan into a plastic bag and freeze.

When frozen, cut into squares and serve with whipped cream.

Fantastic Fresh Raspberry Pie

Serves 6 to 8

4	cups raspberries
1	cup sugar
⅓	cup Chambord (raspberry liqueur)
4	tablespoons cornstarch
1	tablespoon fresh lemon juice
	pastry for a 2-crust pie (page 168)
3	tablespoons butter
4	very thin lemon slices

Preheat oven to 425 degrees.

Place raspberries in mixing bowl and cover with sugar. Combine Chambord and cornstarch in a small bowl; mix until smooth and stir in lemon juice. Spoon Chambord mixture over berries.

Line a 9-inch pie pan with half of pastry. Carefully spoon berries into pastry-lined pan, dot with butter and arrange lemon slices over center of berries. Roll out remaining pastry and cut into 1/2-inch wide strips. Arrange pastry strips over berries in a lattice pattern and crimp edges.

Place pie on middle rack of oven and bake 15 minutes. Lower heat to 350 degrees and bake another 30 to 40 minutes.

Fresh Apricot Pie

Serves 6 to 8

2½ to 3	pounds fresh apricots
1½	cups sugar
3½	tablespoons tapioca
1	teaspoon cinnamon
	pastry for a 2-crust pie (page 168)
3	tablespoons butter

Preheat oven to 350 degrees.

Wash apricots, remove seeds and cut into quarters. Place apricots in a large pot and cover with sugar. Do not *add* water. Slowly bring apricots and sugar to a boil, reduce heat immediately and allow to cool to room temperature. A lot of liquid will form on the cooked apricots. If too much juice has formed, remove some (save for ice cream topping). Mix tapioca and cinnamon with apricots. Line a 9-inch pie pan with crust and fill with apricot mixture. Dot with butter and cover with top pie crust. Bake 50 to 60 minutes until crust is golden brown and fruit is bubbly.

Lemon Meringue Pie

Serves 8 to 10

Filling:

1½	cups sugar
5½	tablespoons cornstarch
1½	cups water
3	egg yolks (4 if small), beaten
½	stick butter
5	tablespoons fresh lemon juice
½	tablespoon lemon zest
1	teaspoon vanilla or almond extract
1	9-inch baked pie shell (page 168)

Meringue:

	3 or 4 egg whites, depending on size
¼	teaspoon cream of tartar
6	tablespoons sugar

NOTE: **All utensils must be free from oil. To be sure, mix 1 tablespoon salt moistened with a little vinegar, rub on all utensils, rinse, and dry thoroughly.**

Preheat oven to 400 degrees.

In a 3-quart sauce pan, mix sugar and cornstarch, gradually adding water. Cook over medium heat, stirring constantly, until thickened and boil 1 minute. Slowly blend 1 cup of hot mixture into the eggs, stirring constantly. Stir this into mixture in sauce pan, return to a boil and boil 1 minute longer. The mixture will be very thick. Add remaining ingredients. Cool slightly and pour into baked pie shell. The filling will be high.

Meringue:

Have egg whites at room temperature to beat until frothy. Add cream of tartar, beating 1 minute longer. Gradually add sugar, a little at a time until stiff peaks form and meringue is glossy. Spread over filling in pie crust, smoothing out to edge of crust. (Unless the filling is completely sealed to the crust by its meringue the pie will weep.) Bake 8 to 10 minutes, or until meringue is lightly browned. Allow pie to cool in a draft-free place.

When preparing a pie with a meringue topping, make sure the meringue touches the sides of the crust all around otherwise the meringue will shrink.

Fruit Ice Cream

A delicious, healthy, non-fattening ice-cream.
Serves 8 to 10

1	cup crushed pineapple
1	papaya or 1 peach
2	bananas
8	dried apricots, soaked in water overnight or at least several hours
3	tablespoons sunflower seeds
¼	cup honey
¼	cup sesame oil
¼	cup tahini or ¼ cup sesame seeds toasted and ground fine

Liquefy all ingredients in a blender. Pour into a 13 x 9-inch dish and freeze to a semi-solid state.

Strawberry Orange Sorbet

Yield: 2 quarts

3	pints ripe strawberries, cleaned and stems removed
1¾	cups orange juice
½	cup lemon juice
1⅓	cups sugar
¼	teaspoon salt

Using a food processor or blender mix all ingredients well. Freeze mixture in a 13 x 9-inch pan for 4 hours, stirring occasionally.

Process frozen mixture in small amounts until light and fluffy. Cover pan with aluminum foil and return to freezer for 3 more hours. When sorbet is frozen transfer to plastic containers and store in freezer.

Can be served in meringue shells for a light dessert, or in sherbet glasses before an entrée.

Fresh Mint Sherbet

Yield: 1 gallon

3   cups sugar

4   cups water

4   cups fresh mint

2   6-ounce cans frozen orange juice concentrate

¾   cup fresh lemon juice

1   pint half and half

1   pint whipping cream

     green food coloring

Make a simple syrup by boiling sugar and water 5 minutes. Chop mint and add to syrup. Dilute 1 can orange juice as directed and combine with syrup, 1 can undiluted orange juice concentrate and lemon juice. Refrigerate 24 hours.

Strain mint out of mixture. Add half and half and whipping cream. Tint pale green with food coloring. Freeze in electric or hand freezer.

Raspberry Melon Mold

Serves 10 to 12

2 to 3 pints raspberry sherbet

2   cups crystallized fruit (mostly cherries and pineapple)

1½ jiggers rum or bourbon

3   pints French vanilla ice cream

     mint leaves for garnish

Use a 12 cup melon-shaped mold or a large round mold that can be put in freezer.

Soften raspberry sherbet and line the mold with it, pressing firmly against the sides and bottom. Leave the center hollow, cover with foil and return to the freezer.

Cut up crystallized fruit and soak in rum or bourbon for about 1 hour. Fold fruit into ice cream and fill the center of the mold. Cover well and return to freezer. When ready to serve unmold on platter and garnish with mint leaves.

A very pretty presentation.

Custard Sauce

Makes any cake special.
Yield: approximately 2 cups

3   egg yolks

3   tablespoons sugar

¾   cup scalded milk

1   teaspoon vanilla

½   cup whipping cream

In a small bowl beat egg yolks and sugar until creamy. Gradually beat in the scalded milk. Put mixture into saucepan and cook over a low fire until thickened, stirring constantly. Add vanilla.

Beat whipping cream until stiff and fold into custard just before serving over pound or angel food cake.

Date-Nut Topping

Yield: 1½ cups

½   cup cooked dates

½   cup corn syrup, light or dark

¼   cup brown sugar

¼   cup water

⅛   teaspoon salt

½   teaspoon vanilla

½   cup chopped nuts

⅓   teaspoon lemon juice

Combine dates, syrup, brown sugar, water and salt. Bring to a boil, stirring constantly. Cook for about 2 minutes. Remove from fire; add vanilla, nuts and lemon juice. Mix well. Cool.

Will keep in refrigerator several weeks. Serve at room temperature over ice cream.

Fruit Sauce

Yield: 1½ cups

	juice of 2 oranges
	juice of 1 lemon
1	**cup sugar**
1	**egg**
	zest of 2 oranges

Mix all ingredients, except orange zest, in top of a double boiler. Cook over medium heat until mixture coats spoon. Cool to room temperature and add orange zest. Refrigerate before serving.

May be used over fresh fruit salad, pound or angel food cake.

Note: Sauce will stay fresh up to 1 week in the refrigerator.

Orange Sauce

Yield: 2 cups

¾	**cup sugar**
2	**egg yolks**
1	**tablespoon flour**
	juice of 1 large orange
	zest of 1 large orange
1	**cup whipping cream, whipped**

In a saucepan combine sugar, egg yolks and flour. Add orange juice and zest, mixing well. Stir constantly over low heat until thickened. Remove from heat and cool. Fold whipped cream into cooled mixture and refrigerate.

Serve over angel food or pound cake.

Praline Sauce

Great for little Christmas gifts.
Yield: 3½ cups

1½	**cups light brown sugar**
⅔	**cup white corn syrup**
½	**stick butter**
1	**5-ounce can evaporated milk**
1	**cup chopped pecans**

Mix first 3 ingredients in a saucepan and over low heat, bring to boiling point. Remove from stove and cool. When lukewarm, add evaporated milk, blend well and add chopped pecans. Store in a jar in refrigerator.

Sauce is delicious served over vanilla ice cream.

Raspberry Sauce

Especially delicious with Chocolate Truffle Cake!
Yield: approximately 1½ cups

1	**10-ounce package frozen raspberries**
2	**tablespoons currant jelly**
⅛	**teaspoon lemon juice**
1	**tablespoon kirsch liqueur (optional)**
1	**tablespoon cornstarch dissolved in 2 tablespoons of water**

Heat berries, add jelly, lemon juice, liqueur and cornstarch solution. Bring to a boil, remove from heat and strain. Cool in refrigerator.

Serve at room temperature over ice cream or pudding. To serve with cake, put a tablespoon of sauce on a plate, then place a slice of cake on top.

Gold Brick Fudge

4	cups sugar
1	can condensed milk
1	cup evaporated milk
2	12-ounce packages semi-sweet chocolate chips
1	6-ounce package milk chocolate bits
1	jar marshmallow cream
1	stick butter
1	teaspoon vanilla
2	cups chopped nuts

Combine sugar and both milks in a saucepan. Bring slowly to rolling boil. Let boil 8 minutes, no longer, to the soft ball stage, stirring constantly to keep milk from scorching. Remove from heat, add chocolate chips, marshmallow cream and butter. Stir until melted and well blended. Add nuts and vanilla. Spread in a large ungreased pan. Cool and cut into squares.

Truffles

Yield: 3 dozen

12	ounces semi-sweet chocolate
4	egg yolks
⅓	cup of a good coffee liqueur
⅔	cups unsalted butter
	sifted unsweetened cocoa
	ground almonds

Melt chocolate in top of a double boiler over simmering water. Remove from heat; cool to room temperature. Add yolks one at a time, stirring constantly until thoroughly blended. Mix in coffee liqueur; return to simmering water for 2 to 3 minutes, stirring constantly. Pour mixture into bowl of electric mixer. Beat in butter a tablespoon at a time. Continue beating until fluffy in texture. Cover with plastic wrap, refrigerate 4 to 5 hours or overnight.

Roll into 3/4-inch balls, then in cocoa or nuts (or both). Refrigerate until ready to serve.

To freeze, place in a container with waxed paper between layers.

Heavenly Chocolate

1	12-ounce package semi-sweet chocolate chips
½	stick butter or margarine
1	teaspoon vanilla
2	beaten eggs
1	package small (or cut-up large) colored marshmallows
1	cup coarsely-chopped nuts

Melt chocolate chips and butter in double boiler, add vanilla. Cool slightly, add beaten eggs slowly. Pour over nuts and marshmallows. Grease hands and shape mixture into rolls. Wrap in waxed paper and refrigerate several hours or overnight. Slice.

Very pretty and excellent for Christmas gifts.

Divinity

Yield: 1½ pounds

½   **cup light corn syrup**
2½   **cups granulated sugar**
¼   **teaspoon salt**
½   **cup water**
2   **egg whites**
1   **teaspoon vanilla**
1   **cup coarsely chopped nuts**

In a saucepan mix corn syrup, sugar, salt and water. Cook, stirring, until sugar is dissolved. Continue cooking, without stirring, until 248 degrees registers on a candy thermometer, or until small amount of mixture dropped into cold water forms a firm ball. *Make divinity only on days when humidity is low. When cooking the syrup, wrap a clean, damp cloth around a fork and use back of fork to clean crystals that form on pan.*

Beat egg whites until stiff but not dry. Pour about half of syrup slowly over whites, beating constantly. Cook remainder until 272 degrees is registered on candy thermometer, or until a small amount of mixture dropped into cold water forms hard but not brittle threads. Add slowly to first mixture and beat until mixture holds its shape. Add vanilla and nuts. Drop by dessert spoonfuls onto wax paper, or spread in a buttered 9-inch square pan.

Variations:

Seafoam: Follow divinity recipe, substituting light brown sugar for granulated.

Chocolate: Follow divinity recipe, using a 6-ounce package semi-sweet chocolate pieces. Beat until mixture begins to hold its shape. Add vanilla, chocolate and nuts.

Holiday: Follow divinity recipe, adding 1/4 cup each of chopped candied cherries and pineapples with the nuts.

Ginger: Follow divinity recipe using 6 tablespoons water and 2 tablespoons preserved ginger syrup for the liquid. Add 1/2 cup finely diced ginger with nuts.

Pecan Toffee

1   **cup butter (no substitutes)**
1   **cup sugar**
¼   **cup water**
½   **teaspoon salt**
3   **squares semi-sweet chocolate**
1   **cup coarsely chopped pecans**

Combine butter, sugar, water and salt in a heavy saucepan. Cook, stirring constantly to a hard crack stage (300 degrees), watching carefully. Immediately pour into an ungreased 9 x 13-inch pan. Cool until hard.

Melt chocolate over hot, not boiling, water. Spread on toffee, sprinkle with nuts and press them down on chocolate. Let candy set for 2 or 3 hours. Break into bite-size pieces.

Quick N'Easy Pralines

Yield: 16

1½ cups light brown sugar, tightly packed
¼ cup evaporated milk
3 tablespoons butter
1 tablespoon cream sherry
1 cup broken pecans

In a 2-quart saucepan on medium heat boil brown sugar and evaporated milk for 6 minutes, then add butter and boil for 2 more minutes. Add sherry and remove from heat. Add pecans and stir until mixed. Drop by tablespoons onto waxed paper.

Chocolate Caramels

Yield: 81 squares

1 cup white Karo syrup
3 cups sugar
2 tablespoons cream
2 tablespoons butter
3 squares bitter chocolate
1 cup chopped nuts
1 teaspoon vanilla

In a heavy saucepan, cook Karo and sugar together for 10 minutes. Add cream, butter and chocolate. Stir as little as possible. Cook until brittle (300 to 310 degrees). Add nuts and vanilla. Beat a few minutes. Pour into a well-buttered 9-inch square cake pan. Score into 1-inch pieces with a knife. When cool, cut apart and wrap each piece in waxed paper.

Do not attempt to make caramels on a rainy day!

Gordon's Butter Mints

1 cup sugar
½ cup water
¼ stick butter
3 drops oil of peppermint (available in pharmacies or specialty shops)
3 drops green or red food coloring (or more to obtain desired colors)

Place all ingredients in a saucepan and cook without stirring until it registers 225 degrees on a candy thermometer. Turn out onto a well-buttered marble slab. Butter hands well and pull the candy. Add oil of peppermint and food coloring while pulling. When candy becomes opaque, cut strips into 3/4-inch pieces. Put in a tightly covered tin lined with wax paper for 24 hours so that candy will become creamy.

It is wise not to make these mints on a rainy or muggy day!

Café Brûlot

New Orleans' famous coffee!
Yield: About 10 demi-tasse cups

4	cinnamon sticks, in halves OR
	½ teaspoon ground cinnamon
4	whole allspice berries OR
	½ teaspoon ground allspice
10	whole cloves
6	tablespoons sugar
8	3-inch strips lemon peel
4	3-inch strips orange peel
1½	cups brandy, at room temperature
½	cup Curaçao (optional)
1	quart freshly brewed hot black coffee

Combine the cinnamon, allspice, cloves, sugar, lemon and orange peel in a warm brûlot bowl or chafing dish. Crush the ingredients slightly with the back of a ladle.

Heat 1 cup of the brandy with Curaçao in a saucepan until lukewarm and add to the brûlot bowl or chafing dish. Ignite remaining 1/2 cup brandy and lower it into the bowl or chafing dish while it is still flaming to set the entire contents aflame. Add the hot coffee gradually while stirring until the flame subsides. Ladle into brûlot or demi-tasse cups.

Coffee Punch

Makes 40 servings

1	ounce instant coffee
2	cups sugar
2	cups boiling water
1	gallon cold milk
½	gallon chocolate ice cream
½	gallon coffee ice cream

Combine coffee, sugar and boiling water. Cool thoroughly and chill in refrigerator. (May be done a day ahead.)

When ready to serve, let ice cream soften for 15 to 20 minutes. In a large punch bowl, combine coffee mixture and milk. Add large spoonfuls of both flavors of ice cream and stir gently. Serve in punch cups with a bit of each flavor ice cream.

Irish Coffee

Yield: 1 serving

1	jigger and 1 tablespoon Irish whiskey
1	teaspoon sugar
	hot freshly brewed coffee
	whipped cream to garnish

Pour 1 jigger of Irish whiskey into an 8-ounce stemmed or Irish coffee glass. Heat and ignite the whiskey. Add a teaspoon of sugar and fill glass to within an inch or two of the top with coffee.

Fill a tablespoon with Irish whiskey, heat and allow the whiskey flames to run down the insides of the glass. Float whipped cream on top and serve.

Brandy Milk Punch

Yield: 1 serving

1¼	ounce brandy
3	ounces half and half
1	teaspoon confectioners sugar
¼	teaspoon vanilla
¼	teaspoon ground nutmeg

Combine brandy, half and half, sugar and vanilla in shaker with ice cubes. Shake well and strain into an Old Fashion glass, top with ground nutmeg.

Mardi Gras Punch

Serves 14

1 6-ounce can frozen orange juice concentrate, thawed
1 6-ounce can frozen lemonade concentrate, thawed
1 quart chilled apple juice
2 quarts chilled ginger ale
  Fruit pieces, cut up oranges, strawberries blueberries, limes, mint OR
  Sherbets—raspberry, orange, lime and lemon (optional)

Combine concentrates. Use half of mixture to make ice cubes with pieces of cut up fruit. If using sherbet, do not make ice cubes. Refrigerate remaining concentrates until ready to use.

To serve, stir remaining concentrates and apple juice together in a large punch bowl, add ginger ale. Float fruit-filled ice cubes or scoops of sherbet in punch.

Nectar Syrup

Yield: approximately 16 ounces

2 cups sugar
1 cup water
1 13-ounce can evaporated milk
2 tablespons vanilla extract
2 tablespoons almond extract
¼ cup club soda
  red food coloring
  vanilla ice cream (optional)

Mix sugar, water and evaporated milk in a saucepan, bring to a boil, then simmer 10 minutes without stirring. Cool, add vanilla and almond extracts. Add food coloring to make nectar syrup a luscious shade of pink.

For a delicious drink, add a small amount of club soda.

Optional: A scoop of vanilla ice cream may be added to drink.

Spicy Hot Tea

Serves 14 to 16

10 cups water
2 cups sugar
2 oranges, sliced
2 lemons, sliced
10 whole cloves
10 whole allspice
4 teaspoons tea leaves

Combine 8 cups water, sugar, lemon and orange slices, cloves and allspice and boil for 10 minutes. Strain and reserve liquid. Steep tea in 2 cups boiling water for 5 minutes. Add this to spiced liquid and strain to remove tea leaves. More boiling water may be added if tea is too strong. Should be very hot when served.

May also be served very cold.

Simple Syrup

2½ cups sugar
¾ cup white corn syrup
1¼ cups water

Bring ingredients to a boil in saucepan, swirl to completely dissolve sugar. Cover and boil for 2 minutes, uncover and continue boiling for another 2 minutes. Remove from heat. Syrup can be refrigerated for a period of time.

Keep on hand for drinks.

Georges Braque (French, 1882-1963)
LANDSCAPE AT L'ESTAQUE *1906*
oil on canvas
Bequest of Victor K. Kiam

From the early days of the 19th century, portrait artists, wildlife painters, and painters of genre scenes followed the example of other well trained European artists who were lured to New Orleans. This tradition continues and today New Orleans is a mecca for artists who, with Louisiana's native sons and daughters, produce a thriving and innovative art scene that spans every continent and medium. From the colorful sidewalk artists in Jackson Square, to the 20th-century works in the permanent collection of the New Orleans Museum of Art, from the rich gallery life on Royal and Magazine Streets, to the outstanding Fine Arts Departments of the local universities, New Orleans is a haven and a wellspring for artists who want to stop here for a few months, or years, or a lifetime.

Wayne Amedee (American, born 1946)
CALIENTE
monotype
27 x 35"

Salad Primavera

Serves 12

4	cups uncooked rice
1	thread saffron
1	6-pound roasted chicken or 2 3-pound barbecued chickens
1	pound thinly sliced ham
2	10-ounce boxes frozen cut green beans
2	10-ounce boxes frozen green peas
½	cup mayonnaise
½	cup tarragon vinegar
1	cup olive oil
2	teaspoons Creole mustard
	salt and ground pepper to taste
1	cup chopped green onions
2	cups diced celery
1	¾-ounce jar small capers, drained
2	4-ounce jars pimientos, drained
1	2½-ounce can black olives, drained and sliced
1	8-ounce can water chestnuts, drained and sliced
1	head Romaine lettuce

Cook rice according to package directions, adding saffron to water.

While rice is cooking remove chicken from bones and cut into bite-size chunks. Cut ham into bite-size pieces. Cook beans and peas just until crisp.

Make vinaigrette sauce with mayonnaise, vinegar, olive oil, mustard, salt and ground pepper. Set aside.

When rice is cooked and cooled put in a large bowl, add remaining ingredients, except lettuce, and mix thoroughly. Stir vinaigrette and add to rice in bowl, mixing well. Refrigerate. Serve on bed of Romaine lettuce.

E. John Bullard
Museum Director

Killer Cheesecake

Serves 8 to 10

4	8-ounce containers whipped cream cheese
16	ounces sour cream
1	stick unsalted butter
5	eggs
2	tablespoons cornstarch
1¼	cups sugar
1¼	teaspoons vanilla
1	teaspoon lemon juice

Preheat oven to 375 degrees.

Let cream cheese, sour cream, butter and eggs stand at room temperature for approximately one hour.

In a large bowl combine cream cheese, butter and sour cream together, blend in cornstarch, sugar, vanilla and lemon juice. Beat at high speed with an electric mixer until well blended. Beat in eggs 1 at a time and continue beating until mixture is very smooth. Grease a 9½-inch springform pan and pour mixture into same. Place in a larger pan filled with enough warm water to come halfway up side of cake pan. Bake for 1 hour or until top is golden brown. Turn oven off, let cake cool in oven with door open for 1 hour. Remove and let stand for 2 hours. Cover and refrigerate for at least 6 hours before serving.

William Fagaly
Assistant Director for Art

Onion Tart

Serves 6 to 8

8   medium yellow onions, thinly sliced
2   tablespoons butter and 2 tablespoons
     bacon drippings (don't substitute drippings)
⅓ to ½ cup grated Swiss or Gruyère cheese
1   egg, well beaten
     salt and freshly ground pepper
1   9-inch pie crust (page 168)

Using a heavy iron or enamel pot, sauté onions in butter and bacon drippings for about 35 minutes. Stir often and cook with lid on, until onions are golden.

When onions are cooked, remove from fire, stir in grated cheese, then beaten egg. Season to taste with salt and pepper. Turn into pie crust and bake at 375 degrees until brown on top, about 30 minutes.

Tart is good hot or cold.

Wayne Amedee
Artist

Grilled Redfish Filets

Serves 6

6   fresh redfish filets
1   tablespoon lemon juice
1   tablespoon lime juice
     dash of soy sauce
2   tablespoons olive oil
     hickory chips soaked in water
     herbes de Provence
     salt and pepper

Using the freshest redfish, wash and pat dry. Combine lemon and lime juice, soy sauce and olive oil and sprinkle over fish. Let this remain at room temperature for no more than 20 or 30 minutes.

Meanwhile prepare a charcoal fire and when ready then throw on soaked hickory chips. Spray grill with a non-stick spray so fish won't stick.

Sprinkle filets with herbes de Provence, salt and pepper and place on grill. Cook 3 or 4 minutes on each side and serve immediately.

Wayne Amedee
Artist

Cream of Wheat Dumplings

Serves 2

¼   stick unsalted butter, melted
2   eggs
2   tablespoons grated Parmesan cheese
     dash of salt
     dash of ground nutmeg
     instant Cream of Wheat
4   cups boiling water

In a small bowl combine butter, eggs, cheese, salt and nutmeg, stir until well mixed. Slowly add instant Cream of Wheat, stirring constantly, to the consistency of paste. Set aside for 1/2 hour.

Use a tablespoon to form mixture into dumplings, drop into a pan of boiling water and continue to boil for several minutes, depending on whether you prefer dumplings to be firm or tender. When ready, remove pan from heat and let dumplings remain in water for 3 to 4 minutes. Remove from water and drain.

Dumplings may be served in soup or hot consommé with a bit of Parmesan sprinkled on top, or served hot as an appetizer or side dish with a sprinkle of Parmesan cheese and warm browned butter on top.

Oscar de Mejo
Artist

Henry Casselli (American, born 1946)
WHITE GOWN
watercolor
29½ x 21½"
Silver Medal; American Watercolor Society, 1986, New York
Private Collection.

Oscar DeMejo (American, born in Italy 1911)
YORKTOWN CELEBRATION
acrylic on canvas
36 x 48"
Courtesy of Nahan Galleries.

Crawfish Dip or Ball

Serves 8 to 10

Homemade mayonnaise:

1	egg
	juice of half a medium-size lemon
¼	teaspoon dry mustard
⅓	teaspoon salt
1	teaspoon Worcestershire sauce
1	cup olive oil

Break egg into blender container, add lemon juice, mustard, salt, Worcestershire sauce and 1/4 cup olive oil. Cover and blend at low speed. Remove cover and immediately pour in remaining oil in a steady stream, continuing to blend at low speed. May be stored in covered jar in refrigerator for several weeks.

Crawfish Ball:

12	ounces cream cheese, softened
15	green onions, finely chopped
	juice of 1 large lemon
5	tablespoons homemade mayonnaise
1	teaspoon Worcestershire sauce
1	teaspoon garlic powder
1	teaspoon cayenne
1	pound cooked, peeled crawfish tails, coarsely chopped
	salt and pepper to taste

Combine 12 ounces cream cheese with green onions, lemon juice, mayonnaise, Worcestershire sauce, garlic powder and cayenne. Mash until well mixed and smooth. Add chopped crawfish tails, mix well and season with salt and pepper to taste. Mixture may be placed in a bowl to serve as a dip, or rolled into a ball and garnished. Refrigerate.

Garnish:

½	pint whipping cream
4	ounces cream cheese, softened
¼	teaspoon paprika
¼	cup chopped pecans
2	tablespoons chopped fresh parsley

To garnish ball, whip cream and combine with softened cream cheese. Stir in paprika and mix until smooth and spreadable. 'Ice' chilled crawfish ball with cream cheese mixture, roll in chopped pecans and parsley to decorate.

Jan Gilbert
Artist

Chicken Imperial

Serves 6

6	chicken breasts
	salt and pepper to taste
1½	sticks butter
	chopped garlic and parsley to taste
1½	cups Italian breadcrumbs

Preheat oven to 350 degrees.

Wash and pat dry chicken breasts. Rub breasts on both sides with salt and pepper. Melt butter, add garlic and parsley and stir about 2 minutes.

Dip chicken in butter mixture and then dip in breadcrumbs. Shake off excess breadcrumbs and bake chicken 1 hour.

For extra moist chicken it is essential to pour any remaining butter in pan over chicken breasts before baking.

Henry Casselli
Artist

'Underground' Salad

Serves 6 to 8

12	new potatoes
6	Jerusalem artichokes (sunchokes) similar in size to potatoes
1	tablespoon salt or to taste
6	drops Louisiana hot sauce or to taste
3 to 4	green onions, including green tops, chopped
1	cup chopped fresh parsley or watercress
⅓	cup olive oil
¼	cup tarragon vinegar
2	tablespoons green herb mustard or other delicate mustard
2	hard-boiled eggs, peeled and quartered, for garnish

In a large pot, place potatoes and artichokes with sufficient water to cover. Add salt and hot sauce. Boil 25 minutes or until both can be pierced easily with a dull table knife. Drain and cool. Peel artichokes and slice into 1/4-inch thick slices. Do the same with the potatoes, leaving skins on if you choose. Place both in a large bowl, add onions and parsley.

In a separate bowl, combine olive oil, vinegar and mustard. Pour over potatoes and artichokes, mix gently with a fork without mashing. Garnish with eggs, or mix eggs into salad immediately before serving.

George Dureau
Artist

Ginger Garlic Chicken

Serves 4

1	medium or large fryer chicken
1	tablespoon or more grated fresh ginger
2 or 3	cloves garlic, grated or pressed
2	tablespoons soy sauce
2	tablespoons oil
2	slices bacon
Optional:	4 small onions, peeled 2 or 3 carrots, peeled

Rinse well and pat dry chicken. Rub chicken well inside and out with ginger, garlic, soy sauce and oil. Place in a large plastic bag or covered dish and marinate overnight.

Preheat oven to 350 degrees.

Drain chicken, tie legs and fold wings back. Place in a greased roasting pan or oven dish with breast side up (on top of a bed of onions and carrots, if desired). Lay bacon slices on top of chicken breast to self-baste. Cover loosely with foil and bake 45 minutes, or until thigh is cooked. Baste 2 or 3 times. Remove foil to brown, if necessary.

May be served hot, cold, or at room temperature. Good picnic item with potatoes or 'Underground Salad.'

George Dureau
Artist

George Dureau (American, born 1930)
WALK IN THE WOODS
ST. FRANCISVILLE
oil on canvas
86 x 76"
From the Collection of Drs. Wesley and Norman Galen.

Robert Gordy (American, 1933-1986)
RIMBAUD'S DREAM #2
acrylic on canvas
82 x 64"
Collection of New Orleans Museum of Art.

Summer Pasta

Serves 4

½	pound spaghetti or other pasta, cooked al dente
5	tablespoons olive oil
3	cloves garlic, minced
½	cup chopped fresh basil
½	cup chopped fresh parsley
½	cup minced black olives
1	3-ounce jar water packed pimientos, drained
⅔	cup black walnuts or pine nuts
1	pound medium shrimp, boiled, peeled and deveined OR 1 pound ham, cubed
	grated Parmesan cheese for garnish

Heat olive oil and garlic in a large frying pan and stir in cooked pasta. Remove from heat and toss in basil, parsley, olives, pimientos and nuts. Toss in cooked shrimp, or good cubed ham if you prefer. Serve grated Parmesan cheese in a bowl to be used for garnish.

Serve with Creole tomatoes in a vinaigrette dressing (page 44). Excellent with cold roast pork loin or sliced roast beef.

Robert Gordy
Artist

Fried Grits

2	cups cold gelled day old grits, cut into 1 to 1½-inch thick by 2-inch long pieces
2	eggs, beaten until frothy, with salt and pepper to taste
	butter for frying
	maple syrup and butter (optional)

Dip pieces of grits in egg batter and fry in butter until golden. Serve hot plain, or with butter and maple syrup.

Grits Casserole

Serves 8

3	cups water
¾	teaspoon salt
1	cup uncooked grits
	dash garlic powder
½	stick butter cut into small pieces
¼	cup milk
2	eggs, lightly beaten
	cayenne pepper to taste
1	cup grated sharp Cheddar cheese

Preheat oven to 350 degrees.

Bring water and salt to a boil in a saucepan. Add grits slowly while stirring and simmer uncovered until tender, about 15 minutes. Add remaining ingredients to the cooked grits and stir until well combined. Pour into a buttered 1½-quart casserole and bake 35 minutes or until set.

Ida Kohlmeyer
Artist

Ida Kohlmeyer (American, born 1912)
SEMIOTIC BLUE
mixed media
72 x 72"
Courtesy of Arthur Roger Gallery.

Max Papart (French, born 1911)
SEDUCTION
oil on canvas
162 x 130 cm.
Courtesy of Nahan Galleries.

George Schmidt (American, born 1944)
JOHN ROBICHAUX'S ORCHESTRA
oil on canvas
72 x 96"
From the Collection of Con and Mary Demmas.

French Potatoes

Serves 6

20   **medium-size pink skin potatoes**
1   **teaspoon salt**
     corn oil

Scrub potatoes well with a brush. Place potatoes in a large pot with cold water to cover, add salt and bring to a boil. Remove potatoes from boiling water while they are still very firm. (Check with a fork; it should enter, but very firmly.) Rinse potatoes with cold water, peel and set aside until they are very cool.

Cut potatoes into squares and put them in a non-stick frying pan. Add just enough corn oil to moisten potatoes and bottom of the pan. Cook on high heat for about 10 minutes, stirring from time to time. When they begin to brown, lower heat and let the potatoes brown slowly, stirring once in a while. Cook about 20 minutes. Add more corn oil only if necessary. Serve within 5 to 10 minutes.

Max Papart
Artist

Crabmeat Bequia (beck-wee)

Serves 4

9   **tablespoons plain low fat yogurt**
1½ **tablespoons fresh lemon juice (lime juice may be substituted for variety)**
½   **teaspoon dill weed**
1   **tablespoon vinegar (raspberry or other flavored vinegars may be substituted for an interesting variation)**
12   **ounces lump crabmeat, chilled**
1   **teaspoon olive oil**
     Boston or garden lettuce
     assorted cold vegetables (cucumber slices, tomato wedges, broccoli and cauliflower florettes)

In a medium-size bowl, using a wooden spoon, combine yogurt, lemon juice, dill weed and vinegar.

In a separate bowl lightly toss crabmeat in olive oil. On a large serving plate, arrange lettuce, place crabmeat in center, cover with yogurt sauce. Arrange vegetables in groups around crabmeat.

Emery Clark
Artist

Alsatian Sauerkraut with Meat Sauce

Serves 4 to 6

2   **pounds sauerkraut (the kind in glass jars)**
1   **large onion, chopped**
1   **large carrot, sliced**
½   **pound bacon, blanched**
4   **sprigs parsley**
1   **bay leaf**
     peppercorns to taste
¼   **cup gin**
1   **cup dry white wine**
3   **cups beef bouillon**
2   **pounds meat of your choice (such as pork chops, sausage, ham, etc.—that has been previously browned or cooked)**

Preheat oven to 325 degrees.

Drain sauerkraut, rinse to taste; squeeze and separate. In a frying pan sauté onions and carrots without browning. Combine sauerkraut, onions, carrot, parsley, bay leaf, bacon and peppercorns and cook 10 minutes. Add gin, wine and bouillon to cover sauerkraut and simmer on top of stove. Place mixture in an ovenproof casserole, top with a round of buttered wax paper, cover and put in pre-heated oven for approximately 5 hours or until liquid has been absorbed by sauerkraut. About 1/2 hour before finished, add meat of your choice. (Be sure that meat is browned or cooked before addition so that both meat and sauerkraut finishing cooking together.)

Serve with beer or chilled Reisling wine, boiled potatoes and mustard.

George Schmidt
Artist

Alligator a l'Indienne

Serves 4

2	pounds alligator meat*
4	cups water
3	lemons
1	small bag crab boil mix
1½	tablespoons salt
1	teaspoon white pepper
3	tablespoons butter
½	cup finely chopped onion
½	cup chopped celery
½	cup finely chopped parsley
1	pinch thyme
½	bay leaf
1	pinch, even smaller, of mace
2	tablespoons flour
½	teaspoon good quality curry powder
2	cups chicken stock, consommé or bouillon
¼	cup coconut milk made by blanching 1/4 cup shredded coconut in milk and straining
1	cup white wine
1	cup cream
2	tablespoons lemon juice
1	cup long grain rice
1	ripe mango (optional)
1	jar top quality chutney

Cut fresh alligator meat into 1-inch cubes. Braise for an hour in a courtbouillon made with 4 cups water, 2 lemons cut into halves, crab boil, a teaspoon each of salt and white pepper. Keep pot cover cracked so that water will reduce to nothing by the end of the cooking time.

Discard lemons and crab boil. Remove meat to a deep platter and set aside. Prepare cream curry sauce by cooking onions in butter until translucent, then adding celery, parsley, thyme, bay leaf and mace. When onions become pale golden, add flour and curry powder. Stir over high heat 2 or 3 minutes until flour begins to color. Pour in stock and coconut milk. Blend with a wire whisk as you bring to a boil. Quickly reduce heat to a low simmer, cook 45 minutes, add wine and blend.

Strain sauce through a medium-gauge wire strainer, using the back of a wooden spoon to press pulp against sides and bottom of the strainer. Discard pulp.

Before serving reheat sauce. When warm mix in cream and lemon juice, then pour over meat. Serve immediately.

Accompany with ample servings of chutney. A tropical adaptation is to add the chopped meat of a ripe mango to the chutney.

Chicken may be substituted for alligator.

Rice as prepared in India:

Bring 2 quarts of water and 1 tablespoon salt to a boil in a 3-quart pot. Pour in rice, stirring immediately. Bring back to boil, reduce heat to maintain gentle boil. Cook uncovered for 15 minutes. Drain rice into a colander and rinse with cold running water. Remove rice to the center of a napkin or large kitchen cloth. Fold corners over to cover rice and place in a warm place to dry out 15 to 30 minutes.

George Febres
Artist

Theo Tobiasse (French, born 1927)
HOMMAGE TO BOTTICELLI
oil on canvas
195 x 130 cm.
Courtesy of Nahan Galleries.

Robert Warren (American, born 1933)
Series: A Garden of Brushes
Title: JOURNEY AT DUSK
acrylic on canvas
75 x 90"
Courtesy of Galerie Simonne Stern.

Latkes Français

Serves 20

12	large potatoes
3	onions, grated
4	eggs
1	cup flour
½	teaspoon baking powder
1 to 2 teaspoons salt	
	vegetable oil
	optional: applesauce or sour cream

Grate potatoes and squeeze with paper towels until all the liquid is out. Do the same with the onions. Add eggs, flour, baking powder and salt. Form into patties. Fry in vegetable oil over medium heat until crispy brown on both sides.

Serve hot with applesauce or sour cream.

Theo Tobiasse
Artist

Crevettes Garlic

Serves 2

¼	pound margarine
3	tablespoons vegetable oil
½	cup fresh parsley
2	cloves garlic
2	bay leaves
	pinch of salt
	pinch of pepper
½	teaspoon oregano
1	pound large shrimp, peeled and deveined
1	cup cooked rice

Put margarine and vegetable oil in a large frying pan on top of the stove. While heating, add all the other seasonings. Simmer over medium heat for 5 minutes. Add shrimp and cook on medium heat 5 minutes, stirring often. Reduce heat and simmer for 10 minutes to absorb flavor.

Serve over rice.

James Coignard
Artist

Tabbouleh

Serves 6 to 8

1	cup bulgur wheat
½	cup water
⅓	cup olive oil or to taste
⅓	cup lemon juice or to taste
1	teaspoon salt or to taste
1	teaspoon ground allspice
1	clove garlic, minced
1	bunch green onions
⅓	cup fresh mint leaves
2	cups parsley sprigs
2	tomatoes
1	head Romaine lettuce
2	ripe avocados
½	lemon

In a covered saucepan, boil water and bulgur, lower heat and simmer 5 minutes. Wheat should remain crunchy. Drain any remaining water. In a mixing bowl, combine wheat, olive oil, lemon juice, salt, allspice and garlic.

Cut green onions into 1-inch lengths. In a food processor, using on/off motion, combine green onions, mint leaves and parsley. Stir into bulgur mixture.

Cut tomatoes into 1/4-inch cubes, add to bulgur mixture and thoroughly combine all ingredients. Cover and chill for 1 hour before serving.

On a large serving plate, arrange lettuce. Peel and slice avocados, arrange on outer edge of plate, and squeeze lemon juice over them. Place Tabbouleh in center.

Robert Warrens
Artist

Poached Figs

At my wife Patsy's insistence, I propose forthwith a recipe for that most senuous fruit, the New Orleans backyard fig. The particular ones that gave birth to this recipe came plump and purple-ripe (*à point*, the French might say) from friend Dell Weller, who, upon hearing what I had done to them, allowed as how he thought I ought have left well enough alone ("Why make a fuss?" sneered he) and just put a little sugar and cream on them, but I seldom leave well enough alone. Anyway, he didn't experience them this way, so what does he know? In order to follow my decadent example, you need, to make enough for six people:

Some figs (perfect and flavorful and ripe, or don't bother, right?) about three dozen, to be exact.

About 2/3 cup dry pear wine (the rest is quite nice to drink) or maybe something like *Gewurtztraminer*. Some time I might even try *retsina*.

Some honey. If you are so lucky as to lay your hands on some German fennel honey, prepare to swoon (it is like no other in the world) and use about a tablespoon full. Otherwise, just use a good raw honey, maybe half again as much.

The zest (the outer colored layer, without any of the bitter inner white) of a whole orange, peeled carefully and thinly from the orange with a good sharp knife, then sliced into inch or inch-and-a-half long very skinny julienne strips.

Put the wine and the honey and the orange peel julienne into a wide-bottomed enameled saucepan or casserole and bring it to a boil. Put the raw figs into it, stem-end up, preferably (so you won't have to move them around) in a single layer. Put the lid on ajar and poach them gently for about 6 or 7 minutes, being sure to stop well short of their turning to mush. Lift them out (carefully, they will be a bit fragile) with a slotted spoon and set them aside while you boil the liquid quickly down to a thin syrup. On each dessert plate place 5 or 6 figs, stem-end up, and pour some syrup over them. Include some zest with each. Beside them place a perfect slice of Cremolatte Gorgonzola or creamy-mild goat cheese and serve. If you are, like me, given to overkill, garnish each plate with a handful of fresh black raspberries or blackberries (the seasons happily coincide) and pour a flute of champagne.

Franklin Adams
Artist

Squasherole

Serves 4 to 6

1	**medium-large spaghetti squash**
4	**tablespoons margarine (1/2 stick)**
1	**cup chopped onions**
2 to 3	**cloves garlic, crushed**
½	**pound fresh mushrooms, sliced**
½	**cup chopped fresh parsley**
1	**teaspoon basil**
½	**teaspoon oregano**
	pinches of thyme, ground caraway
2	**tomatoes, chopped**
1	**cup cottage cheese**
1	**cup grated Mozzarella cheese**
1	**cup bread crumbs**
¼	**cup sunflower seeds, reserve 2 teaspoons**
¼	**teaspoon cayenne pepper**
	salt and pepper to taste
⅓	**cup grated Parmesan cheese**

Preheat oven to 375 degrees.

Cut spaghetti squash in half lengthwise and remove seeds. Place cut side down on buttered baking dish and bake 30 minutes. For microwave, place cut side down in baking dish with 1/2-inch water, cook 5 minutes, rotate and cook 5 more minutes.

While squash cooks, melt margarine in a medium saucepan and sauté onions, garlic, mushrooms, parsley, basil, oregano, thyme and caraway until onions are tender. Add tomatoes and cook 5 minutes. Remove from heat.

When squash is cooked and cooled, scrape insides with a fork (this will form spaghetti-like strips). In a large bowl combine all ingredients except 2 teaspoons sunflower seeds and Parmesan cheese. Place mixture in a buttered casserole and top with sunflower seeds and Parmesan cheese. Bake 35 minutes.

Kenneth Nahan, Jr.
Artist

Orange and Onion Salad

If *la nouvelle cuisine* has done nothing else (actually it has done a lot, like remind us of the importance of good fresh ingredients) it has taught us to be brave (admittedly sometimes to the threshold of silliness) about combining things in what might once have been thought weird ways. Its tenets have thus afforded me the luxury of presenting such a dish as this with more impunity than once I might. Myself, I tend to like salad (a simpler one of greens at any rate) "after" in the French habit, but this one to my thinking does nicely "before." Try it and say *merci* to the likes of Paul Bocuse and the Fréres Troisgros, et al for paving the way. If you have seen recipes for similar salads (I myself have) be assured nevertheless that this one is at least more or less a product of what the anthropologists call independent invention, as distinct from cultural diffusion. For six servings you will need:

3   big or 4 smaller navel oranges

2   big or 3 small purple onions

2   rounded tablespoons of pine nuts (piñola)

2   tablespoons good *balsamico* vinegar
      from Modena, Italy

      A shy half-cup of good fresh oil, maybe
      mixed safflower and extra virgin olive,
      or safflower and walnut

2 or 3 generous fistfuls of fresh basil leaves
      washed spun dry, chopped very coarsely

1   small medium turnip, scrubbed
      but unpeeled (except for "hairs" and
      stem-end hard spot), cut into very fine
      julienne strips

½   teaspoon grated zest of orange

      fresh-ground black pepper

      salt at the table

Grate the zest from one of the oranges until you have what you need. Put the grated zest in the bottom of a wide salad bowl, then proceed to slice the oranges, perpendicular to the stem axis, about 1/4 to 3/8-inch thick. Hold the slices up to bright light to spot seeds, and get rid of them. Squeeze the juice from the end slices into the bowl with the zest. Peel the slices by laying them flat and turning them as you slice the peeling off with downward cuts, leaving no white pulp. Lay the slices in the bowl.

Peel the onions and slice them thinly (about 1/8-inch), pull the slices apart into rings and place them in the bowl.

Scrub the turnip, cut it into strips, place them in the bowl.

Whisk together the oil and vinegar and some fresh-grated pepper and pour the mixture over the oranges, onions and turnip strips, then toss gently enough not to break up the orange slices, but so everything is coated. Schedule things so that this mix can sit and fester in its marinade for at least half an hour.

Brown the pine nuts in a skillet, in a teaspoon of whatever oil you've used for the dressing, but only until they are medium tan and not blackened. A word or two about pine nuts: 1) They have something like seventeen times the flavor if thus browned and 2) they get nasty-rancid in flavor (as do oils) if not fresh, so leave them out if they aren't, replace maybe with (equally fresh) walnuts. Drain the browned nuts on a paper towel or bag.

Chop the basil (it will seem a lot, but it's the salad's "greens," not just seasoning), then add it and the pine nuts at the last minute to the other ingredients, toss again gently and serve with crusty bread on the side.

Franklin Adams
Artist

Orange Chicken

Serves 4 to 6

6   boned chicken breasts with skin on
      juice of 1 lemon

1½   teaspoons garlic salt

¼   teaspoon pepper

½   teaspoon cinnamon

2   tablespoons butter

2   tablespoons olive oil

1½ to 2 cups orange juice

¼   teaspoon oregano

1½   cups wild rice, cooked

Pour lemon juice over chicken breasts, sprinkle with garlic salt, pepper and cinnamon, let stand for 30 minutes.

In a 10-inch skillet over medium fire, heat butter and olive oil, place chicken skin side down and brown. Turn pieces over, add orange juice and sprinkle with oregano. Cook over low heat for 35 minutes or until tender and gravy forms. If gravy gets too thick, add more orange juice and stir well. Serve with cooked rice.

Richard Johnson
Artist

François Boucher (French, 1703-1770)
WOMAN WITH A CAT *1730-1732*
oil on canvas
Museum Purchase through Women's Volunteer Committee Funds.

VI. Lagniappe

Lagniappe is commonly used in New Orleans and Southern Louisiana to indicate "a little something extra."

Making a Roux:

| 2 | tablespoons butter, shortening, or bacon fat |
| 2 | tablespoons flour |

Using a thick pot, heat butter, shortening or bacon fat until bubbly. Remove from heat. Add flour, mix well and return to pot to medium-low heat. Cook, stirring constantly, until the desired color roux is obtained. A white roux looks "straw" yellow—cooking time approximately 2 minutes. A golden roux looks "golden" yellow—cooking time approximately 4 minutes. When quantity of ingredients is doubled, also double the cooking time.

Add only hot liquid to a hot roux.

Making a Brown Roux:

A thick pot is a must. However, a black cast-iron pot gives the best results. The best rouxs are made from ingredients of equal proportions:

| 2 | tablespoons butter, shortening, or bacon fat |
| 2 | tablespoons flour |

Bring oil to medium hot. Add flour slowly, stirring constantly. Mixture will darken the longer it is cooked. However, care is to be taken not to go beyond a "dark brown" color as roux will burn and the burnt taste will be noticeable.

If butter is too hot when flour is added, causing sauce to be too thin, you can use this method to salvage it. For 1½ cups sauce, melt 2 tablespoons buttter over low heat in a separate pan. Stir in 2 tablespoons flour and whisk until blended. Over low heat, gradually stir sauce into this new roux, stirring constantly until sauce thickens.

Making a Brown Gravy:

2	tablespoons butter
½	cup sliced carrots
½	cup chopped onions
1	teaspoon dried thyme
1	bay leaf
1½	cups hot water
½	cup dry white wine (optional)

In a medium saucepan, melt butter and sauté carrots, onions, thyme and bay leaf until carrots and onions are tender. Remove bay leaf and purée vegetables. Follow directions for making a brown roux, add hot water, stir and mix well until thoroughly blended. Add puréed vegetables. Add wine and heat thoroughly. Slowly add more hot water, if necessary, to obtain desired consistency.

Cream Sauce

Yield: 2 cups

1	stick butter
½	cup flour
1½	cups milk
¾	teaspoon salt
	red pepper to taste
¼	teaspoon paprika
1	teaspoon minced parsley

In medium saucepan, melt butter over moderate heat. Stir in flour carefully, blending well. Do not allow it to brown. Gradually stir in milk to prevent lumps. Add salt, pepper, paprika and parsley, stirring occasionally until thick.

For an extra-shiny, velvety sauce, whisk in 2 tablespoons cold butter (butter can be flavored with herbs, if desired) just before serving. Do not bring sauce to boil after adding butter or emulsion will separate.

Clear Chicken Stock

Yield: 1½ pints

1	quart water
1	chicken carcass
1	onion, unpeeled, quartered
2	cloves garlic, halved
1	small carrot with top

bouquet of herbs: bay leaf, parsley and thyme
    tied together

Optional: 1 tomato
         1 cup potato peel
         2 ribs of celery with leaves
         1 lemon, cut in half

In a large pot combine water with all ingredients and bring to a simmer. Skim, then transfer to a 325 degree oven. Cook, covered, for 1 hour. Strain through a fine sieve.

For stronger stock, boil bones 10 minutes before placing in the oven.

Can be frozen in small containers and used as needed in soups or gravies.

Béchamel sauce may be frozen in polystyrene cups. This will enable you to tear cup away when sauce is to be used. Sauce may appear curdled, but can be restored by reheating over low heat just to boiling.

Fish Stock

Yield: 1¾ quarts

3	pounds fish bones, heads and tails, do not use oily fish such as mackerel, salmon, etc.
1	medium onion, coarsely chopped
2	carrots with tops, cut in large slices
3	ribs celery with leaves, coarsely chopped
5	sprigs parsley
1	large or 2 medium bay leaves
½	teaspoon thyme
10	whole black peppercorns
2	quarts dry white wine or dry vermouth
2	quarts water

Thoroughly rinse fish bones, making sure that gills are removed. Place all ingredients in a large stockpot and bring to a boil. Reduce heat and simmer uncovered for 30 minutes. Skim once or twice.

Line a large strainer with wet cheesecloth and ladle hot stock into strainer. Let bones and vegetables sit in strainer for about 15 minutes; do not press juices out of mixture.

Refrigerate stock in jars, or divide in quantities as desired and freeze.

Quickie Stock

Yield: 1 quart

3	cups chopped meat
5	cups cold water
3	carrots
2	onions with 2 cloves stuck in each
2	leeks
1	teaspoon salt
3	peppercorns
	bouquet garni

Cover the meat with water. Bring to a boil and add vegetables and seasoning. Skim frequently. Simmer 1 hour. Strain and refrigerate. Remove fat the next day, then freeze. It is important after defrosting stock to reboil before using.

JELLY, JAM AND PRESERVE POINTERS

Have ready a kettle large enough to hold four times the volume of the juice and sugar.

Do not pare any fruit except pineapple because fruit skin is rich in pectin.

Most fruit extractions yield better jellies with 3/4 cup of sugar per cup of extraction. If the sugar is added before the juice is boiled, the jelly strength is not decreased.

Seal by covering with a thin layer of paraffin. Tilt the glass so that the paraffin touches the edge all around. The jelly should be completely covered, but the layer of paraffin no thicker than 1/8 inch. A thick layer will pull away from the edge.

Jelly test: Dip a cold fork into the boiling juice. If when lifted the fork is coated with the syrup and drops remain suspended from the tines, the jelly stage has been reached.

Process test: If jars with sealing lids are used, paraffin is not necessary. Fill the sterilized jars with hot jam, seal and process in water bath for 15 minutes at simmering temperature.

Mayhaw Jam

**enough mayhaw berries to yield
2 pounds pulp**

water for cooking berries

1½ **pounds sugar**

Wash and sort mayhaw berries. Cook until soft in a covered pan with just enough water to keep from burning. Press through a colander, bring to a boil, add sugar and continue cooking rapidly until the mixture flakes from the spoon in the jelly test. It will be necessary to stir the jam often to prevent scorching, but do not stir rapidly or beat the mixture. When the jam reaches the jelly stage, remove from fire and let stand 5 minutes, stirring gently at frequent intervals to dissolve jam. Pour into sterilized jars and process at simmering temperature 15 minutes. Do not boil.

Strawberry Jam

2 **pounds strawberries**

1½ **pounds sugar**

1 **cup water**

Follow directions for making Mayhaw jam, using less sugar if strawberries are overripe.

Fig Preserves

6 **quarts fresh figs**

1 **cup baking soda to 6 quarts boiling water**

4 **quarts water**

6 **pounds sugar**

Select firm fruit, discard all overripe figs. Sprinkle one cupful of baking soda over figs and cover with 6 quarts boiling water. Allow them to stand 10 minutes for very ripe figs, a shorter time for firm underripe figs. Drain off soda solution and rinse figs well in clear cold water. Let the figs drain while preparing syrup.

Mix sugar and 4 quarts of water, boil 10 minutes and skim. Add well-drained figs gradually so as not to cool the syrup. Cook rapidly until figs are clear and tender, about 2 hours. When the figs are transparent, lift them out carefully and place in shallow pans. If syrup is not thick enough, continue boiling until it is thick, then pour over figs. Let stand overnight.

Pack the figs in cold sterilized jars. Fill each jar with syrup. Seal, process 25 minutes at simmering temperature. *If figs are underripe, use a larger amount of water for the syrup.*

Sealing with paraffin: Melt paraffin over low heat or over boiling water and pour a thin layer over the jelly. Use just enough to cover the surface completely. Tilt the glass slightly and rotate it to be sure the entire surface is covered, then place dry cover on glass.

Cranberry Jalapeño Jelly

Yield: 8 half-pint jars

6	fresh jalapeño peppers
7	cups sugar
2½	cups cranberry juice cocktail
6	ounces liquid fruit pectin
1	cup vinegar

Wear rubber gloves. Quarter and seed peppers. Chop finely and place in a 4-quart pot with sugar and cranberry juice. Bring to a full boil. Add pectin and return to boil. Add vinegar and stir. Remove from fire and let cool. Pour into jelly glasses and seal. (See sealing instructions for Mulberry Jam.

Serve on cream cheese and crackers.

Drunk Cranberries

Yield: 1 quart

1	pound fresh cranberries
2	cups sugar
4	tablespoons brandy

Preheat oven to 350 degrees.

Wash and drain cranberries and place in a rectangular baking pan or casserole. Pour sugar over cranberries. Seal with aluminum foil and bake for 1 hour. Remove from oven and let cool, covered. When cool, add brandy. Pour mixture into a sterilized quart jar and refrigerate.

Will keep in the refrigerator for several weeks. Serve with meats or fowl.

Mulberry Jam

Yield: 4 pints

8	half-pint glass jars with lids
3	quarts mulberries
6	cups sugar
1	small orange
1	lemon
1	package paraffin wax for sealing

Boil jars and lids and leave in water until ready to use.

Wash berries, remove imperfect ones. The tiny stems can be removed by pressing berries through a wire strainer. Cook for 10 minutes before adding sugar. Quarter the orange and lemon. Peel orange and lemon, set pulp aside. Cut rind into thin slices with a knife or scissors. Cook in very little water until tender. Add orange and lemon juice and pulp. Cook a few more minutes. Add to berries and cook over a medium flame, adding sugar a little at a time, stirring frequently from the bottom of the pot with a wooden spoon. Skim foam and seeds as they rise to the top. The jam requires constant attention for little or no water is used. When the jam drips from the spoon onto a saucer and does not run (approximately 30 minutes), it is ready for the jars.

Melt paraffin in double boiler (it is highly flammable and must not be melted over open flame). Spoon jam into jars within 1/2 inch of the top. Press down jam with a knife or spoon to remove air bubbles or pockets. Wipe edges of jars with clean cloth. Pour melted paraffin 1/4 inch from the top. Allow to cool. Screw on tops.

The jam is excellent on bread or as a sauce for vanilla ice cream. It has a pear-like taste with an after taste of orange.

Old-Fashioned Corn Relish

Yields 1⅔ cups

¼   cup sugar
½   cup vinegar
½   teaspoon salt
¼   teaspoon Tabasco
½   teaspoon celery seed
¼   teaspoon mustard seed
1   cup (12 ounces) whole kernel corn
2   tablespoons chopped green pepper
1   tablespoon minced onion

In a medium-size saucepan, combine sugar, vinegar, salt, Tabasco and celery seed, bring to boil and boil about 2 minutes. Add mustard seed, corn and green pepper, stir thoroughly and remove from heat. Allow mixture to cool before placing in container. Chill before serving. Flavor improves on standing.

Artichoke Relish

Yield: 8 to 10 pints

3   quarts Jerusalem artichokes (sunchokes), well scrubbed
1   quart onions, peeled and chopped
1   large cauliflower, washed and cut into flowerets
6   green peppers, deseeded and chopped
1   gallon water
2   cups salt

Sauce:

1   cup flour
6   tablespoons dry mustard
1   tablespoon turmeric
2   quarts vinegar
4   cups sugar

Mix vegetables together and cover with salt and water. Let stand 24 hours. Drain well.

Mix flour, dry mustard, turmeric and add a small amount of vinegar to make a paste. Heat remaining vinegar and pour over mustard mixture. Boil in a large pot until thickened, stirring constantly. Add vegetables, bring to a boil, then seal in hot sterilized jars.

Cinnamon Cucumber Pickles

Yields about 1 gallon

Do NOT use any aluminum cookware.

4   pounds medium-size cucumbers
1   cup powdered lime
½   cup vinegar
1½   teaspoons red food coloring
1   teaspoon alum
4   cinnamon sticks
1   cup vinegar
1   cup water
5   cups sugar
2   packages (regular-small) "Red Hot" cinnamon candies
    whole cloves, as needed—
    4 per each pint-size jar

Peel cucumbers and cut into 1/2-inch slices, remove seed centers to form rings. Place cucumber rings in a saucepan or bowl, sprinkle lime over rings and add sufficient water to cover. Soak for 4 hours. Drain and wash well. Return rings to container, add ice water to cover and soak for 3 hours. Drain again.

In a large non-aluminum pot, combine 1/2 cup vinegar, 1½ teaspoons red food coloring, alum and enough water to cover cucumber rings. Simmer for 2 hours on very low heat. Drain and discard water.

Combine 4 cinnamon sticks, 1 cup vinegar, 1 cup water, sugar and "Red Hot" candies, pour over cucumber rings and bring to boil. Remove from heat, fill jars with pickle rings and liquid and add whole cloves as needed. Adjust lids and process 5 minutes in boiling water bath.

HERBS: are parts of plants, especially the leaves, grown in temperate zones.

Basil: Member of the mint family. A very aromatic, delicate herb which lacks bitterness. Used in soups, sauces and omelettes, it is especially good with tomato dishes and salads. A must in tomato sauces (gravies).

Bay Leaf: From the Turkish laurel tree. Widely used in Creole dishes, casseroles, soups, and stews—one or two leaves at a time. Should be removed at end of cooking.

Bouquet Garni: The most widely-used of all herbal additions to casseroles, stews and soups. Tie together a bay leaf, two or three sprigs of parsley and a sprig of thyme. Remove at end of cooking.

Dill: A plant with aromatic seeds and leaves, similar to caraway in flavor, but milder and sweeter. Widely used in pickling process and often combined with other ingredients for salad dressings.

Fennel: A member of the parsley family with sweet licorice-like flavor, imported from India. Often used in fish dishes, including soups. Sprigs are often inserted into cuts in the flesh of mullet and other fish being grilled. The sprigs catch fire and impart a powerful aroma to the fish.

Fines Herbes: A mixture of 1 tablespoon each of chervil, chives, tarragon, and parsley.

Filé: The Choctaw Indians were the first to use an ingredient made from leaves of the sassafras tree. This powdered ingredient, greenish in color, is what we know as filé. A teaspoon or two of filé added to gumbo when cooking is completed is sufficient to impart a delicate flavor and thicken the liquid. Filé may be used with or without okra.

Marjoram: Extremely aromatic. A member of the mint family, useful in casseroles and marinades, often with rosemary and thyme. Can be used very sparingly as garnish on salads. Highly recommended for all lamb and mutton dishes.

Parsley: The chopped fresh leaves and tender stalks make a splendid garnish for canapes, salads, fish, eggs, potatoes, poultry and meat.

Rosemary: Use this one sparingly, for it is very pungent. Extremely good with lamb. Also for use with pork, fish dishes and wild game. If you use a sprig of fresh leaves, remove at end of cooking time for the leaves are spikey in the mouth.

Sage: Minty, spicy and aromatic when it comes from Dalmatia. Often used with veal, and particularly good with pork. Be very careful with it, for the flavor can easily overpower all others in the dish.

Tarragon: Often called the prince of herbs. Usually encountered in tarragon vinegar for use on salads, but the chopped fresh herb is delightful in omelettes as part of the fines herbes, and is very good sprinkled lightly over chicken, fish, salmon and lamb chops.

Thyme: Like many other good things, best used a little at a time. Excellent in Creole dishes. A favorite of French chefs for soups, stews and gumbos.

All oven temperatures in recipes are expressed in Farenheit.

To convert Farenheit to Celsius

Subtract 32
Multiply by 5
Divide by 9

To convert Celsius to Farenheit

Multiply by 9
Divide by 5
Subtract by 32

For calorie watchers
and those on diabetic diet:

Proportional Substitutions For Sugar

1 teaspoon Sweet and Low =	1/4 cup sugar
1⅓ teaspoons Sweet and Low =	1/3 cup sugar
2 teaspoons Sweet and Low =	1/2 cup sugar
4 teaspoons Sweet and Low =	1 cup sugar

SPICES: are parts of plants, especially the dried seeds and barks, grown in tropical zones.

Cardamom: The dried fruit of a plant of the ginger family, native to India. A favorite of Scandanavians who use it in their pastries and cakes. Crack 2 or 3 seeds into after dinner demi-tasse and stir with a cinnamon stick for a change. Also adds flavor to hot fruit punches.

Cayenne: This pepper gets its name from the Cayenne region of Africa from whence it came. It's hot!!! Gives zest and zip to sauces for fish and sea-foods. Frequently used in the water when boiling crabs, shrimp and crawfish.

Cinnamon: One of the most aromatic of spices and a must in all apple desserts, bread and rice puddings, stewed fruits and pies. A nice compliment to mashed sweet potatoes, pumpkin, brioche (Creole coffee cake), certain breads and cookies.

Cloves: Whole cloves are hand-picked, unopened buds of Madagascar's clove tree, warming to the taste. Insert into ham or pork roast before baking, boiled tongue, pickled peaches, and baked apples. Use in cheesecloth bag with other spices (cinnamon stick, allspice, ginger) to flavor stews and fruit preserves. Ground cloves are sweet and pungent; wonderful in puddings—rice, plum and chocolate. Use in fruit cake, gingerbread, apple, mincemeat and pumpkin pies and certain breads. Add a dash to bean, cream of pea or tomato soups and sprinkle on top of cottage cheese for fruit salads. Zesty in tea or hot spiced wine. Insert in oranges and dry to add fragrance to holiday decorations.

Curry: Curry powder was "invented" in India and is now popular world-wide. A combination of turmeric, curry leaves, garlic, pepper, ginger and other strong spices. Use to make curry sauces for shrimp, lobster, fish, lamb, veal, chicken, turkey, eggs, rice. Use carefully.

Nutmeg: Ground nutmeg, imported from Indonesia, is a favorite for topping drinks; sprinkle over milkshakes, eggnogs, milk punches, vanilla ice cream, whipped cream. Use in custards, puddings, fruit and pumpkin pies, cookies and coffee cakes.

Pepper: A most widely used spice—fresh ground black peppercorns add an exciting flavor to salads and steaks. White pepper—fresh ground white peppercorns should be used in sauces and light colored foods where dark specks would detract from the appearance. White pepper can be substituted for black pepper in any recipe, although it does have a milder flavor.

Saffron: A deep orange-colored substance from the dried aromatic stigmas of the crocus plant, used as flavoring and coloring in foods.

Vanilla: Vanilla bean is the podlike, immature capsule of the climbing tropical American orchid with fragrant, greenish-yellow flowers. The vanilla bean is sometimes used as flavoring in certain confections; however, the vanilla extract is more commonly used in cakes, cookies, puddings, ice cream, sauces. The true vanilla extract is much preferred over imitation vanilla flavoring.

Hints on Basic Ingredients

BUTTER:
Unsalted butter: to be used in hot butter sauces, such as hollandaise, and in sweet sauces and creams. The majority of pastry recipes call for unsalted butter. Salted butter will brown and burn when subjected to high heat; however, when combined with equal amounts of oil, browning will be minimized.

CLARIFIED BUTTER: is obtained by melting butter over medium heat. Allow this liquified/clarified butter to stand for about 30 minutes. Using a spoon, remove the foamy topping (casein), then spoon, do not pour, the deep-yellow clarified butter into a jar and store in the refrigerator. The casein which was removed may be used in vegetables. The whey remaining on the bottom of the pan is not usable; however, some of the butterfat is mixed with the whey. Place this mixture in a small container—a fruit juice glass or custard cup—and refrigerate. When the butter has solidified on top, remove and add to the jar of clarified butter.

The remaining whey is to be discarded. Butter can be clarified 1 or 2 pounds at a time and kept fresh in the refrigerator for 2 or 3 weeks. May even be stored in small glass jars in the freezer.

When clarified butter is used in panfrying, a much more appetizing and clean-looking food results.

WHIPPED CREAM: Of prime importance when whipping, is to have the cream, as well as the bowl and beaters well chilled and beat the cream in a bowl set in a container of ice cubes. If using an electric mixer, follow the manufacturer's directions. However, using a hand whisk will result in a much better whipped cream.

To decorate cakes, pies, custards, etc., cream should be whipped until stiff.

For combining into Bavarian creams, frozen souffles, and all mousses, the cream should be whipped until it mounds and will fall softly from the whisk or beater.

Equivalents:

1 cup raw rice = about 3 cups cooked
1 cup uncooked macaroni = about 2 to 2½ cups cooked
1 cup uncooked noodles = about 1¾ cups cooked
3 teaspoons = 1 tablespoon
2 tablespoons = 1 fluid ounce
4 tablespoons = 1/4 cup
8 tablespoons = 1/2 cup or 4 ounces
16 tablespoons = 1 cup or 8 ounces
1 cup = 1/2 pint or 8 ounces
2 cups = 1 pint or 16 ounces
2 pints = 1 quart
4 quarts = 1 gallon
2 large eggs = 3 small eggs
1 pound sifted flour = 4 cups

1 pound confectioners sugar = 4 to 4½ cups
1 pound brown sugar = 2¼ to 2½ cups
1 pound granulated sugar = 2 to 2¼ cups
1 pound butter or margarine = 4 sticks or 2 cups
1 cup butter or margarine = 2 sticks
1 tablespoon butter or margarine = 1/8 stick
4 tablespoons butter or margarine = 1/2 stick
8 tablespoons butter or margarine = 1 stick
1 pound cheese = 4 cups grated
2 slices bread = 1 cup soft crumbs
20 crackers, about 2 inches = 1 cup crumbs
25 to 30 vanilla wafers = 1 cup crumbs
1 tablespoon fresh herbs = 1½ teaspoons dried herbs
1 small clove garlic = 1/8 teaspoon garlic powder

Ingredient Substitutions:

According to the U.S. Department of Agriculture, the following ingredient substitutions may be made.

Recipe Ingredient:	Substitution:
1 cup fresh milk	1/2 cup evaporated milk, plus 1/2 cup water, or 4 tablespoons nonfat dry milk, plus 1 cup water and 2 teaspoons butter or margarine
1 cup buttermilk or sour milk	1 tablespoon vinegar or lemon juice plus enough fresh milk to make 1 cup (let stand for 5 minutes) or 1¾ teaspoons cream of tartar plus 1 cup fresh milk
1 cup yogurt	1 cup buttermilk
1 cup light or coffee cream	3 tablespoons butter plus 3/4 cup of milk or 1 can evaporated milk—may be used in sauces, baked goods and candies
1 cup heavy cream	1/2 cup butter plus 3/4 cup fresh milk (do not use for whipping)
1 cup whipping cream	1 can evaporated milk, well-chilled, plus a bit of lemon juice, may be substituted in gelatin-type salads
1 cup butter	1 cup margarine or 14 tablespoons hydrogenated shortening plus 1/2 teaspoon salt
1 cup sifted cake flour	1 cup sifted all-purpose flour minus 2 tablespoons
1 tablespoon flour (for thickening)	1/2 tablespoon cornstarch or 1 tablespoon quick-cooking tapioca
1 cup self-rising flour	1 cup all-purpose flour plus 1 teaspoon baking powder and 1/2 teaspoon salt
1 teaspoon baking powder	1/4 teaspoon baking soda plus 1/2 teaspoon cream of tartar **or** in lieu of cream of tartar, add 1/2 teaspoon vinegar or lemon juice to liquid in recipe
1 cup corn syrup	1 cup sugar plus 1/4 cup water
1 ounce square of chocolate	3 tablespoons cocoa plus 1 tablespoon fat

We appreciate the hundreds of recipes that have been submitted to the Committee. However, we regret that due to similarity and lack of space, we were unable to include each and every one. Each recipe in the book was tested three times before acceptance, and we hope that many among our 300 favorite recipes will become your favorites.

COOKBOOK CO-CHAIRMEN:	Toni Feinman
	Adele Adatto
COMPILER OF RECIPES:	Jerry Ingolia, Chairman
	Katherine Bernstein, Assistant
EDITING:	Rose Feingold
	Rosemary Calongne
	Rosemarie Fowler
	Gerry Little
MARKETING CO-CHAIRMEN:	Ilonka Band
	Lura Harrison
CHAIRMAN, WOMEN'S VOLUNTEER COMMITTEE:	Genie England.

Contributors, Testers and Committee Members

Anne Abbott
Linda Adams
Adele Adatto
Bebe Adatto
Lil Adatto
Deanny Albrecht
Christine Alexander
Myra Ancira
Amy Armbruster
Linda Armbruster
Miriam Armbruster
Paul Armbruster
Mrs. William Armbruster
Lynn Armstrong
Janet Aschaffenburg
Mrs. R. W. Ausband

Jan Bagwell
Marguerite Ballard
Cherie Banos
Sue Barnard
Lee Barnes
Clyda Barrett
Mary Elaine Bernard
Katherine Bernstein
Jean Boebel
Lindy Boggs
Dorothy Boutchard
Lou Boyd
Beatrice Boyer
Mary Frances Bruner
Barbara Buchanan
Emajean Buechner

Bethany Bultman
Ann Burka
Elise Burnett

Adele Cahn
Joanne Caldcleugh
Kathleen Calongne
Rosemary Calongne
Angela Carpenter
Margie Case
Adelaide Charbonnet
Rosie Charbonnet
Leah Chase
Charlene Coco
Elinor Cohen
Mrs. Robert A. Cole
Florence Colley
Marjorie Colomb
Jeannie Connell
Doris Cucurullo
Jerri Cullinan
Jeanne Cumberland

Mariruth Datzman
Kathleen Davis
Marjorie Davis
Lloyd Deano
Lois deLoup
Mary Denechaud
Helen Derbes
Cindy Dewhirst
Mrs. Edward Diefenthal

Regina Dillon
Mary Doiron
Lib Duffy
Mrs. Larry Dunaway
Sarah Dunbar
Diane Dupin
Ann Dupy

Phyllis Eagan
Mickey Easterling
Marion Ecuyer
Jim Edgie
Irving Eisenberg
Betty Ellis
Tipping Ellis
Genie England
Taylor Ensenat

William Fagaly
George Febres
Rose Feingold
Kim Feinman
Meg Feinman
Toni Feinman
Chip Fleming
Debra Fleming
Marylisa Fleming
Estelle Fletcher
Louyse Font
Rose Fontenot
Ruth Forsythe
Rosemarie Fowler

Jean Frank
Hella Franklin
Robert Franklin
Mary Fratello
Mollie Fried
Winifred Fried
Jocelyn Fromherz
Zella Funck

Eva Geismar
Julie Glover
Renna Godchaux
Sherrie Goodman
Gayonne Goodyear
Betty Gray
Mrs. Prentice Gray
Jo Ann Greenberg
Frank Gromoskas
Betty Grussendorf
Earline Guice
Margaret Guidry

Elise Hamilton
Marjorie Hardie
Leo Haspel
Shirley Haspel
Dierdre Hayden
Beverly Hegre
Sandra Heller
Linda Heno
Kathy Hershberger
Janice Heymann
Jean Hill
Jane Hobson
Martha Hughes
Marie Hymel

Jerry Ingolia

Lorre Lei Jackson
Barbara Jacobs
Susan Jacobs
Eileen Jeffer
Sally Jellin
George Jordan
Carolyn Jung
Charles Jung III

Katherine Kammer
Connie Kaufman
Jennifer Keller
Lynn Keller
Christine Kelley
Cindy Kemery

Chef Chris Kerageorgiou
Ragan Kimbrell
Elizabeth King
Jane Kohlmann
Yvonne Kotteman
Adele Kuhn

Doris Laborde
Edie LaBounty
Beverly LaPeyronnie
Donna Lafferty
Andree Lago
Jeannette Laguaite
Monica Lambert
Dale Leiter
Billie Leitz
Natalie Leon
Ethel LeRuth
Renee Levy
Gerry Little
Jackie Littleton
Pomeroy Lowry
Dellie Lozes
Martha Lozes
Elizabeth Luke

Mrs. Clyde Maddox
Joyce Majeste
Louise Manning
Chef Michael Marcais
Sharon Marty
Judy Massey
Raymond Mathon
Fran Mayer
Caroline Mayerson
Justine McCarthy
Richard McCarthy
Betty McDermott
Stanley McDermott, Jr.
Carol McNeal
Mrs. W. Gordon McNeely
Mrs. V. N. McNeely
Mary Elise Meriam
Dr. Alvin Merlin
Carol Merlin
Hazel Merrill
Doris Messina
Nancy Michiels
Loraine Morsch
Beverly Muller
Mrs. W. Gordon Mundock

Gladys Niles
Bertha Rose Novick
Jo Ann Nungesser

Occhipinti's Restaurant
Vivian Oglesby
Lillian Opotowsky
Lois Oster
Mrs. Stanford J. Otto
Marjory Ourso
Sheila Owen

Barbara Pate
Cora Pazant
Mimi Pelias
Bettie Pendley
Elise Plauche
Anita Plous
Lloyd Poissenot
Phyllis Ponder
Chef Gunter Preuss

Adaline Rabin
Maurice Ravet
Peggy Read
Beverly Reese
Mickey Regard
Edwina Reisfeld
Margaret Richards
Sandy Robert
Mary Rogers
Regina Romano
Beth Rosen
Carol Lise Rosen
Nan Rosenberg
Marilyn Rosenson
Aline Rothschild
Leonie Rothschild
Beth Ryan

Denise St. Pierre
Ann Satcher
Dorothy Schlesinger
Ruth Schlesinger
Yvonne Schultz
Jan Scotto
Joe Sheldon
Nancy Sherar
Toy Siddall
Mercedes Silverman
E. D. Sites
Mrs. Gary Sod
Marion Sontheimer

Joe Spencer
Katherine Springer
Mary Sprow
Kathleen Stassi
Garrett Stearns
Enola Steinwinder
Odette Sternberg
Fannie Stewart
Sylvia Suter
David Swoyer
Ann Swicord

Jennie Tarabulus
Jean Taylor
Nickie Thorne-Thomsen
Jackie Toledano
Yvette Trahant

June Tucci
Lucille Tumminello
Rosa Tumminello

Mrs. William Ulmer

Helene Volker
Elaine Vuyosevick

Maxine Wachenheim
Cindy Wakefield
Samuel Wall
Marita Walsh
Bonnie Warren
Marguerite Watson
Fay Beth Wedig

Joel Weinstock
Dee Wellon
Bettie Widmaier
Linda Wiener
Dee William
Jean Winters
Grace Witsell
Cindy Woessner
Yvonne Wogan
Albert J. Wolf, Jr.
Cristina Wysocki

Margot Yuspeh

Rita Zanki
Joan Zaslow

Special thanks to members of Le Vatel Club de la Nouvelle Orleans.

The Women's Volunteer Committee thanks all the NOMA staff members who gave unstintingly
of their time and expertise.

GENERAL INDEX

GENERAL INDEX

GENERAL INDEX

GENERAL INDEX

GENERAL INDEX

MAIL TO: ARTIST'S PALATE COOKBOOK, W.V.C.—NEW ORLEANS MUSEUM OF ART,
P.O. BOX 19123, NEW ORLEANS, LOUISIANA 70179   (504) 488-2631

Please send_____copies of ARTIST'S PALATE COOKBOOK @ $19.95 each $_____

Postage and Handling in Continental U.S. @ $2.00 each   _____

Louisiana Residents add 80¢ each Sales Tax   _____

New Orleans Residents add $1.80 each Sales Tax   _____

TOTAL ENCLOSED $_____

NAME_____

ADDRESS_____

CITY_____STATE_____ZIP_____

Charge to: Acct. #_____ Exp. Date_____

☐ VISA
☐ MASTERCARD_____   Daytime
                        Signature   Phone (_____)_____

Make checks payable to: ARTIST'S PALATE COOKBOOK

MAIL TO: ARTIST'S PALATE COOKBOOK, W.V.C.—NEW ORLEANS MUSEUM OF ART,
P.O. BOX 19123, NEW ORLEANS, LOUISIANA 70179   (504) 488-2631

Please send_____copies of ARTIST'S PALATE COOKBOOK @ $19.95 each $_____

Postage and Handling in Continental U.S. @ $2.00 each   _____

Louisiana Residents add 80¢ each Sales Tax   _____

New Orleans Residents add $1.80 each Sales Tax   _____

TOTAL ENCLOSED $_____

NAME_____

ADDRESS_____

CITY_____STATE_____ZIP_____

Charge to: Acct. #_____ Exp. Date_____

☐ VISA
☐ MASTERCARD_____   Daytime
                        Signature   Phone (_____)_____

Make checks payable to: ARTIST'S PALATE COOKBOOK

MAIL TO: ARTIST'S PALATE COOKBOOK, W.V.C.—NEW ORLEANS MUSEUM OF ART,
P.O. BOX 19123, NEW ORLEANS, LOUISIANA 70179   (504) 488-2631

Please send_____copies of ARTIST'S PALATE COOKBOOK @ $19.95 each $_____

Postage and Handling in Continental U.S. @ $2.00 each   _____

Louisiana Residents add 80¢ each Sales Tax   _____

New Orleans Residents add $1.80 each Sales Tax   _____

TOTAL ENCLOSED $_____

NAME_____

ADDRESS_____

CITY_____STATE_____ZIP_____

Charge to: Acct. #_____ Exp. Date_____

☐ VISA
☐ MASTERCARD_____   Daytime
                        Signature   Phone (_____)_____

Make checks payable to: ARTIST'S PALATE COOKBOOK